I0214154

The Drama Teacher's Survival Guide

A complete handbook for play production

Margaret F. Johnson

MERIWETHER PUBLISHING
A division of Pioneer Drama Service, Inc.
Denver, Colorado

Meriwether Publishing
A division of Pioneer Drama Service, Inc.
PO Box 4267
Englewood, CO 80155

www.pioneerdrama.com

Editor: Arthur L. Zapel
Cover and book design: Jan Melvin

Printed in the United States of America
First Edition / Hardcover ISBN: 978-1-56608-253-2

The Library of Congress has cataloged the paperback edition as follows:

Johnson, Margaret (Margaret Friedl)
The drama teacher's survival guide : a complete tool kit for theatre arts / by Margaret F. Johnson
p. cm.
Includes bibliographical references.
ISBN 978-1-56608-141-2 (pbk. : alk. paper)
1. Drama—Study and teaching (Secondary) I. Title.
PN1701.J64 2007
792.071'2—dc22

2006034585

1 2 3 20 21 22

Dedication

This text was shaped and colored by the hundreds of students with whom I had the privilege of working over my thirty-seven years at Sentinel High School and it is impossible to list them all by name. Without their loving support and willingness to try everything I threw at them, I might not have refined many of the technical ideas I have included in this manuscript, and the book would not have happened.

But there is one individual who was there by my side every year, one who supported me through all my productions, designing sets and costumes, painting scenery, building a lighting booth, wiring the intercom, and photographing shows. I dedicate this book to my best friend and husband, Ron.

Table of Contents

Acknowledgments and Credits

Drawings:

All of the drawings and many of the designs were created by Tom Valach, a dear friend and former student.

My Wonderful Readers:

Bill Raoul, Katherine Stewart, Gayle Carlisle, Eleanor Harder, Kim McKelvey, Tim Dennison, Helen Kozlowski, from the University of Montana — Mike Monsos, Beverly Chin and her class, as well as Jillian Campana and her class — Ondine Brandt, Georgiana Graf, Michele Nokleby and especially Tammi Allison and Tom Valach.

Photographs:

Every photograph, whether taken as slides, stills, or video, was taken by my husband, Ron Johnson. There is no way I could have done this book without his expertise.

Introduction

Yea! You're ready to be a teacher! You're about to embark on a wonderful journey involving students as a drama director!

You are overwhelmed! You're not sure what this entails. This book is about how one person can run a successful extracurricular drama program, from administrative detail and play selection to the actual performance before an audience. This is not intended as a manual or a comprehensive study of stagecraft but rather a collection of suggestions and vignettes of personal experiences garnered from putting on school plays for thirty-seven years.

All you have been told is that you as the drama teacher will put on plays. But what is this thing you are considering?

What is drama?

Drama is the most stimulating, fulfilling, creative, loving environment you will ever encounter. You have the chance to work with students on a one-on-one basis and as a group while creating, even for one night, one of the most exciting evenings of your teaching career. You and your students will go on a journey. You will be bringing a play script to life so the audience can enjoy an evening of theatre. Putting on a play is like having a baby. Your nine months of waiting is encapsulated into about eight weeks, but the end result is worth the time and effort.

What is the job of the high school drama director?

Description

What does a high school drama director do? A director in the professional theatre may work closely with the playwright in matters of interpretation, but will leave the technical jobs of costuming, lighting, makeup, props, publicity, and scenery to designers and the financial worries to the producer. This director's primary concern is to analyze the play and prepare it for performance. A high school director certainly has to analyze the play, but you must do much more. You fulfill a combination of duties. You are a **director** who understands the play's meaning, gives actors actions while they are delivering their lines, and suggestions on how to say their lines. You are a **designer** who creates the theatrical environment by deciding the color and shape of the performing space as well as costumes, makeup, props, and lighting effects. You are a **producer** who coordinates the use of the facility and determines the budget. In other words, the high school drama director controls every aspect of the production.

"What does being the high school drama teacher entail?" you ask hesitantly. It involves many things. The major ones include the expectations of your administration, your contract, and your extra-duty pay.

Expectations of your administration

Before you can agree to take this job, you need to ask your administration the following questions (with great tact, of course). You will want their answers before you give your final decision. Write down their answers for future reference.

"Help! I have already signed my contract and said I would be the drama director. Can I now go back and ask these questions and talk about the contract?" You bet! Just tell your administration you want to be clear about their expectations and the pay for this duty.

✓ **How much money is in the drama department account, and how is it funded?** You need at least enough money to buy scripts, pay royalties, and advertise your production (see Chapter 2). Is the extracurricular drama program funded through the general operational budget? If it is, what is the exact amount? Or is it funded through the sale of student activity cards (student funds)? These student funds support the athletic department and the school newspaper. If the drama department is included in the activity card, ask the following questions:

  ✗ What percentage of the funds does the drama department get from the card?

  ✗ How much does it amount to?

  ✗ Do the students come to see the play free if they have one of these cards? (Answers are needed in Chapter 2.)

On the other hand, if the drama department has no funds or if there has not been any money set aside for you to use, ask your administration how to fund a drama department without any money. (Of course, it goes without saying that this is approached with finesse and the utmost charm!)

Any activity worth doing costs money. Present the administration with the three basic items needed to produce any play: **scripts, royalties,** and **publicity**. All three require an outlay of money. (See Chapter 2 for specifics.) Compare these theatre basics to the basic items needed for athletics: helmets, uniforms, playing fields, referees, and travel. Why? Most public schools have an athletic department that is very important. You are very important, too. You are not trying to antagonize the athletic department, only put yourself on the same level. You are just as good, aren't you?

Remind the administration that they are thinking of hiring you or have hired you to be their drama director. They think the drama program is worth your time and effort. They also want a quality program that is a good educational experience for the students. Otherwise, they wouldn't want to hire you.

Therefore, the administration needs to come up with the money for this quality educational program or there cannot be a program.

- ✓ **How many hours do they expect you to spend on each production?** A ninety-minute production will require eighty to one hundred hours. (This includes preparation, rehearsal, and performance.)
- ✓ **How many plays are you to do for the year?** Generally, a school has two plays a year, one in the fall and one in the spring.
- ✓ **Is there any restriction on the type of play performed?** Some communities are very conservative, and the material presented in a play must not upset them.
- ✓ **Must one of the plays be a musical?** Sometimes the music department is involved with the drama department on one of the plays. Musicals have many added responsibilities and require considerably more hours but can be a great experience. If this is your school's policy, you must check with the music people and find out their procedure. Be sure everything is explained before you agree to anything.
- ✓ **Are the plays to make money?** For obvious reasons, the drama department must pay for itself and not run in the red. If the drama department is to pay its own way and make money, ask where the profit goes. Does it go back into student funds and end up supporting the school activities, or can it be reinvested in equipment or future productions for the drama department?
- ✓ **Is the drama department to pay rental on the theatre space, custodians, and/or security?** Most schools provide the space, electricity, custodians, and security for their extracurricular events. It never hurts, however, to check and see what is expected. Each school district is different.
- ✓ **Is there an adult assistant to help you? If not, is there money available for you to hire one?** Most drama departments have an assistant. This is generally someone who has theatre knowledge and/or "knows the ropes," which can be invaluable.
- ✓ **Have you seen the area you are to perform in, and is it satisfactory for play production?** Is it a theatre, a multipurpose room, or a gym? Each has its own strengths and weaknesses. A multipurpose room is just that, used for everything in general and nothing in particular. Almost exclusively, the athletic department uses a gym for practices and games. A theatre is often used for lectures, music, and movies. How the facility is kept up can tell you a great deal about the administration's attitude toward the drama department. However, it can also indicate your predecessors' and custodians' attitudes as well.
- ✓ **Will this area be available, with no interruptions from anyone, for the last three weeks of rehearsal and performance for each play?** You *must* have this much time to insure that your students become familiar with the

performing space and for you to deal with any technical aspects such as lighting, set, and sound. *This is the minimum amount of time you need.* Try to get more time. Ideally, you should be able to use this space for your entire rehearsal and performance time.

Now is the time for you to seriously consider taking the job. Look at the answers to the above questions. If you agree to take the job, or have already agreed, you have accepted the answers and made a personal commitment to do the best you can. If you have not said you will take the job, do not take it — yet. If you have, just be sure that you have a personal financial agreement with the school.

The contract/written agreement

This extracurricular duty must have a separate contract, often called an **Extra-Duty Contract** or **Written Agreement**, stating that you are to direct the school play or plays. Unfortunately, in this day and age, oral agreements are not enough. Each district has its own form depending on the teacher's union and the current contract language.

If an extra-duty contract or written agreement has not been given, check immediately with your school's personnel office, the activity director (often one of the vice principals or the principal, depending on the size of your school), or the teachers' union to see why you were not offered one. If the football or basketball coach has an extra-duty contract or written agreement, you also must have one.

This extra-duty contract or written agreement comes with extra-duty pay. If the athletic coaches are paid, you must be paid, too. Your time and energy are valuable commodities. Don't ever give them away. This payment will never be equal to the amount of hours required to direct a play. You, on the other hand, are certainly not going to do it for free.

After signing your teaching contract and receiving your extra-duty contract or written agreement, you are officially the high school drama director.

"OK, I am a high school drama director," you exclaim with great pride, and then it hits you. "Oh, dear, how can one person do all of this with no experience in theatre, possibly limited equipment, and eager students?" you ask, wondering if you have made one big mistake. No, you haven't made a mistake. You have agreed to go on a creative theatrical journey with eager students. All you need is a little encouragement, time, and basic theatre knowledge.

Three qualities a drama teacher needs

"So, how do I go about it?" School theatre can be successfully taught with the same qualities every successful teacher has: **organization, enthusiasm,** and **imagination**.

Organization

The key element of theatre directing is organization. Neither you nor your students want to waste time. The point of this book is to help you organize your job as director, making it easier and much more enjoyable.

You will not do it alone. You need actors, crew folks, and assistants. It is working with others that makes this job not only easier but also very rewarding.

If you are fortunate enough to have adults who are familiar with the various technical jobs of theatre and are willing to help, hold on to them. They can often work as advisers to you and your students.

Using students as crew heads of the various technical aspects of a show can lift many burdens from your shoulders. Of course, students need constant guidance, prodding, and praise. There are times when it might be easier to do it yourself, but remember that you are in educational theatre, trying to teach students to be more responsible and reliable. Most students welcome the challenge. If you feel that they can do the job, most of the battle is won. (Chapters 5-12 help with much of the organization you will need for a successful show.)

Enthusiasm

Enthusiasm cannot be taught or learned from a book. If you enjoy what you are doing, everyone else will, too. Convince yourself that you can present the play you selected, and your students will follow your example. Enthusiasm is contagious. As teachers, we all understand that if we believe in what we teach, we can convince most students that our classroom information is important. Persuading students to do theatre is much easier. Most everyone wants to be a star or to have something to do with the production of a play even if he or she may be too timid to say so. Part of the success of your production will come from this infatuation with theatre.

Enthusiasm takes energy! No one likes to be taught by robots that sit chained behind their desk with a book, never changing the inflection of their voice or gestures. Likewise, no one likes to be directed by someone who sits in the performing area saying nothing or who socializes with friends when they should be paying attention to the actors who are on-stage giving their all. As you work with your students, you need to get involved with the play. They need to feel your energy, whether it is while you are on-stage giving directions or in the back of the theatre critiquing their efforts. Actors get their energy from you.

Be a cheerleader!

First and foremost, cheer for you. You must take care of yourself. Be your own cheerleader. In order to have energy, you must stay healthy. You will be totally drained when you come home from work. Lie down, rest, and eat your veggies! Truly, you must take this suggestion very seriously. When we do not feel well, have not eaten, and/or are tired, we are not energetic, but grouchy, grumpy, and cantankerous. In other words we are ill-tempered. No one will want to be around us, and we will not have any enthusiasm.

Remember, theatre is a *doing* activity. You need to cheerlead to get everybody going. Never let your students just sit back and watch. Get them involved. This means that you are involved, too. Using rehearsal activities or games allows students a chance to explore the play and not say, "I can't." Games create wonderful energy and the students gain a deeper understanding of the play and its characters. (See Chapter 10.)

Imagination

"Imagination is more important than knowledge," Albert Einstein stated, and this has become my motto. It is also the basis for theatre. The actors must believe in their characters and what they do in the play. You, as the director, must believe in the play and the fact that your actors can accomplish anything. And, finally, the audience must believe in the story you are telling.

You and your students are creating illusions of time, place, and character. The audience knows that in reality the period is not the 1900s, that this is not an expensive New York apartment, or that the fifteen-year-old student is not fifty. They are using their imaginations because you and your students have created that illusion — you have believed. Then, and only then, will the audience believe.

Imagination allows us to overcome limitations. All drama directors need are:

✓ A play worth doing;

✓ Students who want to act;

✓ An audience to view the play;

✓ A place to perform;

✓ Something for your actors to sit on and wear; and

✓ Lights so that everyone can be seen.

If you have a well-equipped theatre, all the better, but remember, often the results are more effective when you have limited technical facilities and funds. This book looks at theatre problems imaginatively. Keep it simple and do it well.

Final note

Working together gives theatre the extremely unique and special feeling of family. This book underlines this feeling of family, this feeling of community, this working together between you as a director and your students as actors and technicians to create a special, magical world that each will remember always. Do not consider this book the sole source of information. Become familiar with standard practice by obtaining information from the books suggested in the Further Reading section (on pages 254-255) and checking the Internet. Taking additional theatre workshops and courses is a must. Consider this book only "a lifeboat sailing on the sea of extracurricular terror!"

Prologue:

Checking Out the Responsibilities

Chapter 1

Starting Out

What do I do first?

You have begun your school year. You have your classes, your room, and your keys, and you have met the faculty. "Now, what do I do first as the new drama director?" Apply several key phrases, reserve the theatre facility, and schedule the dates and times needed for play practice and performance.

Key words and phrases for success

There are four key words and phrases all successful drama directors know and use.

✓ One is **diplomacy**. Remember how you asked the questions in the introduction? You will encounter many stumbling blocks as you begin this journey. Pick your battles. You will not win any popularity contest if you are in the office every day with a problem. Decide which problems or battles you will fight for. Give in when you can, but not all the time. Nor should you find a problem with everything. Sometimes it may take a great deal of endurance.

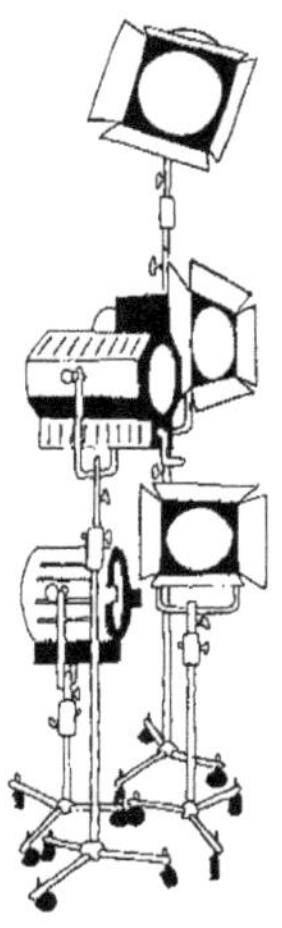

My first major battle happened twelve years after I started teaching. I don't think you should wait that long, but I picked one that I felt was extremely important and that I wanted to win.

For years our school's philosophy was that the community's use of the building came first. The theatre was rented out all year to outside groups, particularly dance groups in the spring, which would take over every inch of the area. I was never consulted. The mindset was, "We have to be nice to the public; they pay our wages!"

I always tried to follow my own advice and requisition the theatre for all practices and performances, but the secretary would pay no attention to my dates. I would go down faithfully in the spring, turn in my dates for the following year, and mention — discreetly and tactfully — that my plays required sets and lights that could not be changed. Slowly, the events in the fall stopped coming, but I still had to contend with the spring events.

> I had finally had enough when we were required to strike our complete set one night before opening *Stalag 17* for a dance concert that wanted the lights and the set pieces moved, not just offstage, but completely out of the backstage area. I came unglued and went to my principal. I think I can safely say that I did not use my best diplomatic tone. This was the first time he had seen my wrath. My major point was, "This was a school activity, and shouldn't it take precedent over a dance group from outside of school?"
>
> That night, he marched into the theatre (he was an ex-football coach and in excellent condition) and told the dance lady to take what she was given and to be happy with it. He then proceeded to tell her everything I had done to get ready for her recital.
>
> The following year, the theatre was mine and only mine, provided I requisitioned it. Our philosophy had finally changed. Today, our students and their activities come first; the community comes second.

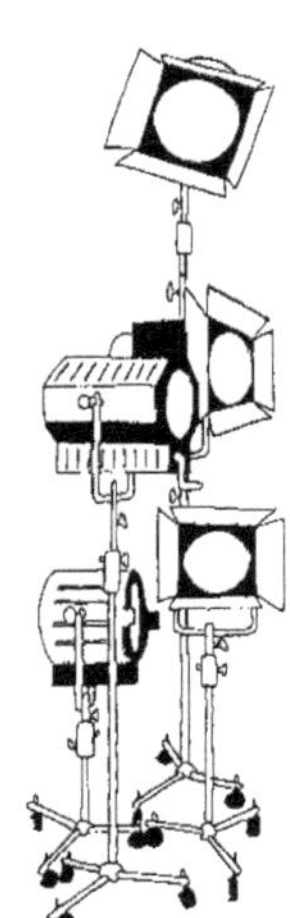

Often, you share the same facility with the athletic department. Scheduling can be a problem, but attacking the system does not work. Working within it is best. Use diplomacy. Get your program off on an equal footing. Go to games, participate in assemblies. Do not schedule your first play the same night as the biggest game of the season.

✓ Theatre is a paradox: both **flexible** and **inflexible**. You will be using these two words throughout your year. The first is *flexible*. You are flexible anytime and every time you can be, whether it is with letting others use the theatre facilities or making allowances for student's needs early in the rehearsal process. During the rehearsal period, your directing of the show may change — movement, props, and sometimes even entrances and exits will change because they will not or do not work. You must be flexible.

But sometimes you need to be inflexible. Become inflexible (with diplomacy) when asking actors to have their lines memorized, be prompt at all rehearsals, and be present for final rehearsals. You should also be inflexible in not letting anyone use the theatre facility the last three weeks prior to a production.

✓ **Make friends!** Becoming an ally with the principal's secretary, the records clerk, the custodians, and the athletic department is extremely important. In the school setting, the hierarchy is set before you enter its doors. These are the folks who run the school:

 ✗ The person who is familiar with everything and runs most of it is the principal's secretary. She is the one who knows everyone.

 ✗ The records clerk (or business person) is the one who helps you with your finances. Often he or she will let you purchase things even if there is little money in your budget because he or she understands that you will bring it in when your play is produced.

✗ The custodians are in charge!

- ✎ They have the keys;
- ✎ They have knowledge about electricity;
- ✎ They have tools and extension cords, mops and cleaning stuff.

These folks have all things we need in the drama biz. Bringing them brownies or chocolate chip cookies always helps!

✓ **Ally yourself with the athletic department!** In ninety percent of schools, athletics comes first. Do not let this intimidate you. Theatre is similar to athletics; you do many of the same things. You both ask students to put in extra time after school. You both work closely with students, often one-on-one. You also both work as a group or "team" to produce the best product you can, whether it be the first place football squad or a fine play. There is pressure to win in athletics, but you produce a play for the public, which is a reflection of the school and you. The quality of your production is always important. Comparing yourself to the athletic department should not cause animosity. It lets the administration recognize that both areas are important to students and parents and deserve equal consideration.

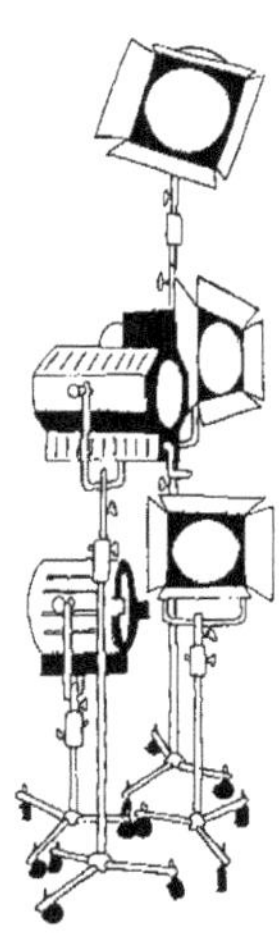

Quite by accident, my first play required that a jury be selected from the audience. Our head football coach was not only selected but made the foreman. The head wrestling and basketball coaches I met almost every day in the lounge during our unscheduled coffee break. I went to games when I could, even sold tickets when I was not rehearsing, and finally ended up handling the concessions during games and matches. When our various teams were headed for playoffs, our play casts would send telegrams wishing them good luck. My drama classes participated with skits for various pep assemblies.

Every year I would have at least three athletes in my drama program. Their coaches and I would work out any scheduling problems. We wanted our students to experience as many activities as possible. I did not realize how important this alliance was until we were doing *Godspell*.

I needed some wrestling mats for our stage floor as I was having the students perform some simple tumbling activities. I went to the head of the physical education department (who was also the wrestling coach) and asked, "Do you have any old mats I can use for the run of my show? It will be over October twentieth, and I know you start wrestling about then."

He was happy to help: "Sure. How many do you want? I'll send the boys down this afternoon." Yes, I got the old mats and several new ones, too. A week later the gymnastic coach traipsed into the theatre after school and announced, "I need those mats right now. Who gave you permission to use them? Did you just help yourself?!" I answered that I had gotten them from the department head. "Well, we'll see about that!" He stormed out of the theatre.

I did not see him again. I found out later he was told, "There are more than enough left for you to use for your program. She has the use of all the mats she wants until she is done with them. Then, and only then, can you use them!"

Scheduling plays

"OK, those are words/phrases I can use, but what must I do first?" You need to schedule your dates for your play performance(s), as well as tryouts and rehearsals, and requisition the theatre area. "Why in the world do I have to schedule my plays now? I don't even know what play I'm going to do!" you question, getting a little agitated. It's OK. Just keep reading. Believe me, if you don't requisition the area early, you will not have it. Other school groups and/or outside groups can come in and use the area. If you have the area requisitioned you can always give it up. The people wanting to use your area can then come to you. This is a place you need to be flexible.

Before considering any dates, you need to think about your actors. Most students you will want to cast are participating in at least one other extracurricular activity, usually music or athletics. You want as many students to be involved in your program as possible. You do not want students to have to choose between activities. This is another place that you need to be flexible. Meet with the activity director or building-use person and get the athletic and music schedules planned for the year. (All athletic events for a year are planned months ahead, and most music teachers set dates for concerts in the spring for the following year.)

If you are required to do two shows, you will want to do a play in the fall. The month of September and the first part of October are not good because you will not have enough time to get acquainted with your students or put a show together. The latter part of October, most of November, and the first part of December are the best dates to choose from.

During the fall there are many activities. In my state we have football, soccer, golf, cross-country, and volleyball, as well as music concerts. For obvious reasons, you cannot perform the week of Thanksgiving or after the fifteenth of December (holiday concerts and family activities take up this time), so what do you have left? The latter part of October (often during the middle of October there are teacher's meetings), three weeks in November, and two weeks in December. From these possible dates, you will need to select several dates. The same process of elimination happens for productions in the winter and spring. For a winter show you may have winter break, basketball, wrestling, gymnastics, and swimming. For the spring you have spring break, district and state music festivals, banquets, prom, final music concerts, track, tennis, softball, and baseball.

Setting dates for production

Next, you, along with your administration, must decide on the specific dates from the list you have selected for your performances. When selecting dates for productions, consider all the options: weekends and weekdays. Performing during the week is good as most athletic events are on weekends. Most shows last about ninety minutes, allowing students to keep up with their homework and not miss school. On the other hand, if games are played during the week, then the weekend is an ideal time to perform plays. Depending on the size of your school and the athletic department, it may be hard to find a free week or weekend. If that is the case, never schedule against a big athletic game or musical event. Attendance will not be good. Again, be flexible. If you are doing a musical, the music teacher will have to be consulted.

With the date(s) set, requisition the play production area (from here on out I will refer to it as the theatre) for at least the last three weeks and tryouts. If necessary, requisition a separate rehearsal space. If at all possible, hold your rehearsals in the theatre. The most important reason for rehearsing in the theatre is you and all your responsibilities. You are just one person doing the high school drama director's many jobs as well as teaching, correcting papers, and eating and sleeping — if you are lucky! Even if you get help, you are still ultimately responsible for every aspect of a production. You need the theatre for as much time as possible to eliminate as many problems as you can before the final dress rehearsal.

Rehearsing a ninety-minute, two- or three-act play takes a long time. You need eight weeks with four rehearsals a week (see Chapter 5). This eight-week rehearsal period runs from tryouts to performance. Most of the time will be in two-hour blocks. (Also see Chapters 5 and 7-11 for rehearsal forms and the various types of rehearsals.)

When you talked about the drama director's job with your administration, you ensured the theatre would be available the last three weeks of the rehearsal period. Why three weeks? If it is the only time you can use the theatre, you will need that much time to put up the set, focus the lights, and allow your actors to adjust to the new location for projection of their characters and their voices. Changes in movement may be needed as well in order to make adjustments for the differences between the rehearsal space and performance space. You will want to rehearse with all the crews and put the show together. Three weeks is the minimum time you need.

Requisitioning building use

You have cleared your specific dates and been told that the area is available. Double check! You do not want the theatre rented out or in use by another group. You will not just requisition the play performance dates, however. You will, I repeat, requisition the theatre for a minimum of three weeks prior to the performance as well as for tryouts. Hopefully you will also be able to requisition it for the entire rehearsal period. If that is not possible, find a suitable rehearsal space and requisition it, too. Even if this area is your classroom, it needs to be requisitioned.

Put the dates and locations of all tryouts, rehearsals, and performances in writing, and keep a copy for yourself. Submit your dates on the Building Use Form to the activity director or principal or their designate (sometimes it is the principal's secretary). Each school has its own form. Find it and fill it out. See Example 1: Building Use Form (page 17).

Be sure the dates are recorded on the school calendar. If they are in writing, it's not as easy for anyone to forget about them. This eliminates problems later on.

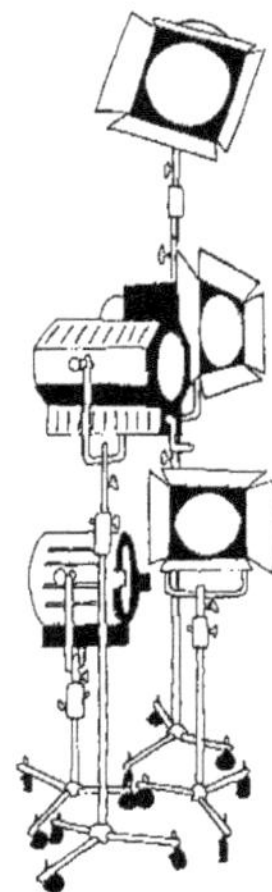

On the first night's rehearsal of my very first play, a very short, bent-over, grizzled old janitor came storming into the theatre informing me, "You don't belong here. You did not ask for this date," as he tried to stuff a slip of paper into my face. It was a copy of my requisition with all the dates I had requested emblazoned on it. I had requisitioned our theatre for the eight weeks of rehearsal long before I had tryouts.

My sturdy five-foot, seven-inch frame towered over this man. "I have requisitioned the theatre!" I told him in no uncertain terms. I took the paper from him and pointed out, "You see, it says October first through fourth, seventh through twelfth, fourteenth through nineteenth, etc."

"Yes," he insisted. "But this is the ninth. It doesn't say the ninth. It only says the seventh and the twelfth of this week."

I could not believe it. This man was really dumb. I then pointed out that the "—" mark meant that it included all the dates between the first and the last. He continued to argue with me. I didn't back down.

I think the only reason he finally harrumphed out of the theatre was that I was bigger than he was. From then on, for several years, I carried a copy of my requisitions with me all the time. I never wanted that to happen again.

Do not change your date

Unless there is a catastrophe, the dates you have set must not change. Your theatre most likely will be needed later, and your publicity will have already gone out. This you must be inflexible about. One of the old sayings in theatre is *the show must go on.* There are a thousand and one reasons to postpone or cancel a production. Do not! Below are examples of things I could have changed my play dates for, but did not. Changing or canceling a show is a little like murder — I have heard it gets easier every time you do it!

- ✓ The first show I ever directed opened the night President Kennedy was assassinated, November 22, 1963.
- ✓ I have had to go on in place of an actress who had her teeth knocked out in a car accident the night before we opened, as well as for students who have not shown up for performances.
- ✓ When an actor's father died (four days before opening night), we continued. He never missed any rehearsals or performances. Coming to rehearsals was a diversion from his sadness.
- ✓ One spring we had a flu epidemic in town. Almost sixty percent of our student body was out with it, including one of my leading ladies. The assistant director went on in her place.

You have learned the requirements for success and requisitioned your tryout, play rehearsal, and performance dates. At this point, you need to be concerned about your budget. Yes, I know. You want to consider your first play. Well, before you can do that you need to be aware of exactly how much money you have to work with.

Building Use
Sentinel High School

Today's Date ________________

Permission is requested for the use of ________________________

On ________________________ **From** __________ **To** ____________

For the purpose of ________________________

____

____

Signed ________________________

Department ________________________

Example 1: Building Use form

Chapter 2
Budget

The question, "How much money is in the drama department account and how is it funded?" has already been answered by your administration. The first thing you need to do is figure the three expenses that must be paid no matter what play you decide to do. The first two are required: **scripts** and **royalties**. The third, **publicity**, has to be considered a necessary expense because you need to spend money in order to make money.

Expenses that must be paid

Scripts

Cost of scripts

You need to buy enough scripts so that each person with a speaking role has one script. You also will need at least four more: one for you, one for your assistant (see Chapter 6), and two for the technical crew (lights and sound). Scripts vary in price from five to nine dollars each. The average number of students in a production is sixteen to twenty, so the cost ranges from $80 to $136, not including postage.

"Why buy all those scripts? I can copy them," you offer, knowing it can save money. *Photocopying scripts without permission is stealing.* If you duplicate a script, you are taking something that belongs to the playwright. This is how he makes his living — he writes plays. You are also breaking federal copyright laws.

What is copyright law?

Copyrights are licensing agreements with the author, the author's personal agent, or a royalty house or licensing agency (which may or may not be a play publisher) acting on behalf of the author. Copyright laws not only pertain to the scripts but to the royalty as well (see Chapter 3). Anything published before 1923 is in public domain; anything published between 1923 and 1977 has a term of ninety-five years where the copyright is valid. After 1978, the copyright is based on the life of the author plus seventy years.

Under copyright law you are forbidden to change the title of a play, to revise whole scenes, or to make minor revisions that will change the theme, plot, or aesthetic effect of the play. The key word is *change*. Any handling of copyrighted material must conform to the letter of whatever restrictions are set by the playwright.

Scripts in the public domain are not subject to legal restriction, but honesty requires that an adaptation be labeled for the audience for what it is, and that revision is done only if the result is an improvement on the original or if the revision is desirable. There is no rule of thumb. If you have any specific questions, check the Internet. A good site is http://www.angelfire.com/or/Copyright4Producers/.

Four ways to help pay for scripts

There are four ways to help pay for the cost of scripts:

✓ **Buying scripts through the English department.** Present the name of the play to the head of the department and see if there is enough money in the English supply budget to buy these scripts. The students cover their scripts and write their stage directions in pencil. After the production, erase and uncover the scripts. The scripts may then be used as a text for the drama section in English. Buy a minimum of thirty scripts for classroom use.

✓ **Sharing scripts.** Actors playing smaller roles can share one script. Example: one actor appears in ACT I and another in ACT II, or two appear in ACT I but not on the same pages.

✓ **Using the director's script for the light or sound person.** Although it is only one script, every little bit helps.

✓ **Borrowing scripts from a school that has done the play you are considering.** Contact them and see if they have kept their scripts. If they have, ask if you can borrow them. Have your students cover them and return them promptly after your production, erased of all your marks.

Royalty

A royalty is the money that must be paid for the right to perform a play. A performance royalty is due any time a play is performed in whole or in part for an audience, whether or not the audience pays admission, and no matter how small the audience might be. Typically, royalties are a set amount paid before the production. They may vary in price, from seventy to ninety dollars for the first performance to forty-five to seventy-five dollars for the succeeding performances. It is illegal to take someone else's work, perform it, and not pay for it. You, personally, can be sued, as can the school, if the royalty is not paid.

This money goes to the author for writing the play and to the publisher for printing and handling the play. Paying a royalty fee and receiving performance rights means that you have permission to use the playwright's property. The playwright is entitled to be paid whether or not you choose to charge admission.

By writing the publishers and explaining why you are doing a benefit performance or presenting the play for free, you can sometimes obtain a lower royalty. Mentioning the size of your theatre space might also get you a reduced rate. Some publishers sell royalty-free, one-act plays.

Publicity

Publicity — tickets, programs, posters, and free advertising — is necessary for each play produced. First, check the paper supplies in the teacher's workroom and the art room — with the art teacher's permission, of course — and the school copying machine before figuring any costs. Sometimes the administration will let you use these free of charge. If not, price the paper at local office supply stores and investigate other possibilities in the community. An instant copy store can make things look professional for a reasonable price. Here is a great place to use your student assistant (see Chapter 6). Going to a regular printer gives you great copies, but it is very expensive.

Another free option is to find out if the school has a printing area that does their bulk printing. If they do, personally check it out. Each printing staff has forms to fill out and ways they want the final copy. Follow their instructions to the letter.

Income

You have figured specifically what you need to spend on your three basics; the next order of business is to see how much money you can anticipate making. If your money is funded through the general operational budget, you already know exactly how much money you have to work with. Take that amount and subtract the amount of your three basic requirements discussed above. Whatever is left is the amount you can spend on the other technical aspects of your first show. Remember, however, you want to keep money in reserve. You may have to finance another play later on in the year or next year.

Two ways of anticipating income from student funds

If you are funded by student funds, there are two ways of anticipating income:

✓ The best way is to see what happened in the past. Go back to the first question you asked your administration. Let's assume they told you the drama department was funded through the sale of activity cards, and you already know what percentage you receive from each activity card. Check with the business clerk or the person who keeps the books. Ask the clerk to make a copy of last year's income from the activity cards, the door receipts, and the drama department's expenses. Hopefully you will find a poster or the business clerk will know the cost of last year's play's tickets. Take the total of the door receipts and divide it by the cost of the play ticket. These numbers might not be an absolute guide, but they will give you some idea of how many people attended last year's play as well as the ticket price. This helps you figure your income for your first show apart from student activity cards. Hopefully you can count on at least the same number of people attending your play.

You have just figured your anticipated income. Next, you will need to know how many activity cards were sold for the current year so you will know how much money you actually have to work with and you can make a comparison with last year.

✓ Another way of anticipating income is by using the formula below. Taking some of the information used above you can figure how much you can make on one production.

Production Formula

Present budget	$0
+ Price of one ticket (or price for a movie ticket)	$5
X Average attendance per night previous year	125
X Number of performances	2
= Total amount monies anticipated (gross)	$1250

Ticket price

"How do I know what to charge for an individual ticket?" you utter, wondering when you can select your play and not realizing you needed a strong business sense as well as organization, enthusiasm, and imagination! Always keep in mind the cost of a movie ticket. Your price should be comparable or higher, depending on the show.

Four ways to help defray cost of production

There are ways to help supplement your drama department budget. Four are listed below along with a great way to enlarge your audience base.

✓ Enlarge your audience by performing a preview of your show for all English classes. This can be done opening day or the day before. It creates interest and gets the entire school excited for the upcoming evening performance. There are two ways of doing this:

✗ Present a ten-minute cutting, allowing your student assistant or you to announce information about it, introduce everyone in the cast, and urge them to come and enjoy.

✗ Present an act or a thirty- to forty-minute scene. Tantalize your audience.

✓ Consider selling homemade cookies or candy before your play and during the intermission. All the money you make is profit. Be sure you have cleared this with the administration and the custodial department. Most schools have policies about food in the building.

✓ Have a school bake sale. Sell homemade goodies during lunch and after school. Crispy rice bars are inexpensive to make and are a hit with most teenagers. Again, checking with the administration, cooks, and/or janitors is necessary.

✓ Some states allow schools to have raffles or a "50-50." This "50-50," or magic pot, is also a raffle. You buy a raffle ticket for a given amount when you come to the play, put your name on it, and place it in the pot. At the end of the show, a name is drawn from the pot. The person whose name is drawn gets half of the money raised from the raffle tickets, and the drama department gets the rest. This must be cleared not only with the administration but also with the county attorney.

✓ Work through the English department. Present one of the year's productions as part of the English curriculum. Have the English department purchase your scripts. Your goal, however, is to get their support by having their students see your productions. You want to make going to the play the thing to do. By experiencing live theatre, students learn that theatre can be enjoyable, fun, and even educational. These students become part of the theatre experience.

  ✗ Sell tickets through English teachers for a set amount. The amount can be less than your general admission price, as all the students in your school will attend the show. Every student takes English, as it is a requirement for graduation. A two-day run (one-half of the full-length show each day) is best. This is a guaranteed income. (This does affect royalty because you are doing the show many more times. Writing the publisher and explaining your situation can reduce the cost. Just be sure that you charge enough to cover the additional royalty expense.)

These are a few of the shows I have done for our English classes:

Ten Little Indians

And So Ad Infinitum

Arsenic and Old Lace

The Diary of Anne Frank

A Flea in Her Ear

Gaslight

The Merry Wives of Windsor

A Midsummer Night's Dream

Much Ado About Nothing

Nicholas Nickleby

Night of January 16th

Our Town

Romeo and Juliet

The Savage Dilemma

Stalag 17

The Taming of the Shrew

The Curious Savage

The Imaginary Invalid

The Trojan Women

If, once you determine the cost of the three basics — scripts, royalty, and publicity — you think there is not sufficient money for your drama department, see the administration or the business clerk. Show the individual the figures and explain that you have not yet considered the costs of any technical aspects you may want to work with. Ask them if they have any thoughts on what you should do to raise money. If they do not have any ideas, suggest one of the two options listed below.

✓ If students buying an activity ticket see the play free, suggest that the students — with activity cards — pay to see the play but receive a discount. If the ticket price was five dollars, the student cost with an activity card would be three dollars. Reducing the rate to one dollar apiece does not give you much money to work with.

✓ If there isn't enough money set aside for the drama department and the administration does not want you to try any moneymakers, get their approval to go in the red with your first show. Always keep in mind that you have discussed this with your administration and they understand that you *must* have the money for the three basics — scripts, royalty, and publicity — or there will be no high school drama department.

You have just figured on paper your expenses and income. You now need to become familiar with your school's business office procedures because you will need to purchase scripts, pay royalties, and buy "stuff" for the technical effects, if any. But first, remember to make friends. And do not forget the sweets!

Purchase orders

What procedure must you follow to purchase the scripts and play royalty as well as other equipment for the drama department? **Purchase order forms!** A school purchase order is a form designed by the business office to purchase items for all areas of the school from athletics to desks and tables. When using your drama department funds, follow the business office procedures to the letter.

✓ Get the purchase order, fill it out, and have it approved. This means that the person who is in charge of finances usually must see what you are buying and put his or her signature on the form. Mail the purchase order to the company or call them. Various play publishers have catalogs (see Chapter 3) and toll-free numbers you can use to place your order. They will ask for your purchase order number. Calling the company allows you to have your scripts quickly. You can also pay for the royalty when the bill comes for the scripts, which saves the school from writing two checks.

  ✗ When purchasing other supplies, such as paper for publicity, have students find out where to buy the items by calling around and getting the best prices. Again, before you buy anything, fill out the purchase order and get it authorized.

✗ Do not go out on your own, buy something, and then fill out the purchase order. You probably will not be reimbursed for that expenditure.

Each school has its own purchase order form. Become very familiar with it! As I tell my students, fall in love with it — it is your friend. See Example 2: Purchase Order Form (page 25).

Petty cash

One of the handiest things a school drama director can have is money on hand to purchase the small things that invariably come up, usually at the last minute. There are always changes that require additional expenses when you don't have time to get a purchase order. You can take the money out of your own pocket, but reimbursement is generally not possible. Having a **petty cash** fund takes the worry out of this last minute shopping. Petty cash is ready money that you have signed out for in one lump sum. One hundred dollars is a good amount. When money is needed, take the amount out of this fund and return a receipt for it. When the play is over, return the money you did not use and the receipts for all the rest. No advanced budget planning can cover everything. If your business clerk will allow such an account, it is a god-send.

Record expenses

Keep a very complete record in a file folder of all your expenses. Put the name of the play on top and all purchase orders, programs, letters, rehearsal schedules, and tryout sheets inside. Write on the inside a list of all the costs, all the profits, and the number of people who attended. This not only helps you when figuring future budgets but also is necessary information for the bookkeeper.

Other technical aspects

You next need to consider the cost of costumes, lighting, makeup, props, sets, etc. It is impossible to indicate what percentage to spend on these technical areas because each play has different requirements. A period show usually costs more for costumes than the set, whereas, in a play with two sets, the reverse is true. If money is available you will have to decide where you want to spend it. Fill out the purchase orders for supplies, have them signed, purchase the supplies, leave a copy of the purchase order with the respective companies, and return the receipts to the business clerk. The company will then either send a bill or the school will go ahead and pay the bill. See Example 3: 1999 Budget for *A Midsummer Night's Dream* (page 26). (For the purposes of this book, examples from *A Midsummer Night's Dream* will be used throughout.)

If you have only enough money for your three basics, do not worry about anything else. Do your first play without spending money for anything technical. You will have a wonderful production because you are relying on organization, enthusiasm, and imagination rather than other things.

"Whew! When do I get into the actual drama stuff?" you ask seeing folders, purchase order forms, calculators, and printouts strewn all over your desk. Read on, Macduff!

PURCHASE ORDER

SENTINEL HIGH SCHOOL ANYTOWN, USA

FOR PROMPT PAYMENT

Please refer to Order No.
and send statement to:

Sentinel High School
Principal
123 Main St.
Anytown, USA

ORDER NO. ________

Check No. ________

Amt. Pd. ________

Date Pd. ________

Company________________________________

Address________________________________

____

Description of Purchase	Unit cost	Total

Requested By:____________________ Approved:____________________
(Not valid without authorized signature)

Activity____________________ Date____________________

Example 2: Purchase Order form

1999 Budget for *A Midsummer Night's Dream*

Basics	
Publicity	$10.00
Royalty	0.00
Scripts	140.00
Subtotal	$150.00
Various Technical Aspects	
Costumes	
Black fabric	$54.32
Lamé	79.26
Mylar wrapping paper	58.00
Netting	26.67
Sewing materials	14.34
Sweatshirts (4)	80.00
Unitards (6)	252.00
Lighting	
Blue-green gels	62.50
Makeup	
Silver face paint and iridescent shadows	45.98
Miscellaneous	
Videotape	7.95
Set	
Black plastic	24.98
Christmas Decorations	176.00
Glitter	23.95
Spray adhesive	32.95
Subtotal	$938.90
Total	$1088.90

Things I had in stock

Costumes — Workmen's outfits, 3 Wedding gowns, 3 Tuxes, Pyramis and Thisbe costumes, Props, Donkey head

Set — Platforms, Coat rack, Trees, Shower curtains

Example 3: 1999 Budget for *A Midsummer Night's Dream*

Act I:

Preparing the Script

Chapter 3

Play Choice

Finally, you get to select your play! But first you need to know some of the lingo. Like many other trades and occupations, the theatre has its own colorful language. Below are a few terms you will need to know when starting to read your plays.

General terms

Amateur: One who works in the theatre without pay.

Aside: Lines spoken by an actor to the audience, not noticed by other characters on-stage.

Audition: Process where the director of a production asks performers to show what they can do (how they would play a specific role). Often very nerve-wracking for both the director and the performers but can be a fairly painless process with organization. There are two major types of auditions:

Cattle Call: The type of audition at which many actors are present. We do not call it this in school; "Cattle Call" is a professional term.

Interview Audition: Private audition — one-on-one — opposite of Cattle Call.

Blocking: Putting actions to the words in the script.

Bomb: A theatrical dud.

Book: Play manuscript.

Center Stage: The middle of the stage.

Chorus: Group of singers, dancers, or speakers working in unison.

Director: One who plans and directs the play for production. In a school, the director teaches a full day of classes and does everything else that is needed.

Downstage: Toward the audience.

Below: Downstage of (as in "Cross below the sofa").

Flop: Theatre production that fails.

Gypsy: A dancer who goes from musical show to musical show, often in the chorus.

House: Where the audience sits. Often referred to as "the audience."

In the Red: Losing money on the show.

Jury: First-night audience.

Knockout: Sure-fire hit.

Lines: Speeches of the play.

Monolog: Protracted speech by one person.

Panning: Unfavorable reviewing.

Plant: Person stationed in audience who has function in play, *or* line, idea, or character that significantly foreshadows some important element coming later in play.

Prompt Book/Prompt Script: Script marked with directions and cues for use by your student assistant director.

Scene: Division of an act; usually refers to short section where there is change of characters.

Script: Typewritten or printed copy of play.

Sides: Pages of manuscript paper holding just one actor's lines and cues.

Stage Directions: Instructions in script of play. Usually they are the directions given in the first production and used with the first set design and the author's permission.

Stage Left: Actor's left when facing audience.

Stage Manager: Person responsible for play in production; calls cues for actors, lights, sound, set changes.

Stage Right: Actor's right when facing audience.

Stage Superstitions:

Bad Luck:

Being wished good luck;

Whistling in dressing room;

Using old rabbit's foot for new makeup;

Opening telegrams before first performance.

Good Luck:

Pocketful of coins;

Cat backstage;

Wearing old shoes associated with a hit;

Wishing player bad luck ("Break a leg").

Turkey: Theatrical flop or "bomb."

Upstage: Toward rear stage.

Above: Upstage of (as in the direction, "Cross above the sofa").

Two types of plays

Now you can start your reading. There are two general types of plays: **non-royalty** and **royalty**. One of the three basic costs you must consider is a royalty. There are some plays, however, that do not require a royalty. These are called non-royalty plays.

Non-royalty

Non-royalty plays usually fall into two categories: those written strictly for schools and those written by playwrights who are long since dead.

✓ A play is a variety of interesting and unique characters telling a story. The differences between a good and poor script are the characters and the story the characters tell.

We must care about the characters. Are they trivial, dealing with stereotypes, saying and doing stereotypical things?

✗ The cheerleader or jock who is really stupid: "Yeah man, like right on!"

✗ The brain who is a nerd.

✗ The plain girl who turns out to be the Homecoming Queen.

These characters are not appealing or unique nor are the stories they tell interesting. Careful reading and analysis will determine whether a play's characters and story have the qualities you want. There are some good school plays, which deal with teenagers and their problems, discussed later in this chapter.

✓ Plays written by playwrights whose plays were written before 1923 are plays in public domain (the author and his or her descendants are dead; therefore, no one receives the royalty). Usually these plays are classics and are certainly worth considering.

Royalty

A royalty is the money you pay to the author/publisher for the right to perform a play. These plays are those that have been written since 1923, (see Chapter 2) and are considered modern. Generally, if a play has a royalty, it has much more worth; as the saying goes, "you get what you pay for."

Start viewing and reading

Good play selection is only as strong as your background in dramatic literature. Ideally, the best way to start is by seeing every play you can. If you are in a very small community this may not be possible, nor do you have much time when school starts, but make it a point to view any local productions you can. It is the best way to gain a background in dramatic literature. Seeing professional productions is even better. School directors cannot always duplicate these productions, but you certainly can derive worthwhile things (the period, costumes, setting, characterizations) from viewing them. Watching videos of productions is the next best thing to being there. Again, you probably cannot duplicate what you see, but you certainly can get a wonderful visual idea of what one director, a technical staff, and many actors and actresses did with a specific production. Also check your local television schedule. There are channels that feature old movies, many based on plays not available through local video stores.

A quick way of obtaining a limited background of the vast number of plays available is to read play catalogs. Catalogs have short descriptions that list the characters, type of sets, a brief summary of the plot, the price of each script, and the royalty for the play. Most publishers mail free catalogs to schools every year. If you do not have them, write the companies listed at the end of this chapter and ask for current catalogs.

An even quicker way to become familiar with these catalogs is to go on the Internet and look up the publisher. Below is a list of play publishers and their contact information.

Anchorage Press, Inc.: PO Box 2901, Louisville, KY 40201. (502) 583-2288. www.applays.com — great children's shows.

Baker's Plays: PO Box 699222, Quincy, MA 02269-9222. (617) 745-0805. www.bakersplays.com

Contemporary Drama Service: 885 Elkton Drive, Colorado Springs, CO 80907. (800) 937-5297. www.contemporarydrama.com — has a wide selection of plays for middle grades.

Dramatic Publishing Co.: PO Box 129, Woodstock, IL 60098-0129. (800) 448-7469. www.dramaticpublishing.com — has many selections for middle grades.

Dramatists Play Service: 440 Park Ave. S., New York, NY 10016. (212) 683-8960. www.dramatists.com

Meriwether Publishing Ltd.: 885 Elkton Drive, Colorado Springs, CO 80907. (800) 937-5297. www.meriwether.com

Pioneer Drama Service, Inc.: PO Box 4267, Englewood, CO 80155. (800) 333-7262. www.pioneerdrama.com

Playscripts, Inc.: 325 West 38th St., Suite 305, New York, NY 10018. (866) 639-7529. www.playscripts.com

Plays, the Drama Magazine for Young People: PO Box 600160, Newton, MA 02460. www.playsmag.com

Samuel French, Inc.: 45 W. 25th St., New York, NY 10010. (212) 206-8990. www.samuelfrench.com

Find copies of plays individually and in collections in your school and public libraries. The interlibrary loan is available nearly everywhere. If you are near a large city, investigate its libraries or contact other local drama teachers and try to exchange scripts with them. Ask local universities and/or colleges if they have scripts to lend you. If you borrow any scripts, be sure to return them.

"OK, I've read many plays, but what am I looking for?" you ask. For your first production, look for a good story, a simple set, easy-to-make costumes, and, most of all, interesting characters.

"What?" Yes, the most important thing to look for in a school script is **characterization**.

A good script for students has colorful characters that can be played several ways because these characters have many dimensions. Your students need to be able to try a variety of ways to discover, create, and bring to life the characters they are playing. If the play you've chosen has wonderful characters, you have great freedom as a director to explore the best way to "tell the story." A weak script, however, doesn't allow your actors any freedom to interpret their parts. The characters are one-dimensional and can be directed and played in only one way. Their dialog is simple, based on stereotypes. There is nothing to explore!

Play list

"OK, so where is the list of plays for me to choose from?" Often, experienced drama directors suggest, "Use the classics!" Everyone recognizes these tried and true plays of the past, those great comedies of the 1930-50s: *You Can't Take It with You, Arsenic and Old Lace*, and *Harvey*. They certainly contain fascinating characters and have strong scripts. However, for inexperienced school directors, they can be extremely difficult to produce. Why? They generally require:

✓ Complicated sets as part of the plot;

✓ At least one of the pivotal characters is older — difficult for inexperienced actors to play convincingly;

✓ Dialog that represents the period in which the play was written; and/or

✓ Critical timing.

The last on this list — critical timing — is the key. The pace of these shows has to be fast, frantic, and fun. Also, great attention must be paid to the language. These are period pieces, and the integrity of the lines as written must be kept, word for word. This also ties into the pacing.

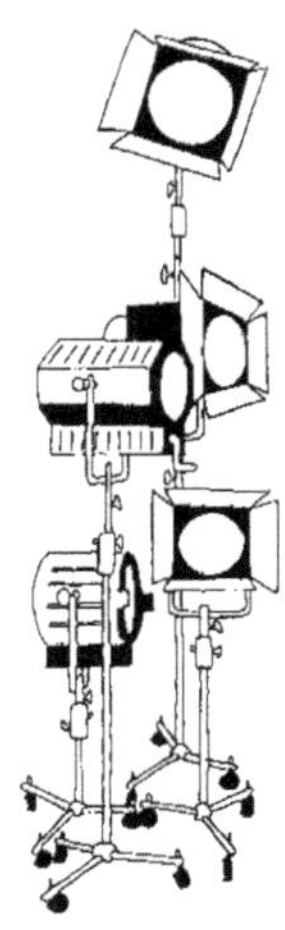

> I directed two of these classics written over sixty-five years ago twice, once in the 1970s and once in the early 1990s. Both required complicated sets. When I first directed *The Bat,* I did not cut any lines but only had one ten-minute intermission — it was a full three-act play. The show ran two hours. The audience loved it. It was too long, however, for the audience of the 90s. They became very restless (the exposition took the entire first act — thirty-eight minutes). It was no longer a good show for school unless it could be cut to an hour and a half.
>
> The second time I directed *Arsenic and Old Lace,* I took my own advice and trimmed it. By watching the movie, I got ideas on how to cut the show to one hour and thirty-three minutes without any intermission. It was just long enough. It still had the wonderful appeal of the original but not the length. I did not update it; I just did some careful editing with help from the experts who filmed it.

The second suggestion often given by experienced directors is, "Do teenage problem plays — no set, and the kids can play themselves!" Teenage plays deal with situations students can understand emotionally and feature characters close in age to themselves. Generally, these are plays made up of many vignettes featuring ensemble casts. This gives directors flexibility in cast size while giving nearly every actor an equal status in the play. The worst choices for your first show are plays that deal with sexuality, drug abuse, anorexia, incest, and/or suicide — worthy subjects for all of us, but not for a first show by a new director.

If the actors are playing these types of characters, they may become very self-conscious and not do their best, or they may be mistaken for their character. Acting involves taking risks. If characters have problems and the students playing them do such a good job, will the audience forget they are actors playing a role and start thinking they are the person they are portraying?

As the major characters are teenagers, casting can be very difficult. You do not want your actors to play themselves. This is called **typecasting**. Sometimes it is easier to cast for type rather than working with actors to help them create a whole new person. This doesn't let actors grow. In fact, you should never typecast. You want to challenge your actors and allow them to explore their characters and have new and varied experiences.

These two suggestions about what shows new directors should do are meant well and certainly have merit. To answer your question, "Where is the list of plays for me to choose from?" truthfully there is no sure-fire list of plays that everyone can do. Below is a very small, select list including three of the "oldies" as well as plays that most communities would like and accept. *Arsenic and Old Lace* requires a major set including a staircase. Do not tackle complicated technical shows your first year, but don't be afraid of them, either. If the school would like a musical or has not had any shows for children, Ray and Eleanor Harder's plays are good choices. The writing is clever, the characters colorful, and the music delightful and available on cassette or CD. Their shows appeal to both young and old. Two Shakespearean plays have also been included on the list. Both of them took hours of preparation, including cutting the script to ninety minutes, costuming, and dealing with the language, but any time spent on Shakespeare is well worth the effort. Some of the plays suggested are not what many of us think of as "High Art." That's OK! Remember, our communities, while wanting to be entertained, are very protective of their children.

Suggested plays for new directors

*Plays marked with a + are good for those who have never ever been involved with a theatre production; plays marked with a * are by Tim Kelly or the Harders.*

Comedy/Drama

The Clumsy Custard Horror Show and Ice Cream Clone Review
David and Lisa
The Diary of Anne Frank
Ghostchasers *+
Here and Now
Hurricane Smith and the Garden of the Golden Monkey *+
Is There a Comic in the House?
A Midsummer Night's Dream
Our Town
Romeo and Juliet
The Curious Savage
Night of January 16th
Tom Jones (A refreshing, clean comedy based on the book)
You Ain't Nothin But a Werewolf * (Featuring 50s music)
*Phantom of the Op'ry**
*Lucky, Lucky Hudson and the 12th Street Gang**

Children's shows

Annabelle Broome *
Beauty and the Lonely Beast *
Gold Fever *
Goldilocks and the Christmas Bears *
The Best Christmas Pageant Ever
Winnie the Pooh

Teenage shows

2nd Class +
Class Action +
Love, Death, and the Prom +
Works in Progress +
Check, Please (Jonathan Rand)*

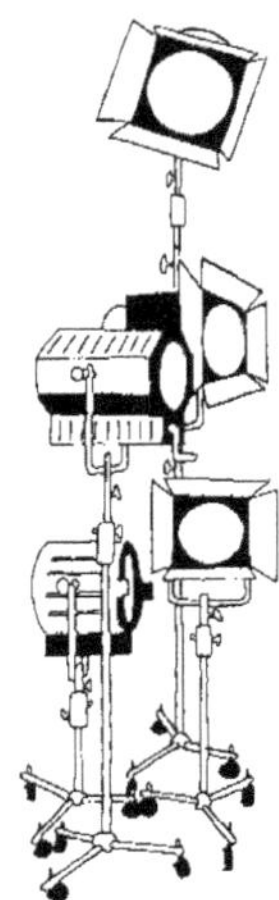

Years ago I would never have suggested nor would I have ever done a play written by Tim Kelly, a very prolific playwright for the amateur market. His plays epitomized what I thought were bad high school plays. They were beneath me. My students were going to get "real theatre," and that did not include his kind of play.

In1986, I needed to find shows for fifteen to twenty actors with parts that could be either men or women. I looked, looked, and looked some more. Tim Kelly's plays state that gender can be changed and roles can be added or doubled depending on the number you have trying out. He allows directors to work with his scripts. This is not a normal situation. As I read the script, it became clear that his strength as a playwright was in creating characterizations that young people could play in many ways and audiences could enjoy.

I recruited two of our teachers and one administrator to be in the play and the rest, as they say, is history. It was a huge success. The students loved being in it, hearing the audience laugh, and receiving applause.

These plays are light entertainment — fun to do and loved by audiences. Tim Kelly's plays can be done with minimal technical work. Also, many of his plays can be straight or musicals (purchasing the cassette tape/CD with all the music already recorded makes it a much easier musical to do).

Each year in March, I continued presenting one of Tim Kelly's plays, and the audiences kept growing. I would do a more artistic play in the fall.

Finally, I went to my principal feeling I had totally betrayed my students and myself by doing "this kind" of theatre. His answer to me was, "What's wrong with everyone having a good time? Isn't that theatre, too?" You decide.

What to consider when selecting a script

Now that you have read some plays, seen some live theatre, and/or viewed some plays on television and video, how do you pick the one that is best for you? Begin by answering the following four questions. Where do you find the answers? Ask fellow teachers and administrators or look in last year's yearbook.

- ✓ **What was done last year?** You don't want to repeat last year's show.
- ✓ **How was it received?** Play receipts from the business office is one way to gauge this.
- ✓ **Who was in the show last year?** Were there more girls than boys in the cast? What class were they in? This gives you some idea of your talent pool for this year. Your choice of play also depends on the number, gender, physical maturity, talent, and training of the actors and actresses available. Last year's play also shows you the students' interest in theatre. Generally, more girls try out than boys (except in a boy's school), so first consider plays that have more girls' roles or roles that can be either male or female. Take care not to select plays strictly on the number of women's roles. Many of these plays fall into the category of "badly written."

✓ **What technical aspects were used? Scenery? Costumes?** By seeing the pictures in the yearbook, you can tell what kind of set and/or costumes were used or the plain fact that there was no scenery, no costumes, no play, no anything!

By answering these pertinent questions, you're ready to consider more things!

With all the scripts available, what is your job? To pick the one play that best suits your actors, your administration, and your community. For your first production, you do not have to wow the audience with elaborate extravaganzas or Shakespeare. When starting out, pick a show that is based on character, has roles that can be played by either sex (because you do not know who is going to try out), and is entertaining. Often you can have one student play two or three roles if you do not have enough actors; be flexible. Selecting plays that stress character and action rather than complicated costumes, lighting, and set is something both inexperienced directors and actors can handle successfully. Remember, the majority of the audience is there to see friends, sons, or daughters, not the niftiest costumes or set you can create.

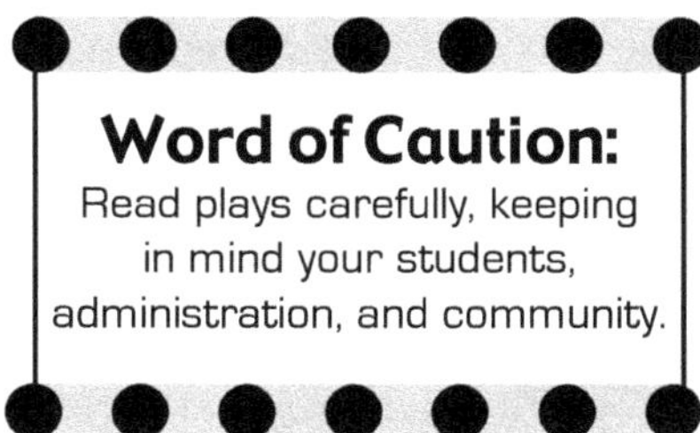

Word of Caution:
Read plays carefully, keeping in mind your students, administration, and community.

If at all possible, pick a show that you are familiar with.

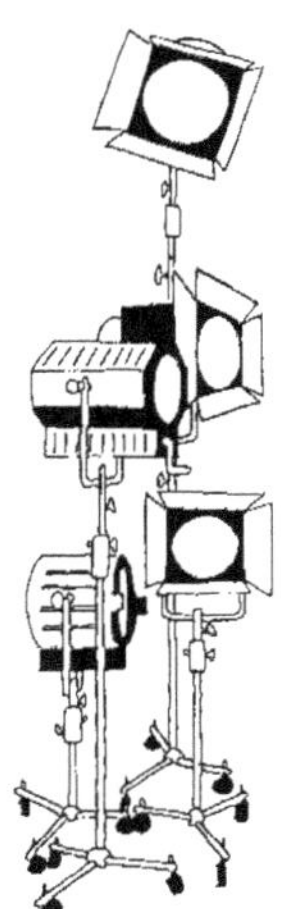

When I began my teaching career, the first show I directed was a courtroom drama. I had done the research and knew the three-act play very well. I liked the play, and it had never been done at Sentinel. I was enthusiastic. (It is the only show I have done five times!) Even if it did open the night of President Kennedy's assassination, I felt good about my production because I knew the show, had created very interesting characters, and the audience loved the gimmick of picking the jury out of the audience.

Be sure that the play you select not only meets your requirements, but also is a show that you really want to do. You are going to be spending a great deal of time with it — a minimum of eight weeks! Remember that you have many people to convince that this show is great and fun and the thing to do: the administration, the students, the faculty, and the community. If you are not totally committed and enthusiastic about it, it is going to be a very long two months. *Enthusiasm! Enthusiasm!*

Student board

Having **student board** members who read and/or watch plays and make suggestions is helpful in selecting plays. It offers an excellent opportunity for students to become more observant and discerning play watchers and readers. It also enables you to hear what interests your students. Take care when listening to students, for often they do not have the background to judge objectively nor do they have the direct responsibility to the principal and the administration. You make the final selection because you are best able to assess which play is best — I repeat — for your actors, your administration, and your community.

Next, you need to consider three more important factors often overlooked when selecting a play: where you will be presenting it, the audience, and the play's length.

Location

Where is the play being performed? The facilities definitely affect the choice of play. The location of the space may limit the size of the audience and influence the budget. The size of the acting area may limit the number of characters in the play. The lighting available may limit shows that require special effects, as well. The construction area may limit plays that require specific types of settings. While considering your limitations, do not become paralyzed with fear. Imagination and creativity (covered in the technical chapters) are designed to help you and your students overcome many obstacles. If you have no limitation then, "The world is your oyster!"

Audience

Consider your audience. The play must captivate them. You never want your audience walking out and shrugging, "so what?" The audience expects and has a right to take something with them when they leave the theatre. The play chosen, therefore, needs to provoke thought, amuse, delight, and/or inform. Remember the audience has — first and foremost — come to be entertained.

Length

The length of the production is extremely important. Television influences people's concentration. Any show lasting longer than two hours, including an intermission, pushes the limits of the audience's attention span. Often, doing a show with no intermission and having it last an hour and fifteen to an hour and thirty minutes works well. Children's shows in particular should never run more than an hour. Even a musical should not last any longer than two hours.

Cuttings

Most play publishing companies define a **cutting** as: a play cut to time, with scenes in original order, with no additions, alterations, or substitutions, and without character or gender changes. They consider written requests for gender changes as a casting consideration only. Usually, cuttings require approval by the publishing company. They can approve most cutting requests shortly after they are received, but changing gender may take much longer and may require the playwright's approval. Because you are working with production deadlines, send your cutting request in early. (Some approvals can take up to eight weeks.) Although the publishing company will make every effort to get your cutting approved, all of their plays and musicals are protected by international copyright law, which means that any alterations, deletions, or substitutions are prohibited by law except with prior written consent of the copyright holder (usually the author).

Most (but not all) authors allow their plays to be cut. Some playwrights feel so strongly about the integrity of their work that they will not approve cuts of any kind, while others will approve a cutting for a school play festival competition only, and still others are happy to oblige almost all cutting requests. Any changes made after your cutting is approved must also be approved.

A few tips

When submitting a cutting request, remember that dialog and characters cannot be added! Changes cannot affect the context or cultural overtones of the play or subvert the playwrights intent. If the play is a dramatization of a screenplay or novel, you cannot add additional characters, music, or dialog from that screenplay or book. You must work with what is in the play. If a play is not written as a musical, it cannot be changed into one by adding "musical numbers." Underscoring and transitional music may be added with discretion if the music is either original, in the public domain, or licensed through the proper agency.

Your first reading

After selecting several plays to examine, begin your evaluation of each play by carefully reading all the information given on sets, costumes, or any special effects for each play. This helps you visualize what everything looks like and gives you an idea of what is technically necessary for your production.

It is best to read a play in one sitting without interruptions. You want to get the total feeling of the play. The people viewing the play will see it in one sitting. Read the script very quickly. You are not studying the play at this time. It should not take you more than two hours to read most scripts. You will do this for each of the plays you have selected. See Example 4: 1st Play Read-Through Form (page 40). A blank form for your use can be found in the Additional Resources section. Keeping forms on all the plays you see and read gives you a wealth of plays to draw from. It takes time to fill out the form, but is well worth the effort.

Administrative approval

Before you make your final decision, present your choice and/or choices to the administration, keeping in mind that a script which primarily deals with characterization allows you to cast a wide variety of students. The more students in your production, the more valid it becomes, not only to the audience but also to the administration, faculty, and students.

You must get the total support of your administration. Open communication is the best way to do this, which means receiving prior approval of your script. It's hard enough to produce the play; you do not need any additional roadblocks once you are in production.

You have been examining several scripts and have a good idea of what you want and can do. Take the script(s) to the administration and ask them to read your choices. After they have read them, make an appointment and discuss the choices with them. Get their feedback. If they have any concerns, you need to hear them now, before anything can happen. Anticipating problems with the administration can be helpful because you both will need to be able to defend your choice. Most administrators will not have any problem with your choices. They hired you as their drama director and assume you know what you are doing. Before you leave the office, you all will select the play you want to do. You now have your administration's approval. You and the administration will defend any comments made by faculty, parents, and/or community members. You have all made the choice. There should be no surprises. If for any reason there is a problem later on, you are ready with answers.

1st Play Read-Through Form

Name of play *A Midsummer Night's Dream* **Publisher** *Performance Form*

Author *William Shakespeare* **Royalty** *$0*

Comments: What is the play about?
Three worlds — the real world, the fairy world, and the workmen's world. Teenagers run from authority (real world) to the woods (fairy world) to escape, and chaos ensues. Actors (workmen) are not bright, are unimaginative, and are putting on a play for the Duke. Girls stay constant in their love for the boys, but the boys change! There is a fight between the King and Queen of the fairies, but in the end all is resolved. The girls get the guys they love, the workmen produce the "worst" play ever performed, and the King and Queen of the fairies live happily ever after. One of the workmen must be a man (Bottom), the fairies must be girls, and possibly adults could play the father, Duke, and Hippolyta. Bottom must sing, dance, wear an Ass's head — be a very versatile actor. Puck needs to be a real character, Can add fight scene between the two boys, and an almost-fight scene between the two girls. Great teenage roles. Pyramis must also be very versatile.

Type of play: Comedy *X* Drama *X* Farce____ Musical____

Length: 1 Act____ 2 Act____ 3 Act____ other *5 Acts*

Scenes: 1 2 3 4 5 (6) more____

Setting: Interior____ Exterior *X*

Where: *Athens and a nearby woods*

When: Future____ Present____ Past *X*

Time: Year *1590s* Spring____ Summer *X* Fall____ Winter____

Time span: *Several days* (minutes-years)

Cast: Men *12* Women *9*

Types: Adults *X* Students *X* Character *X* Children *X* other *fairies*

Does it have: Walls____ Doors____ Windows____ Fireplace____ Chairs *X* Tables *X*
Platforms *X* Staircase____ Bookshelves____ ***OR***
X Can be done on a blank stage just using curtains, suggesting walls, doors, and windows

Costumes:

X Period (clothes which are from a different time period than we live in now)

____Modern (clothes which we wear today)

X Special (elaborate)

General Feeling
What did you feel after reading it? Did you like it? Was it stupid, great, funny, touching, exciting, wordy, dream-like, full of remembrances, light as a feather, or fluffy? (Don't mull this over, just jot down your initial impression. this often becomes your concept or idea for the show. First impressions are seldom wrong.)
Very funny — magical — typical teenage reaction to authority — confusing

What color(s) do you see the play in, if any?
Blues and greens for fairies, brown for workmen, velvet for Duke.
Because we're outside and it is very difficult to recreate the outside, it must be magical, somewhat dark because it takes place at night. also, there are many scenes, so it must be simple. Don't want the show to drag — it's got to move. Maybe using lights is the way to go — do area lighting with very little set.

Example 4: 1st Play Read-Through form. Blank form on page 233.

Chapter 4
Script Exploration

Getting to know the script is the most arduous part of your job. You are going to read and reread the script, taking many notes and thinking theatre. You will also be researching the period in which the play takes place including costumes, architecture, and any other thing for which the script might call. Understanding the script backwards and forwards may be time-consuming, but the rewards are worth it.

Second read-through

Read your script a second time — very carefully. You are trying to translate the play into a theatrical impression that will convey to the audience how you feel about the play. Use your imagination. There are two things to do while you read the script: take notes on characterization and find your concept. This reading takes time because you are envisioning the whole show.

Characterization

Look at the individual characters. Visualize them and take notes. Theatre is a tool that helps individuals understand human nature, learn about themselves, and attempt to solve human problems. This involves personality, activity, sociology, and psychology. In other words, it is a study of people. See Example 5: 2nd Play Read-Through Form (page 47). A blank form for your use can be found in the Additional Resources section. Use one sheet for each character. The following information on each character is just part of the information you will need.

- ✓ Is the character in one scene or every scene?
- ✓ How old is the character?
- ✓ Does the character possess any eccentricities?
- ✓ What does the character wear? Does the costume have to be specially made?

You become the authority by creating — imagining — each character in your head. The insight you feel, see, and internalize will help clarify for you and your actors the characters' needs; therefore you will clarify the play's needs. This research of the play through its characters as well as your visualization will also help your actors imagine and create better characters at tryouts when you tell them what you want.

Finding a concept

"OK, I've drunk my three bottles of pop, broken several sharp pencils, used reams of paper, and filled out the cards on each character. Now what do I do?" You have read the play very thoroughly for the second time and visualized all the characters. You have used your imagination. You were consciously or unconsciously getting a strong feeling about the play and what the playwright was saying. You can now answer the following questions:

- ✓ What came to you when you were done reading the play? What did you imagine?
- ✓ Did you see the show in a color, sound, object, word, and/or phrase? (Was there a line in the play that seemed to express the whole thing?)

The answers will become your **concept**. A concept is the broad idea or theme of the play. This concept may be as concrete as a word like *confinement* for *The Diary of Anne Frank* or *memories* for *I Remember Mama*, or an abstraction such as a feather boa for *Hello, Dolly* or a spider web for *Macbeth*.

The concept can come in many forms. The four listed below are ones I have used before.

- ✓ *David and Lisa,* a play about mentally disturbed teenagers, must be played with very real characters. David is afraid of being touched. He thinks that "a touch can kill." In the end he has to save Lisa, and the only way he can do that is by touching her. We used two hands reaching for each other as our visual concept and two key lines for a more cerebral concept (which helped all the actors find their characters): "It's not important what others think of us, it is important what we think of ourselves," and, "We're all combinations, weak in some areas, strong in others."
- ✓ *Music* was our concept for *The Curious Savage*. The characters in this play live in a rest home for the mentally ill. They are not dangerous or mean, but lovable, endearing, and a little eccentric. Ravel's "Five O' Clock Fox Trot" was perfect.
- ✓ *Annabelle Broom* is a most delightful children's show about a witch whose only desire is to be dressed completely in pink. Obviously the show's concept is the color pink. Annabelle, dressed in gray for most of the show, does, of course, get her wish, coming out in the final scene dressed completely in pink. Staying with color for our concept, we dressed the other witches in appropriate colors: Mable, the head witch, in red; the gossipy Lydia in green; sleepy Maud in blue; and stupid Esther in orange.
- ✓ *Magic* is the key word for *A Midsummer Night's Dream.* The show must be magical. Using purple, green, and silver Mylar wrapping paper for the costumes gave the shimmering illusion of fairies. In my mind, fairies symbolize magic. Creating the forest out of silver Christmas decorations and small white twinkling lights added to the magical effect.

Third read-through

The third read-through of the script includes four very different items: **research, technical aspects, rehearsal segments**, and **tryout scenes**. As you read the play the third time, you will be reading in snatches, going back and forth through the script, time and time again.

Research

Depending on what play you are working on, you will need to do different research, whether it be to look at period costumes, interview a World War II Prisoner of War, read about mental illness, or find a book on "standard practice" to figure out a technical problem. A play always takes place at a given time that must be projected visually to the audience. Each play is unique and requires something different. The script will dictate what you need to know. Take time and find out.

Technical aspects

When an audience enters the theatre with programs in hand, what do they see — a closed curtain, a set, or a blank stage? As the curtain opens and/or the lights come on, what they see — before a word is spoken — establishes where they are or that they are nowhere in particular. Stop and think. When we go to a theatre festival, most schools performing plays do not have a set or special lighting. They all do their plays on the same stage with little or no scenery. Yet we are transported wherever they want us to be. We accept their conventions; the same is true for your production. If you have created colorful, believable characters and we can see them, we will accept anything you choose to do technically.

Before the first actor says a word, what does the author say about where you are? Nearly all plays require certain things, as prescribed by the playwright, i.e. doors, windows, levels, special pieces of furniture, or fixtures. Note the locations suggested by the script. Ask yourself, "Does it have to be there, or are there other possible locations?" You have already visualized and written down information about each character. Now you need to imagine these characters in some setting to tell this story. You also need to include props that help tell the story.

Fill out the 3rd Read-Through "required technical aspects" form (found in the Additional Resources section). See Example 6: 3rd Play Read-Through Form (page 48). This, too, will take a great deal of time, but when you are done, you will know what you need and want for your production. Once the form is filled out, make a floor plan. See Example 7: Floor Plan for *A Midsummer Night's Dream* (page 48). Blank floor plans for your use can be found in the Additional Resources section. This is like making a map of where everything is (doors, windows, chairs, tables, couches, trees, bushes) so your actors will know where to go. You start mapping out your floor plan by answering the following questions:

✓ **How much space is available?** Measure your stage from the act curtain to the back wall and from the edge of the act curtain Stage Right to the edge of the act curtain Stage Left, when the curtain is fully open. Write these measurements down because you will need them very soon.

✓ **What are the sightlines for your stage?** Sit in the front of your audience area as far right as possible; then look at the stage. How much of the offstage area can you see? Especially note how much of the backstage area is exposed near the front curtain line. Next, move to the far left of audience area; repeat the procedure again, moving to the center.

If your stage is in the gym or cafetorium (the area where all the students eat that has a stage at one end; chairs are put up when a play is presented, much like when you do a play in the school gym), you will need to set up a chair where the front row is usually placed for play performances. It might be wise to check with the head custodian since he/she usually is in charge of setting up the chairs. If your auditorium has a balcony, it must be checked as well, particularly from the front-row seat in the center, as you will need to observe what the audience is going to see.

These are called **sightlines** — you have sat in the auditorium and seen what the audience will see. You have sighted! They help you determine how far the act curtain must be closed to hide or mask the backstage area. You may want to experiment with your sightlines by closing the curtain just a little and taking another look at the stage. Be sure to measure how far the curtain is closed.

To make your floor plan:

✓ Look at either the front or the back of your playscript. Often there is a floor plan already designed. You will have to decide if you can use it. If you can, make sure of where you want to specifically put the furniture. If you do not want to use this floor plan, it will at least give you a "jumping off" point for your own floor plan.

✓ With the dimensions you have from your measurement of the stage and the sightlines, begin a rough floor plan of the set. Start with something that looks like a cross between an open triangle and a parallelogram. This allows the majority of the audience to see the action and the actors at all times.

First draw a scale diagram of the stage (one-half inch equals one foot is excellent for this purpose). You need to determine how many doorways or openings you need and the relative importance of each. Now plan the placement of major furniture, etc., depending on how much acting space is needed. You are mainly concerned that furniture placement provides:

✗ Suitable space for your actors to carry on their dialog;

✗ Enough places for your actors to sit; and

✗ No obstruction to the flow of traffic (people coming in and out).

You know that when you block your play (put action to the words the characters say) you will need:

- ✗ Variation of movement to and from an acting area;
- ✗ Variation in your grouping within the acting area; and
- ✗ More than one strong acting area.

Taking into account the largest number of people on your stage at one time, how much space will they need to avoid congestion? Also consider the relationship of frequently-used doorways to the placement of the furniture. Many directors place only furniture that is absolutely necessary on-stage. Their reasoning is that too much furniture clutters the acting and traffic areas. On the other hand, too little furniture may give the stage a barren look and, more importantly, offer insufficient areas for actors to group themselves comfortably. What you want to create is a stage broken up into several playing areas, mostly established by the furniture.

You must be concerned, too, with the placement of bulky pieces of furniture such as sofas. If they are positioned so that they mask the bottom half of actors using important doorways, they limit the theatrical value of entrances and exits.

When you have placed your entrances, exits, and basic furniture, keeping in mind your acting areas, that is just about it! All the rest is just atmosphere or icing on the cake.

Rehearsal segments

You now need to read the script (yes, again!) to devise rehearsal segments and tryout scenes. These rehearsal segments specify the pages that you will rehearse in a given period of time. Generally you can work with about twenty pages during one two-hour rehearsal period. There are several ways of doing this:

- ✓ **Divide your play into approximately twenty-page segments.** You will come out with either three or four. Try to make the segments equal. Having twenty pages or fewer in a one-day rehearsal period allows time to go over scenes more than once. If the segments come out with an uneven number, make the larger segments at the beginning of the play. Having the shorter segments at the end of the play allows more time to work on the most important part of your play — the climax.
- ✓ **Divide your play by the characters that appear in the various scenes.** Actors playing characters who appear in all of the scenes/acts of your play generally attend all the rehearsals. But if a character appears in only one scene or several pages in Act I and Act II, try to put these scenes together so as not waste the actors' time. Start with a character's entrance and go to when they exit. Rehearsing scenes out of sequence will not hurt the show. You will rehearse the play in proper order during the last weeks of the rehearsal period. See Example 8: Rehearsal Segments for *A Midsummer Night's Dream* (page 49).

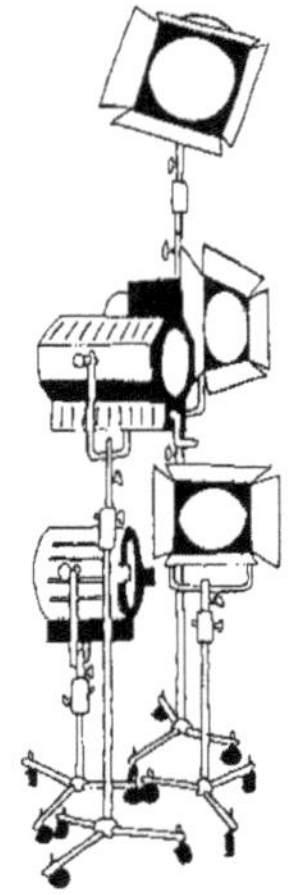

A Midsummer Night's Dream was divided into four segments: the real world with the father and lovers; the lovers with Puck and Oberon; the fairy world with Bottom; and the workmen's world. Each world was rehearsed one day a week for six weeks. Then the show was put together. (See Example 9: *Midsummer* rehearsal schedule on page 50.)

Tryout scenes

Tryout scenes are short scenes from the selected play for students to act/read at tryouts. As you were reading for the rehearsal segments, you also needed to keep in mind the scenes you want to hear at tryouts. These scenes let your actors shine and help you judge who will be best for a given role. Pick scenes that allow you to see and hear your actors "strut their stuff." Do not select scenes with more than four people. It is even better if the scenes involve only two characters. Try very hard never to pick something from the end of the play. You do not want to give anything away. However, if a character must die, laugh, or yell, include that scene in the tryout. This is something special that only that character does and the actor you select must be able to do it. Include the major characters in your scenes. You often will not have scenes for all the characters in the play, but you must have the major characters represented.

Always try to find monologs for several of the characters, even if you have to put several speeches together. There are always those students who do not or cannot find partners, so they will have something they alone can try out for.

Time the tryout segments so they do not exceed two minutes. Reading them out loud yourself is a good way to judge. Tryouts that are less than two minutes are even better. You can tell almost instantly if the actor is good (you do not need two minutes). If you have to sit and listen to these tryouts for several hours, it gets very boring.

Mark the pages you have selected in your script and be ready to copy them. Then you will cut and paste the copy while you are preparing your tryout sheets. Typing the scenes is also possible, but copying them is much faster. You also will want to mark pages or scenes you might like to see at callbacks. (See Chapter 6). These scenes are either too long or have too many characters to be tryout scenes.

Final note

Congratulations! You have completed the most time-consuming part of your preparation: you have studied the script and filled out character cards, you have identified the concept and the required technical aspects, you have researched aspects of the play as required and decided on rehearsal segments and tryout scenes. Whew! You accomplished this with a great deal of time and, more importantly, organization — one of the three essentials mentioned in the introduction. Now you are ready to make your rehearsal schedule and try-out sheets. Yes, I know. You want to get started with the play. You are tired of all this paperwork. Believe me, it will be a godsend. Just hang in there for one more chapter. The fun is about to begin.

2nd Play Read-Through Form
Character Analysis/Costume Card

Play *A Midsummer Night's Dream* **Character's Name** *Bottom/Pyramus*

Description of character in the script: *A weaver*

Gender: Male *X* Female___ Either___

Description of costume in the script: *None*

Age: *25-50* **Occupation:** *A weaver who thinks he can act — other workmen think he can, too*

Character's relationship with others:

Married to__________ Single *X* Divorced from __________ Enemy of __________

Friend of *other craftsmen* Father of______________ Mother of______________

Brother of______________ Sister of______________

Time period of the play: *1590s*

When do they appear in the play?

Act 1/Scenes *2* Act 2/Scenes _____ Act 3/Scenes *1*

Act 4/Scenes *all* Act 5/Scenes *1*

Time span of character's involvement:

Minutes_____ Hours_____ Days *X* Weeks_____ Months_____ Years_____

Adjectives (list at least 2): *Loud, awful actor, boastful, gullible, clown, innocent*

Character's want or goal in life: *To be the finest actor in the world and play all the parts in playlet.*

Character's actions: Act Silly *X* Cry *X* Dance *X* Die *X* Fight *X* Kiss *X*

Laugh *X* Recite poetry *X* Scream___ Shout *X* Sing *X* Fall *X* Jump *X*

Lounge/ Pose *X* Run *X* Sit *X* Walk *X* Other___

Size of role: Large *X* Medium____ Small____

Importance to plot: Major *X* Minor____

Is there a line or phrase that describes the character? *Titania says, "Me thought I was enamoured of an ass."*

Does the character need to change clothes? Yes *X* No____

Why?: *He wears an ass's head and plays "manly" character in playlet*

If the character needs to change costumes can any of the following be used?

Apron_____ Blouse_____ Coat_____ Gloves_____ Hat_____ Purse _____

Shawl_____ Shirt_____ Skirt_____ Sweater_____ Tie_____ Vest_____

Other *something that can be added to make him heroic, possibly armor, a helmet*

Example 5: 2nd Play Read-Through Form. Blank form on page 234.

3rd Play Read-Through Form

Required Technical Aspects: *A Midsummer Night's Dream*

Something for the actors to sit on, either in the woods or the town. Must have two distinct worlds — the real world of Athens and the magical world of the fairies. Something theatrical for the workmen to use when they give their "play."

What do you need?	Yes	How many?	Why?
Furniture			
Benches	✓	?	*Depends on what I have for actors to sit on*
Stools	✓	2	*Depends on what I have for actors to sit on*
Tables	✓	?	*Maybe we need it, have seen it used in other productions*
Other			
Can curtains work?	✓		*As trees*
Props			
Hand props (books, umbrellas, papers, etc.)	✓		*Flower, scrolls, ass's head, book, various costume pieces needed for playlet, lion's head, scarf, dog, etc.*
Set props (drinking glasses, plates, baskets, food, maps, pictures, etc.)	✓		*Wall in playlet, something for all the lovers to sit or perch on while watching playlet. Also, some kind of curtain.*
Lamps	✓		*Used in playlet*
Music	✓		*Elizabethan music for the various dances in the play. The fairies dance several times and the workmen dance after the play. Need music as transition from one world to the other. Sound effects: woods noises, theme songs for the playlet.*
Special effects/ lighting	✓		*The real world needs harsh white light, while the woods need to be lush, magical, green/blue, somewhat dark — need to have area lighting because the set is the same woods but the script calls for different places in the woods. Little white Christmas tree lights and silver Christmas decorations used in the evening scenes. Very magical.*
Platforms/levels	✓	5	*We have them and it adds levels and more interest for the viewer, rather than everything being on the same plane. Also can use one for playlet and the opening scene.*

Example 6: 3rd Play Read-Through Form. Blank form on page 235.

Final floor plan, include everything you have said you need.

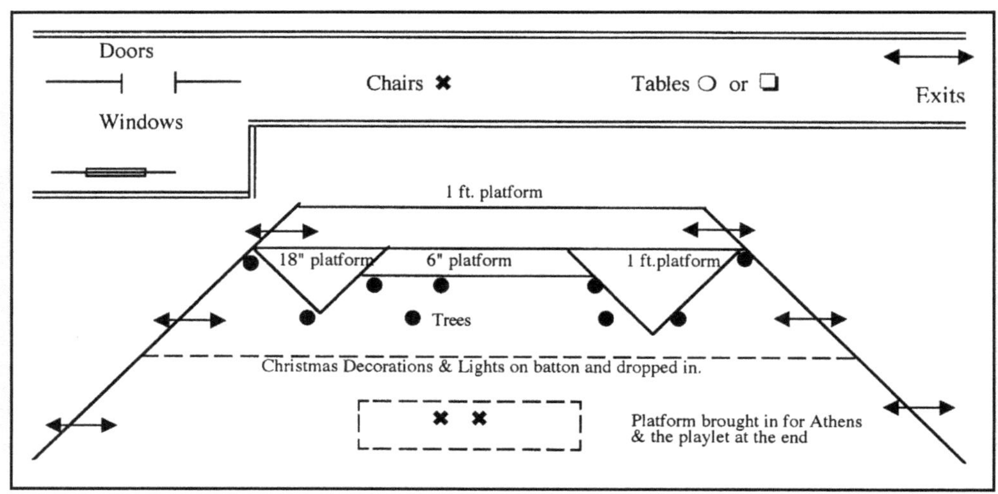

Example 7: Floor plan for *A Midsummer Night's Dream*

The Perfection Form Edition — A parallel text edition was used. It was divided into four sections for rehearsal purposes. Each section or group met one night a week for a number of weeks. Then we put the whole show together and worked with either acts or the full show. These pages are listed without cuts.

Rehearsal Segments for *A Midsummer Night's Dream*

The show is divided into 2 acts: Act I pp. 3-73 and Act II pp. 74-147.

Group 1 LOVERS

7-9 PM

Lysander, Demetrius, Hermia, Helena
pp. 3-17, 39-41, 47-53, 113, 75-89

Group 2 LOVERS and ADULTS

7-8 PM

Lysander, Demetrius, Hermia, Helena, Theseus, Egeus, Philostrate, Hippolyta
pp. 3-17, 107-111, 121-143 (only practicing their lines, not seeing the play within a play)

8-9 PM

Lysander, Demetrius, Hermia, Helena, Oberon, Puck
pp. 49, 71-74, 89-97

Group 3 FAIRIES

7-8 PM

Oberon, Titania, Robin, Head Fairy, Peaseblossom, Cobweb, Moth, Mustardseed, Bottom
pp. 27-31, 45-47, 63-67, 101-105, 143-147

8-9 PM

Oberon, Titania, Robin
pp. 31-39, 43, 69-71, 91-93

Group 4 WORKMEN

7-9 PM

Quince, Bottom, Flute, Snout, Snug, Starveling, Puck
pp. 19-25, 57-63, 115, 125-141

Example 8: Rehearsal Segments for *A Midsummer Night's Dream*

Rehearsal Schedule for *A Midsummer Night's Dream*

January 1999

Monday	Tuesday	Wednesday	Thursday	Friday
4	5	6 Tryouts	7 See movie	8
11 WORKMEN pp. 19-25, 57-63 Read & Cut	12 LOVERS & ADULTS pp. 3-17 Read & Cut	13 LOVERS 1 pp. 39-41, 47-53 Read & Cut	14 FAIRIES pp. 27-31, 45-47, 31-39, 43 Read & Cut	15
18 WORKMEN pp. 19-25, 57-63 Block	19 LOVERS & ADULTS pp. 3-17 Block	20 LOVERS 1 pp. 39-41, 47-53 Block	21 FAIRIES pp. 27-31, 45-47, 31-39, 43 Block	22
25 WORKMEN pp. 19-25, 57-63 Off Book Check publicity	26 LOVERS & ADULTS pp. 3-17 Off Book	27 LOVERS 1 pp. 39-41, 47-53 Off Book Check costumes	28 FAIRIES pp. 27-31, 45-47, 31-39, 43 Off Book	29

February 1999

Monday	Tuesday	Wednesday	Thursday	Friday
1 WORKMEN pp. 19-25, 57-63 Working Check props	2 LOVERS & ADULTS pp. 3-17 Working Tickets due	3 LOVERS 1 pp. 39-41, 47-53 Working	4 FAIRIES pp. 27-31, 45-47, 31-39, 43 Working Program check	5
8 WORKMEN Working Costume check	9 LOVERS & ADULTS Working Costume check	10 LOVERS 1 Working Costume check	11 FAIRIES Working Costume check	12
15 WORKMEN Working Program due	16 LOVERS & ADULTS Working	17 LOVERS 1 Working	18 FAIRIES Working	19
22 ACT 1 Costumes due Lights due	23 ACT 2 Costumes due Lights due	24 ACT 1 Costumes due Lights due	25 ACT 2 Costumes due Lights due	26

March 1999

Monday	Tuesday	Wednesday	Thursday	Friday
1 ALL TECHNICAL EVERYONE	2 ALL TECHNICAL EVERYONE	3 ALL TECHNICAL Performance during school	4 ALL TECHNICAL Performance during school	5 ALL TECHNICAL Performance Evening

Character Groups

LOVERS 1
Lysander, Demetrius, Hermia, Helena

LOVERS and ADULTS
Lysander, Demetrius, Hermia, Helena, Theseus, Egeus, Philostrate, Hippolyta Oberon, Puck

FAIRIES
Oberon, Titania, Robin, Head Fairy, Peaseblossom, Cobweb, Moth, Mustardseed, Bottom

WORKMEN
Quince, Bottom, Flute, Snout, Snug, Starveling, Puck

Example 9: *Midsummer* Rehearsal Schedule

Chapter 5

Rehearsal Schedule Made Easy

Rehearsal schedules

Rehearsal schedules are complicated because you are dealing with all the actors' schedules, your schedule, the schedule for the theatre area, the school's schedule, *and* trying not to waste anyone's time! Your rehearsal schedules must be done before you have tryouts. Giving the rehearsal schedule out before tryouts begin allows students to know the time involved in this extracurricular activity. They can then choose whether or not to make the commitment to your production.

You also want to consider your needs and your actors' needs. A well-planned rehearsal schedule considers everyone's needs and is, at the very least, common courtesy. It will prevent hours of frustration later on in the rehearsal period. Organization of a rehearsal schedule is the real key to successful rehearsals.

Your personal needs

Your own needs must be taken into account first so you don't resent your students or the drama program because you failed to take or make time for yourself. Remember when you were reading your play and discovering your character's wants? This is your want. Before making any rehearsal schedule, consider your personal needs and commitments. You have to take care of yourself, and during the run of your production you need to pamper yourself. Maybe you need to give yourself a night off or early break in one rehearsal. Consider this a treat. Remember, everyone needs a treat every once in a while!

Actors' needs

Next consider your actors. Remember, they have classes to attend every day, homework, jobs, other extracurricular commitments, chores to do at home, and parents' demands. In addition, actors can sit around and do nothing for an hour while waiting for their moment on-stage. There is nothing more distracting than having actors kill time by making noise or getting into trouble backstage because they are bored.

Weekly rehearsal schedule

Organizing segments

Refresh your memory by looking at the segments you decided on in Chapter 4. You divided your play into four segments. These segments become the four days of your rehearsal week. Rehearsing four days a week for a period of six to eight weeks (if you are organized) is enough. Four days of rehearsals per week allows:

✓ Many students to become involved in theatre.

✓ You too have a private life.

Organizing your week

You will need to decide which four days of the week to rehearse by checking the total school calendar and your administration's policy for after school/after supper use of the building. There are five considerations:

✓ Rehearsing during the week may allow you to cast athletes and students who work on weekends.

✓ Rehearsing on Fridays and Saturdays can be a problem if you have weekend athletic events or students with weekend jobs. Administrations may also have rules about building use during the weekends.

✓ Friday and Saturday may be the best time for rehearsals if athletics events occur during the week — with prior approval of the administration, of course!

✓ Saturday morning rehearsals can accommodate schools that have one night during the week for church meetings as well as leaving Friday night open. (Everyone wants Friday night off!)

✓ Sundays are generally not allowed. Most states and administrations have policies about Sunday practices and rehearsing.

Next you must decide the time for your rehearsals. There are three options:

✓ **After School** (two hours between 2 and 5 PM, depending on when your school is dismissed) gives everyone the evenings free, but can limit the students who would be available because of other commitments such as music and athletics. It also makes it easier for students who ride buses to make arrangements for rides home.

✓ **After Supper** (two hours between 5 and 9 PM) allows most students who are engaged in after-school activities to work on your production. Students will have to make arrangements for transportation to and from the school. However, this may not be feasible because some administrations do not want the school building open in the evening.

✓ A combination of the two above.

Length of after school/nightly rehearsals

Two hours

The majority of your rehearsals will be for two hours within the time frames discussed above. You and your students are tired after eight hours of school. Everything can be accomplished in a two hour block of time if you:

✓ Are organized;

✓ Have a goal for each rehearsal;

✓ Start and end on time; and

✓ Work with eighteen- to twenty-page segments each night.

Having the two-hour block is somehow psychological, too. Everyone's attention span is much better, including your own. Two hours of intense concentration is enough!

Three hours

When your rehearsals of the act runs (see page 54) start, about two weeks before you open, the length of your rehearsals will extend to two-and-a-half to three hours. The goal is to put the show together and polish it. Running an act, giving notes, and running it again takes time. Running the whole show takes at least ninety minutes. Then there are notes and technical things that need work. Three hours is not out of the question for the last six to eight rehearsals.

Rehearsal groups

A major play requires approximately twenty-seven to thirty-one rehearsal days. (Shakespeare requires at least four extra days for working with the language.) Put your rehearsals into six groups: **read through, blocking, off book, working, act runs,** and **complete runs.**

"OK I've followed you so far, but what are blocking rehearsals versus working rehearsals? I know what a complete run is as well as a read-through rehearsal, but I'm lost!" That's all right. Let's put the rehearsals together, in order. They are covered in great depth in Chapters 6-11.

Read-through rehearsals (one day)

It is always a good idea to start your production with everyone present for the first rehearsal. You will be reading the whole play (from start to finish) with all the cast and crew. This will be the only time everyone will be together until you start your act runs.

Blocking rehearsals (four to six days)

Blocking is stage movement. This is when you tell the cast where to come in, sit, stand, and/or move. These rehearsals are long and tiring. Having only twenty pages a night for a rehearsal segment makes the job of blocking much easier. It allows you time to block your pages and review them each night. Make sure that the actors are writing down all the blocking in their scripts in pencil so it can be changed or erased with ease. When it comes time to memorize, they are not only to remember their lines but also their blocking. Allow one extra day; sometimes things do not get done, so this allows you a night to catch up on anything not blocked.

Off-book rehearsals (five to six days)

Off-book literally means that the actors go through the segments without using their scripts. The key word for these rehearsals is *memorization*. Your actors are giving the characters life and need to begin developing relationships with other characters. They cannot do that if their heads are in their books.

You need to check that each actor has memorized both their blocking and their lines. This means that the actors do not have any scripts in their hands. These rehearsals are hard, frustrating, and extremely important. You must stick to your guns. No books allowed on-stage during this group of rehearsals or afterwards — ever, ever, ever! No "nanny" blankets for the actors! You are *inflexible* here.

You may include in this rehearsal group at least one day when lines are not required to be memorized. Use it for review of the lines and blocking already memorized. This gives actors extra time to spend on memorizing their last set of lines. The actors need that extra day to catch up, and it saves everyone nights of terrible aggravation. All lines must be memorized by the end of this group.

Working rehearsals (eight to twelve days)

Working rehearsals are fun. You are watching your actors become their characters. You are working with them in developing character and motivation. You will notice that these rehearsals take the most time in the schedule. During these rehearsals you also need to check up on your various crews. Make use of the Basic Rehearsal Schedule in the Additional Resources section of this book (page 237). It lists when to check crew work and when to bring each crew to rehearsal.

First full run-through of the show (one day)

This run-through of the whole show is for you. It puts the show together so you can see what your production looks like. It is also for your crew. They need to see the play. Everyone now needs to give the "final push."

Act runs (four days)

Act runs give you time to go through each act twice a night. You need all of your crew people present in addition to your actors. The crew people are going to run the lights and sound just as your actors are running their lines. These are often called *act run-throughs*. These rehearsals and the complete runs are considered *tech week(s)* as well.

Complete runs (two to three days)

The last two to three rehearsal days are complete runs of the show. These rehearsals include everything: acting, lights, sound, costumes, props, makeup, and curtain call. Review the *Midsummer* Rehearsal Schedule in Example 9 (page 50), noting the different types of rehearsals and various deadlines.

Final notes

Good organization of the rehearsal schedule allows you to spend time with your actors and create better productions with fewer rehearsals. Do remember, however, that some students you may want to cast will have other obligations, and to accommodate their schedule, your schedule may change slightly. Be flexible here.

When you set up your schedule try to have the same segments meet the same day each week. If they meet at different days each week, it can be very confusing. It will not take you long to discover the schedule that works best for you.

"All right, I've researched my script, but why must I have this rehearsal schedule before I've even had tryouts?" Two of the things that you will want to cover at tryouts are:

✓ What you expect; and

✓ The hours the actors are going to be committed.

You will not be able to tell your students these things until you have designed your rehearsal schedule.

Act II:

Getting the Show on the Road

Chapter 6

Tryouts

You have spent hours and hours preparing for this wonderful journey. It is time to get the show on the road. The fun is about to begin. All your hard work will soon be given life. It is two weeks before you start tryouts and you need to determine who will be involved with your program. You need to get ready for your anxious performers. The following steps help with this part of your job.

Before the day of tryouts

Student assistant

You have finished your rehearsal schedule, so what's next? You could use some help. Consider selecting one or more students who will help you. These students could be the student assistant directors, but they can have any name you want to give them. For the duration of this book, I will refer to them as student assistants. Their job is to assist you with:

✓ Tryouts;

✓ Movement (blocking), and

✓ Notes.

The student assistants are persons who will not miss any rehearsals, will listen to you, will follow your directions, and will be respected by the majority of the actors. I could not have done my job without their help. I even had more students wanting to be my student assistants than I had plays for them to assist.

The student assistant's job

Pre-Rehearsal/Show

1. Must be the first one at rehearsal area every night.
2. Make a treat list and post it.
3. Make sure the set is ready to go by 7 PM.
4. Don't get into little cliques and talk about "stuff" (sad, happy, etc.). That can be done after you have left the rehearsal.
5. Have a specific game ready for the actors at 6:55.
6. Always have your script, a spiral binder, and pen/pencil.
7. Write down everything.
8. Help others if they need it.

During the Rehearsal and Show

1. Start the rehearsal on time; don't wait for your director to tell you. Remember he or she has a lot on his or her mind.
2. Take notes.
3. Use your eyes and ears. See and listen. You will catch things the director won't. That is the major reason you are there.
4. Anticipate problems and be ready to deal with them.
5. Help with blocking, line memorization, and running lines.
6. Give suggestions to help the actors achieve what the show needs.
7. Always be positive, but firm. You are a director, not a good buddy. You want the actors' respect.
8. Help any crews that need it.

Opening the House (during night(s) of performance)

1. Make sure all the actors are present.
2. Make sure everything is in its proper place and is working (check with all your crew people and make sure they have done their jobs).
3. Do not run around on the stage after the doors have been opened to the public.

After the Rehearsal and the Show

1. Make sure all your crews have done their "clean up".
2. Make sure all equipment and props are put away — basically strike the stage.
3. Cover the piano (if used) and put it away.
4. Make sure everyone has checked in and out with you. The record needs to be perfect. Find time during the rehearsal to mark attendance of everyone.
5. Don't leave unless your director has excused you.
6. Drive home safely.

Advertise

Now is time to get into action! Time to get enthusiastic. Everyone needs to know about the play and the tryouts. The following suggestions will encourage a good turnout. Here is a good place to use your student assistant.

✓ Put a copy of your play in the library for the students to check out and read.

✓ Place notices in the school newspaper.

✓ Make posters to advertise tryouts. Posters will encourage students to talk about the upcoming production and even persuade them to try out. Often student assistants recruit friends to help. The more students involved in the promotion of the play, the more students will try out. See Example 10: Tryout Poster for *A Midsummer Night's Dream* (page 73).

These posters include tryout information as well as:

✓ Name of play;

✓ Date, time, and place of tryouts;

✓ Number of roles; and

✓ Production dates.

At least one week before tryouts put your tryout sheets (see page 62) outside your door. This gives the actors the opportunity to take the sheets without bothering you.

One week before tryouts put daily notices in the school bulletin announcing play tryouts. These announcements tell students and teachers the important dates, a little about the plot and characters, and the ratio of girls to boys in the cast. Change the announcements daily, making them fun and interesting to pique students' interest. A similar announcement should appear in the school paper.

Consider placing a sign-up sheet in the cafeteria during lunch. While the students are eating and chatting, visit various tables and talk up the play. Ask the students to consider trying out or signing up for a crew on the sign-up sheet. Not all those who sign up will come to auditions, but students will see you pitching your program (being enthusiastic), and word-of-mouth will help spread interest.

Remember, you want to let everyone know they are welcome to try out and/or work crews on your production.

How many days of tryouts?

Plan one day of tryouts and one day for callbacks as you are not aware of the degree of your students' talent. These callbacks literally *call back* those students you want to hear try out again. You can also call everyone back if you want, allowing students to try out again. Having callbacks gives you time to check the list of students who originally tried out with the administration for academic approval (to see if their grades are satisfactory) before you cast your show.

Be aware, however, that having two days of tryouts may present these problems:

✓ I found that everyone either waited until the second night to try out or they came to both nights!

✓ Permitting students to miss a tryout due to an appointment sets a precedent. It makes other things more important to them than your drama program. Do not allow special tryouts for those who cannot make it on the date you have selected. If they are that busy, they probably do not have the time to devote to your program. It is better to have dependability than talent that drifts in and out!

Once you have established your program, select the cast as soon as possible — do it the same night as the tryouts or first thing the next day. You will be very aware of your talent and your administration's requirements, and you will have selected a play that fits their abilities. Waiting is a very hard thing to do. Also, waiting several days to a week can cause you more problems with parents. The longer the wait, the more each student thinks they are going to be cast. They also can think the opposite and get involved with another activity. Get the agony over with!

Prepare tryout sheets

The fairest way to handle tryouts is to have **tryout sheets** available for the actors to pick up before the tryouts. These sheets not only have information about the play but also contain information about the crew. These sheets include the following information:

- ✓ Name of the play, the dates of tryouts and the production;
- ✓ Short summary of the plot. Many students trying out do not or will not have a chance to read the play;
- ✓ Comments about the characters. You need to let your actors know how you perceive each character;
- ✓ Number of parts available for both men and women;
- ✓ Rehearsal information — times, length, location, etc.;
- ✓ The one- to two-minute scenes you selected in your third reading of the script (see Chapter 4);
- ✓ If the tryout piece is to be memorized or not; and
- ✓ What crew work is available and the hours required for each technical job.

See Example 11: Tryout Sheets for *A Midsummer Night's Dream* (pages 74-76).

One of the reasons for having a piece memorized at tryouts is to see if there is some care being taken before tryouts. Also, by not having the script in their hands, actors can "strut their stuff." On the other hand, are you scaring some potentially great performers away by asking for memorization? However, if they cannot memorize a two-minute scene, how can they handle a part in a ninety-minute production? You have to decide what you think is best for your situation.

If memorization is optional, it is always interesting to see who cares enough to put the time in to memorize the piece. This can tell you a great deal about the actor.

There is no set of rules for what to do with your crew. The best advice is to make a list of things that you need each crew to do and be sure that the students know their jobs. Because we are very harried with all the things that have to be done, we sometimes forget to tell our students what we expect and then get mad when something is not done. Decide what is most important to you, make your list, and stick to it. The one thing I would recommend is that the person who takes on the job of House Manager be very trustworthy, as they will be handling money. You want to be able to trust that student with your life, as it were! Below is my list for crews and their specific jobs. I made this into a little booklet that I gave out to prospective crew folks.

Lights

(Needed every night of performance and the last two to three weeks of rehearsal.)

Pre Rehearsal/Show

✓ Turn on work lights.

✓ Set up headsets in booth and backstage; test them.

✓ Turn on light board.

✓ Go through a light check. Once check is done, turn off stage lights.

✓ Before opening the house on performance nights, turn off the work lights, turn on pre-show lights.

During Rehearsal/Show

✓ Make cue sheet as given to you by the director (this is a sheet of paper with lines written down that "cue" when to change the lights).

✓ Follow these cues.

✓ Pay attention, take notes.

✓ Ask questions if you do not understand.

After Rehearsal/Show

✓ Turn off light board and dimmer board — don't forget the switch upstairs.

✓ Make sure all headsets are put away.

✓ Turn off work lights.

Sound

(Needed every night of performance and the last three weeks of rehearsal.)

Pre Rehearsal/Show

✓ Get tape/CDs for show, either from the director, friends, or radio station.

✓ Get headphones, little amp., and three floor microphones.

✓ Open the sound room.

✓ Turn on tape/CD player and amp/mixer. Plug in little amp. and headphones.

✓ Make sure the tape/CD is cued up and any microphones and/or headphones are working.

✓ Start introduction music when instructed by director.

During Rehearsal/Show

✓ Make a cue sheet for your sounds, as determined by your director.

✓ Be ready.

✓ Have sounds cued up before needed.

✓ Do not let actors distract you — stay on task.

After Rehearsal/Show

✓ Strike microphones and return to storage, along with the amp. and headphones.

✓ Rewind the tape/remove CD and store properly.

✓ Turn off the power; lock the sound room.

Video

(Needed every night of performance and at rehearsals from the third week on.)

Pre Rehearsal/Show

✓ Get camera as instructed by director.

✓ Set up tripod in aisle, about six rows back, and plug in power cord.

✓ Attach camera carefully, plug it in, put tape in, and check date information and focus.

During Rehearsal/Show

✓ Ask your director what he or she wants taped. Do not tape when rehearsal has stopped and your director is working with actors.

✓ As you learn the show, follow actors using close-up — video is a close-up medium.

✓ When finished with one run-through, eject tape store properly.

✓ Get another tape and resume taping.

After Rehearsal/Show

✓ Store all equipment.

✓ Turn off all equipment.

✓ Lock up all equipment.

Props

(Needed every night of performance and last two weeks of rehearsals.)

Prep work

(Some of this is done on your own time, but it all must be completed two weeks before production.)

✓ Get prop list from student assistant.

✓ Check all areas where props are stored — see director.

✓ Check with actors who may have useable props.

✓ Get substitute props by third week of rehearsal.

✓ Make/Create props, if necessary.

✓ If necessary, look around town at antique stores, dollar stores, secondhand stores, hobby stores, etc.

✓ Don't spend money without permission from director.

Pre Rehearsal/Show

✓ Make sure all props are where they need to be (on-stage, on prop table, etc.)

During Rehearsal/Show

✓ Assist actors with getting correct props as needed.

✓ Keep prop table organized.

After Rehearsal/Show

✓ Put away all props.

Costumes

(Needed every night the first half of rehearsal period.)

Must be able to:

✓ Baste;

✓ Sew buttons;

✓ Hem;

✓ Use sewing machine;

✓ Read, cut out, and use patterns;

✓ Work with costume coordinator with any other necessary tasks.

Set

(Needed first three weeks of rehearsal.)

Set-building tasks

✓ Primarily painting.

- ✗ When painting, be sure you find out about scenic paint and the various techniques used for theatre.

✓ Use of power tools (drills, stapler) may be necessary.

✓ If you do not know or understand, ask.

House Manager

(Needed every night of performance and the last two weeks of rehearsal.)

Pre Rehearsal/Show

✓ Get list of cast and crew from student assistant.

✓ Make tickets for each night of performance (see Chapter 13: Publicity).

During Rehearsal/Show

✓ Hand out tickets (as designated in Chapter 13).

✓ Come to the last six rehearsals and collect any monies that students have collected from advance ticket sales. Keep track of names and money. Be prepared to give out more tickets if needed.

Tryout information sheet/card

This is a simple form you will make up for each student to fill out the night of tryouts. As the students come in, you will give them your tryout information sheet/card and pencils (more than likely they will not have brought any). This card includes:

✓ Their name;

✓ Parents' name, address, and phone number;

✓ Their class schedule;

✓ Any talents they may have like singing, dancing, playing an instrument;

✓ Their obligations after school and/or after supper; and

✓ Part(s) they are interested in.

Leave room on the sheet or card for your notations. The Tryout Information Sheet can be found on page 238 of the Additional Resources section.

Three things to check

Now that your advertising is going strong, your tryout sheets are complete, and you have your tryout information cards prepared, follow these three steps:

✓ Show your administration your tryout sheets. Explain in detail what you are going to do at tryouts and your goals. Most administrations only want to be sure that every student has the opportunity to try out and that the process is fair. There are some administrators who will not want to be bothered with either reading scripts or checking tryouts and rehearsal schedules. They have hired you for the job and assume you know your craft. This is fine, but always make the gesture. This is where diplomacy comes in handy. Give them the choice. Always offer your administration a copy of anything given to students. If they do not read it, it is their prerogative. You have done your job.

✓ Many schools require students involved in any extracurricular activity to buy an activity ticket and/or pay a participation fee to help defray the cost of the activity. Most schools also require some type of academic approval before students can participate in extracurricular activities. Be sure to check this out. The administration may want to review the cast before it is announced or give you a

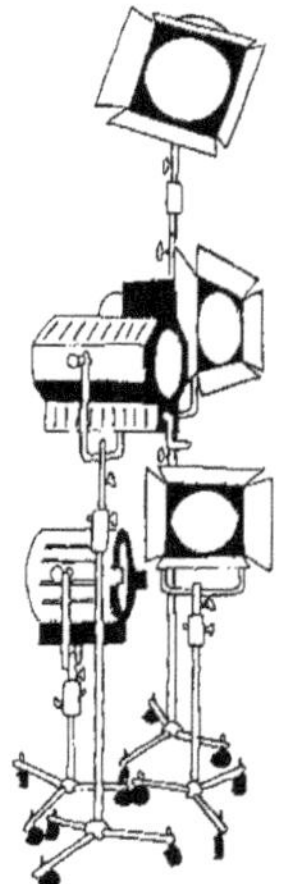

> I decided to do the all male show, *Stalag 17*. Now, this can cause problems, especially today with equal rights and Title 9 (equal opportunity for boys and girls in extracurricular programs). One of my female students asked if she could try out. Without thinking, because I knew I would not cast her, I said "No." Well, did that cause an uproar! She went right down to the administration and said, "This isn't fair!"
>
> I was called to the principal's office that afternoon. He wisely told me to go home and think of how we could solve the problem. He did not suggest that my choice of play was wrong or that the choice be changed to placate the girl's complaint.
>
> The following day I went back to see him and we decided *anyone* could try out. This satisfied the student, her friends who had rallied around her, the administration, and me. We had "all our ducks in a row." On the tryout sheet I stressed the use of girls for all the crews, as well as serving as crew heads. On the night of tryouts, not one girl showed up! Would I have cast a girl in the show? No. But would I have given her the right to try out? Yes.

list of students not eligible due to grades. Follow their instructions. It will eliminate embarrassment for you and the students. Whatever the school policy is, follow it, and be sure that it is covered during tryouts.

✓ Back in Chapter 1, when you requisitioned your area, you also requisitioned the area where you would have tryouts. Check it out and make sure that the space is still available. One never knows!

Day of tryouts

Before you start your tryouts, bring additional tryout sheets (students do lose them), plenty of pencils for students to borrow, your tryout information sheets, and all of your scripts for the play. You might want various students reading scenes that were not covered on your tryout sheet.

Come to tryouts with enthusiasm and an open mind. Be flexible. You never know who is going to try out. You have picked a show that allows you some leeway in gender casting. You also might have to settle for someone who is not what you envisioned for a specific role.

How long should the tryouts take? Usually about two to two-and-a-half hours. It all depends on how many students try out.

Rehearsal schedule

You must also have your rehearsal schedule ready to hand out or discuss with the prospective cast members. It includes:

✓ The production dates;

✓ The weeks of the rehearsal period;

✓ The days of the week you will be rehearsing;

✓ The hours per day you rehearse; and

✓ The time of rehearsals.

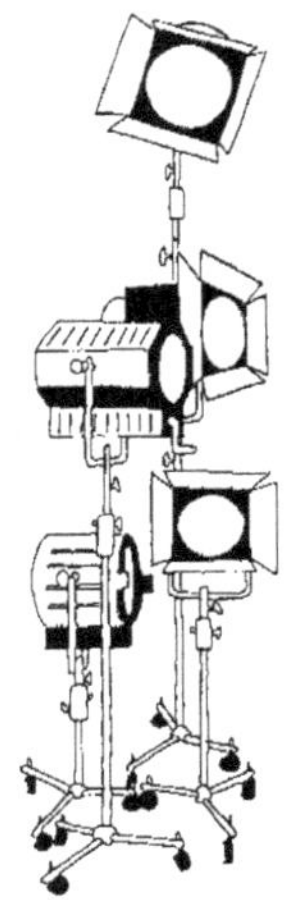

The actor who played Puck in my first *A Midsummer Night's Dream* was about 190 pounds and 6'3". He was not particularly nimble, so we used his size to create a very clumsy, gangly Puck.

Yes, it is true that the students have seen all this information on the tryout sheet, but as we all know, they forget and have to be reminded — often.

Establish your expectations

Begin the tryouts on time, even if students are straggling in. You want them to know from the start that when you say a given time, you mean it. Then do the following:

- ✓ Introduce yourself, your student assistants, and the play. Be enthusiastic. Show them you care about the show. Get them "revved up."
- ✓ Tell the students what you expect from them. This includes:
  - ✗ Those characters needed at every rehearsal;
  - ✗ Those characters who appear less frequently;
  - ✗ The administration's philosophy about the activity ticket and/or the participation fee, as well as eligibility;
  - ✗ The contract, if you are going to initiate it (see Chapter 7); and
  - ✗ That they will be able to read twice for their tryout.
- ✓ Explain your callbacks.

Students who cannot meet the above requirements should not try out. By trying out they understand what you expect, the times involved, and are willing to give their all.

Similarly, if you choose students who indicated on their tryout information card/sheet that they were involved in football, other activities, or work, it is understood that you will not expect them at play rehearsal on days they have other commitments or game days. You have acknowledged that you will not interfere with their commitments. However, students often forget what major activities are coming up — concerts, district/state events, etc. — so you need to be aware of the school calendar as well to remind them of prior commitments.

Two chances to read

After the cards/sheets have been filled out and you have established your expectations, it is time to see the student actors in action. Gather the sheets/cards and call each student up. Plan on each student reading twice. Permit them to read for two different parts when they are called up. Or, you can have everyone read once and then have everyone read again — whichever works for you. By having everyone read once, then a second time, everybody gets a little break between readings, and you are able to see at least two sides of each actor. If they do not have two parts selected, that is fine.

If there are not enough boys to read with all the girls who are trying out, have your student assistants or yourself read the part with the girls. There will always be those few at tryouts who want to read seven thousand times. Do not let them.

What to look for

You have come to this tryout with ideas about each character; you have filled out your character card, using information for the play and your imagination. You know what each character does in the play, their wants, how old they are, and their relationships to others in the play.

How do your actors measure up?

- ✓ Did you ask the actors to have the piece memorized? Did they do it? How well? If not well, could you work with them to accomplish the character you want? If the piece is not memorized, did they know something about the character, or are they reading cold and mispronouncing words with awkward phrasing?
- ✓ Can you hear them?
- ✓ Can you understand them?
- ✓ Was there extra care taken in their tryout? Have they come with some kind of costume or with their hair fixed in a certain way?

Having heard the students read twice for the parts they want, keep in mind that you might not have heard them read for the parts you would select for them. Take a few minutes. Look at your students. Start thinking about your characters and which actors you think would be best for them. Start your casting process.

The casting process

Leave the tryout area and find a quiet place where you can concentrate. (Be sure to put someone reliable — an adult or senior student — in charge of the students in the tryout area. You do not want them wandering all over the building.) Keep in mind one thing: *your show will be no better than the weakest person you cast.* Start by dividing your list of actors into three groups:

- ✓ **Group 1** will be those students you will definitely cast. They are good.
- ✓ **Group 2** will be those students you will need to hear and see again (this will be the largest group).

✓ **Group 3** will be those students whom you definitely will not cast. You have heard enough!

Next, decide which students you want to read for which characters.

Go back to tryouts and, if time permits, call the students up again, giving them a third chance to read, but this time with the part you want to hear from them. Everyone deserves many chances to try out, and the administration loves the fact that each student has more than one chance to be cast. If possible, have all students read again even if you know you will not cast them. Give everyone every chance to shine. This eliminates any possible problems with parents. You have given their child ample opportunity to become involved.

Listen closely to those students you want to hear again. You might even go to the script and have them read a scene you did not have on the tryout sheets. Even though this is a "cold reading," let them show you what they see in the character, vocally and physically. Do keep in mind that some students do not perform a cold reading very well. They stumble, stutter, and are rather bad. All you can do is imagine — just remember how well they did on their prepared piece.

If you are not seeing what you want, give suggestions or stage directions on how to read a line or do an action. Watch how these students react to your direction:

✓ Will they do what you want them to do, or do they say, "I can't do that"?

✓ Can you work with them?

When you are satisfied with all that you have seen and heard, start looking at things like the actor's size, type of voice, dependability, conflicts, and attitude. Jot these things down on your tryout information sheet/card. If you are unsure about some of the things students have written down, ask your student assistant to check with the individual student to clarify any problems.

Announce that you will have callbacks and tell students where to look for the list of names, as well as where and when the callbacks will be. Dismiss everyone. Post the callback list the following afternoon after you have had time to think and check with the administration.

Callbacks

Callbacks are handled the same way as tryouts. The only difference is that the students will be reading for the parts that you have assigned. You have had at least twenty-four hours to do three things:

✓ Select the scenes you want to hear read;

✓ Arrange which students you want to hear reading which characters; and

✓ Check with the administration for eligibility, if needed.

Go through the same process as you did with the first day of tryouts. Callbacks may take two-and-a-half to three hours. You have each actor's tryout information sheet or card from the day or night before, so:

✓ Call roll.

✓ Review your expectations.

✓ Call back the students to read the parts you have selected for them, either from your tryout sheets or the actual script. Be sure to hear everyone you want — sometimes this will mean that you will hear one student several times reading various roles.

✓ Do not be afraid to tell them what you want — direct them. See how they work, not only with you but also with each other. Remember they will be together for the next eight weeks.

✓ Announce to your students when and where the cast list will be posted and the time of the first rehearsal. Be sure to give yourself time to accommodate the administration if you have to check on the academic status of your students. Only then can you post your cast list.

✓ Excuse your students, thanking them for their efforts.

Now it is time to cast your show. "But won't I have tears, anger, and complaints from those who didn't get cast?" That is a distinct possibility. Unfortunately, that is part of your job, so "gird your loins" and start! There is nothing wrong with taking your time the first time you do this. If you need an extra day, take it. You want the best cast possible, especially for your first production. Follow these two steps:

✓ Listen to your student assistants. You have spoken to them in depth about confidentiality. You want to be free to say what you feel and not have it blabbed all over school. They also have the "inside track" on various personalities of which you may not be aware. You not only want the best cast you can have, but you also want your cast members to get along.

✓ Listen to your gut; ninety percent of the time you will be right. You have researched your script, know the show and its requirements, have seen your potential actors, and know their conflicts. You often do not get your ideal, but you have done your homework. You know what the play requires to make it successful. I remind you:

  ✗ Your show will be no better than the weakest person you cast.

  ✗ It is better to cast a person who is dependable than one who has talent but too many commitments.

"OK, I've got my cast list, but I cannot make up my mind between a couple of the actors. They both were very good. They do not have conflicts; they both came to tryouts very prepared. I cannot make a decision. Help!" This is a very valid and difficult part of your job. What do you do? One of three things:

✓ Make the tough decision and cast one of them.

✓ Make the tough decision and cast one of them, but make the other one the understudy. They will come to all rehearsals, write down blocking, and work on character development. Being an understudy is not like being in the play, but it does allow more students to be involved with your production. I personally have never had an understudy, but many directors use them very successfully.

✓ Try double casting. This is when you cast two people in the same role. It is a mixed bag. It certainly allows many more students to become involved in your drama program. It does, however, foster jealousy because of the "Our show is better than yours" syndrome. It also only allows you one-half the time to work with each actor.

After casting the show, some students who are not cast will want to sign up for the crews — let them. Include them in your first rehearsal as well. It is never a good idea to have a wall built up between those who act and those who do technical work. You must all work together to make a successful production.

"OK, I'm brave. I've endured the joy, tears, anger, and complaints. I've 'girded my loins' ... but what if someone drops out? What do I do then?" After you have cast the show, have each of your actors and their parents sign a contract at the first rehearsal (see Chapter 7). Hopefully this will eliminate any dropout problems. If it does not, try one of the following suggestions:

✓ You have other students you did not cast who indicated an interest in the play. They may be working on one of your crews. Contact them.

✓ You have a student assistant who can fill in.

"I can start working on the play!" you shout to the ceiling and anything and anyone within hearing distance. Yes, you can. Congratulations! You did it. Your show is no longer just words on the printed page. It is ready for life. What lies ahead is exciting, exhilarating, and exhausting: the creative part of play production — directing.

Tryout for

A Midsummer Night's Dream

Tuesday, January 6

7PM

Sentinel Little Theatre

Parts for 8 Men, 9 Women,

and 5 who can be either

Production dates: March 3-5

Tryout information: Outside room 155

Example 10: Tryout Poster for *A Midsummer Night's Dream*

Tryout sheets for
A Midsummer Night's Dream
There are 22 parts —
8 for Men, 9 for Women, 5 can be either
January 6th, 7PM, Sentinel Little Theatre

Rehearsals are Monday — Thursday 7-9 PM
Everyone will be needed after February 22nd
Production dates: March 3-5

About the Characters:

The Adults represent authority, both parental and civic. They are the practical ones, very down to earth. THESEUS, EGEUS, PHILOSTRATE, HIPPOLYTA

The Lovers are teenagers and want to escape authority to live the life of freedom and love. LYSANDER, DEMETRIUS, HERMIA, HELENA

The Fairies are anything you would like them to be. they are magical, ethereal, airy, and intangible. OBERON, TITANIA, PUCK, HEAD FAIRY, PEASEBLOSSOM, COBWEB, MOTH, MUSTARDSEED

The Workmen are not magical, ethereal, airy. They are very tangible,not too bright, and extremely unimaginative. BOTTOM, FLUTE, QUINCE, SNOUT, SNUG, STARVELING

About the Crew:

We will need two people on lights; a sound person; folks to help create and sew costumes; a video crew; a publicity crew which includes: tickets, program, and poster; and, a makeup designer.

About the Plot:

Plans for the wedding of Theseus, Duke of Athens, and the Amazon Queen, Hippolyta, whom he has defeated in battle, are being made. Egeus, an Athenian, has promised his daughter Hermia to Demetrius, and although Hermia is in love with Lysander, the Duke orders her to obey her father. The two lovers escape to the forest, followed by Demetrius and Helena, who is in love with Demetrius. Here they are found by Oberon, King of the fairies, his Queen, Titania, with whom he is extremely disgruntled, and the merry Puck. Puck has a magic love-juice that will make the one whose eyelids are anointed fall in love with the first object he sees upon awakening. He uses it somewhat indiscriminately, causing the two boys to change who they are in love with as well as causing Titantia to fall in love with an Ass. A strange comedy ensues, but eventually Demetrius abandons Hermia to Lysander and devotes himself to Helena. At the Duke's wedding feast, which celebrates three weddings: The Duke and Hippolyta; Hermia and Lysander; and Helena and Demetrius. Bottom the Weaver and his group of very unimaginative players present the play (within a play) of "Pyramus and Thisbe," a farce of *Romeo and Juliet.* This playlet is one of the funniest ever written and is the funniest one written by Shakespeare.

The keyword for this production is: *Magical*

Example 11: Tryout Sheets for *A Midsummer Night's Dream* (Page 1)

PUCK

(The chief fairy who gets everything mixed up; can be played by either a man or a woman.)
If we shadows have offended,
Think but this, and all is mended,
That you have but slumber'd here
While these visions did appear.
And this weak and idle theme,
No more yielding but a dream,
Gentles, do not reprehend:
if you pardon, we will mend:
And, as I am an honest Puck,
If we have unearned luck
Now to 'scape the serpent's tongue,
We will make amends ere long;
Else the Puck a liar call;
So, good night unto you all.
Give me your hands, if we be friends,
And Robin shall restore amends.

THISBE

(Played by one of the other workmen in the farce of Romeo and Juliet *— this is "Juliet" who finds her "Romeo" dead. She has just wakened up from her faint. Can be played by either a man or woman.)*
Asleep, my love?
What, dead, my dove?
O Pyramus, arise!
Speak, speak. Quite dumb?
Dead, dead? A tomb
Must cover thy sweet eyes.
These my lips,
This cherry nose,
These yellow cowslip cheeks,
Are gone, are gone:
Lovers, make moan:
His eyes were green as leeks.
Tongue, not a word:
Come, trusty sword;
Come, blade, my breast imbrue:
(Stabs herself)
And, farewell, friends;
Thus Thisbe ends:
Adieu, adieu, adieu.

THESEUS, DUKE OF ATHENS

(One of the adults, not aware of women's rights.)
More strange than true: I never may believe
These antique fables, nor these fairy toys.
Lovers and madmen have such seething brains,
Such shaping fantasies, that apprehend
More than cool reason ever comprehends.
The lunatic, the lover and the poet
Are of imagination all compact:
One sees more devils than vast hell can hold,
That is, the madman: the lover, all as frantic,
Sees Helen's beauty in a brow of Egypt:
The poet's eye, in fine frenzy rolling,
Doth glance from heaven to earth, from earth to heaven;
And as imagination bodies forth
The forms of things unknown, the poet's pen
Turns them to shapes and gives to airy nothing
A local habitation and a name.

QUINCE and BOTTOM:

(Two of the six workmen who are going to put on a play for the Duke on his wedding day. Other than Bottom, the workmen can be played by either men or women.)

QUINCE: Is all our company here?

BOTTOM: You were best to call them generally, man by man, according to the script.

QUINCE: Here is the scroll of every man's name, which is thought fit, through all Athens, to play in our interlude before the duke and the duchess, on his wedding-day at night.

BOTTOM: First, good Peter Quince, say what the play treats on, then read the names of the actors, and so grow to a point.

QUINCE: Marry, our play is, the most lamentable comedy, and most cruel death of Pyramus and Thisbe.

BOTTOM: A very good piece of work, I assure you, and a merry. Now, good Peter Quince, call forth your actors by the scroll. Masters, spread yourselves.

QUINCE: Answer as I call you. Nick Bottom, the weaver.

BOTTOM: Ready. Name what part I am for, and proceed.

QUINCE: You, Nick Bottom, are set down for Pyramus.

BOTTOM: What is Pyramus? A lover, or a tyrant?

QUINCE: A lover, that kills himself most gallant for love.

BOTTOM: That will ask some tears in the true performing of it: if I do it, let the audience look to their eyes; I will move storms, I will condole in some measure. To the rest: yet my chief humour is for a tyrant

BOTTOM (a workman) and TITANIA (Queen of the Fairies)

(Bottom has just been changed into an Ass, so he's wearing an ass's head, but he doesn't know it. Oberon, King of the Fairies, has had Puck put a potion in Titania's eyes so she will fall in love with the first thing she sees.)

BOTTOM: I see their knavery: this is to make an ass of me; to fright me, if they could. I will walk up and down here, and I will sing, that they shall hear I am not afraid.
(Sings.)
The woosel cock so black of hue,
With orange-tawny bill,
The throstle with his note so true,
The wren with little quill, —

TITANIA: What angel wakes me from my flowery bed?
I pray thee, gentle mortal, sing again:
Mine ear is much enamour'd of thy note;
So is mine eye enthralled to thy shape;
On the first view to say, to swear, I love thee.

BOTTOM: Methinks, mistress, you should have little reason for that: and yet, to say the truth, reason and love keep little company together now-a-days.

TITANIA: Thou art as wise as thou art beautiful.

BOTTOM: Not so, neither: but if I had wit enough to get out

Example 11: Tryout Sheets for *A Midsummer Night's Dream* (Page 2)

of this wood, I have enough to serve mine own turn.
TITANIA: Out of this wood do not desire to go:
Thou shalt remain here, whether thou wilt or no.
And I do love thee: therefore, go with me;
I'll give thee fairies to attend on thee,
And I will purge thy mortal grossness so
That thou shalt like an airy spirit go.

DEMETRIUS (who is in love with Herima) and HELENA (who is in love with Demetrius)

(Two of the lovers who have run away to the woods to get away from the authority figures. They find nothing but chaos.)

DEMETRIUS: I love thee not, therefore pursue me not.
Where is Lysander and fair Hermia?
Thou told'st me they were stolen unto this wood;
And here am I.
Hence, get thee gone, and follow me no more.
HELENA: You draw me, you hard-hearted adamant.
Leave you your power to draw,
And I shall have no power to follow you.
DEMETRIUS: Do I entice you? Do I speak you fair?
Or, rather, do I not in plainest truth
Tell you, I do not, nor I cannot love you?
HELENA: And even for that do I love you the more.
I am your spaniel; and, Demetrius,
The more you beat me, I will fawn on you:
What worser place can I beg in your love, —
Than to be used as you use your dog?
DEMETRIUS: Tempt not too much the hatred of my spirit;
For I am sick when I do look on thee.
HELENA: And I am sick when I look not on you.
I'll follow thee and make a heaven of hell,
To die upon the hand I love so well.

LYSANDER (who is in love with Hermia) and HERMIA (who is in love with Lysander)

(The other two lovers who plan to go to the woods to get away from the Duke and Hermia's father because he wants her to marry Demetrius, not Lysander.)

LYSANDER: How now, my love! Why is your cheek so pale?
How chance the roses there do fade so fast?
HERMIA: Belike for want of rain, which I could well
Beteem them from the tempest of my eyes.
LYSANDER: Ay me! for aught that I could ever read,
The course of true love never did run smooth.
HELENA: If then true lovers have been ever cross'd,
It stands as an edict in destiny:
Then let us teach our trial patience.
LYSANDER: A good persuasion: therefore, hear me, Hermia.
I have a widow aunt, a dowager
Of great revenue, and she hath no child:
From Athens is her house remote seven leagues;
And she respects me as her only son.
There, gentle Hermia, may I marry thee;
And to that place the sharp Athenian law
Cannot pursue us. If thou lovest me then,
Steal forth thy father's house to-morrow night;
And in the wood, a league without the town,
Where I did meet thee once with Helena,
To do observance to a morn of May,
There will I stay for thee.
HERMIA: My good Lysander!
I swear to thee, by Cupids strongest bow,
In that same place thou hast appointed me,
To-morrow truly will I meet with thee.
LYSANDER: Keep promise, love. Look, here comes Helena.

Rehearsal Components

Midsummer will be divided into four sections for rehearsal purposes. Each section or group will meet one night a week until February 22nd. Then we will put the whole show together.

Group 1: Lovers

LYSANDER, DEMETRIUS, HERMIA, HELENA

Group 2: Lovers and Adults

LYSANDER, DEMETRIUS, HERMIA, HELENA, THESEUS, EGEUS, PHILOSTRATE, HIPPOLYTA, OBERON, PUCK

Group 3: Fairies

OBERON, TITANIA, PUCK, HEAD FAIRY, PEASEBLOSSOM, COBWEB, MOTH, MUSTARDSEED, BOTTOM

Group 4: Workmen

QUINCE, BOTTOM, FLUTE, SNOUT, SNUG, STARVELING, PUCK

PLEASE HAVE ALL PARTS MEMORIZED — THANKS

Example 11: Tryout Sheets for *A Midsummer Night's Dream* (Page 3)

Chapter 7

First Rehearsal

Now you are getting ready for your first rehearsal. You finally get to work with your students, and you can hardly wait. However, before you start you need to update your rehearsal schedule and contact parents. Then you need to organize the rehearsal with expectations, warm-ups, a read-through of the script, reminders, and your final notes.

Final rehearsal schedule

Before your first rehearsal you need to prepare the final rehearsal schedule. Again we are talking about organization. You and your student assistant have your rehearsal schedule and the information sheets/cards for all the actors and their conflicts, if any. You have cast your show knowing that these conflicts exist. Make any adjustments needed on the schedule, being careful to make the schedule very clear. On this final rehearsal schedule include script page numbers and the characters needed for each rehearsal. Post one of these schedules by your room for easy reference.

Parent support

Including parents and/or guardians is necessary because you need their support and understanding. There are three ways of enlisting their help. Decide which one is best for you.

✓ Give two copies of your rehearsal schedule to your actors and crews — one for themselves and one for their parents. The rehearsal schedule allows parents to know what you expect of their children. Students occasionally use fictitious rehearsals to get out of the house! Sometimes rehearsals run late or you need to have extra rehearsals. If you stick to the schedule, parents are more supportive when adjustments have to be made. If they do not know what is going on, changes cause problems and you can lose an actor or crew person.

✓ Send a letter home to your actors' parents congratulating them about their child making the play, explaining your hopes for the show, and enclosing the rehearsal schedule. This makes the production even more personal. You can have your student assistant write the letter but, of course, you must check it for grammar and accuracy.

✓ Prepare a student-parent contract for both actors and crew. This contract is the best way to eliminate problems and avoid any misunderstandings. The contract includes the rehearsal schedule and your rules and requirements for being a member of the production. It reminds students and parents of their obligation and responsibility to the play. Teaching responsibility to young people usually means that they have to fulfill obligations. (Of course, for your part, you have an obligation to see that students are following the school rules — coming to school daily and maintaining their grades.) Even though parents may not like having to sign a form like this, most do and understand the reason for it.

✗ It is also important to make it clear to the cast and crew that if they do not get the contracts signed within a week (or the time you and your administration agree on), they will be dropped from the cast. This may sound tough, but it can prevent problems later on.

Clear the contract with your administration. They may even want to add something to it. Have it printed on NCR (no carbon required) paper so you can have a copy, the student can have a copy, and the administration can have a copy. See Example 12: Sentinel High School's Theatre Contract (page 82). A blank contract for your use can be found in the Additional Resources section.

Establish expectations — again

When everyone has gathered for the first rehearsal there are four things you do before you start warm-ups and reading the play:

✓ First and foremost, be enthusiastic.

✓ Start on time.

✓ Reintroduce yourself, your student assistant, and the goals for the show. Talk a bit about yourself — tell something that makes you a bit more human. Tell your cast about the show and what you envision the show looking like (the concept).

✓ Pass out the final rehearsal schedule and discuss it. This would also be a good time to reiterate your expectations. Writing them out on the rehearsal schedule would be even better. Everything must be clarified. This is also the time to call your actors' attention to the memorization dates. You will want to point out to them that when you say off book you mean it!

Warm-ups

Allow time during this rehearsal to share in the excitement of undertaking this journey. Play some games. Games not only break the ice but everyone gets to know one another. Warm-ups are easy exercises that get students ready for the work ahead. Actors look forward to these exercises. It makes the transition from home, school, or job to rehearsal easier and much more productive. Spending five minutes at the beginning of each rehearsal with some kind of warm-up gets everyone ready for the rehearsal period. Two that work well are explained below.

- ✓ Everyone is to sit in a circle. Go around the circle and have each student give his or her name and an adjective that would best describe them. You may also add to the game by having them tell why they tried out and give their previous theatre experience. Select one student sitting in the circle, and have him or her go around the circle and try to say everyone's name and one thing about each. Continue until everyone has an idea of who is who.
- ✓ Have everyone sit in a circle and number off. Then you start a rhythm: two claps on the thighs (using both hands), two hand claps together, and then two snaps of fingers. Practice this until everyone can do it. Now comes the tricky part: when the two snaps happen, the person with the number 1 is to say his or her number on the first snap and another student's number on the second snap. Then everyone claps their thighs, claps their hands together and when it comes time for the snaps, the person whose number was called says their number on the first snap and another number in the circle with the second. The trick is to keep a steady rhythm without breaking it because someone does not remember his or her number. If they do not notice when their number is called, have the person who said their number start over.

  In order to make it a bit more difficult, have the person who messes up become the previous number. Of course many people's numbers then change and the trick is to remember your new number. To make it even more difficult, various rules can be put into effect such as no reverse numbers, no number to the direct right or left of you, etc.

I found the games described above in Viola Spolin's *Improvisation for the Theatre*. Two other books that are excellent sources for acting games are: *Theatre Games for Young Performers* by Maria C. Novelly and *More Theatre Games for Young Performers* by Suzi Zimmerman. Both of these books are published by Meriwether Publishing Ltd.

Read-through

After everyone is introduced and feeling comfortable, the actual reading of the play takes place. "Why must I take the first rehearsal to read the play — why not just dive in?" There are two major reasons:

- ✓ As stated earlier, this will be the only time all your actors and crew will be together for a long time. Not all of them know one another or have scripts, so this is a great way to get to know everyone and hear what the show is all about.
- ✓ You need to be sure that all your actors and actress have read the whole script and know what the play is about. You cannot take for granted that they will do it on their own!

Include the crew in this first rehearsal and whenever possible in the rest of the rehearsal process. Have them come into a rehearsal to show you how their crew work is progressing. Do not ever foster the star syndrome. Never, Never,

Never! Everyone shares in the production, and no one is better than anyone else. In a family, everyone is important. So it is with a theatre family.

Do not read the show non-stop. Breaking at the end of an act is a good idea. It lets everybody get a chance to stretch his or her legs and move about. As my students are always hungry, I bring treats and give them out at this time. My student assistant then takes over the job of assigning treats to the cast and crew so that there are treats at every rehearsal. He or she will make a list of each person involved in the play and assign a day he or she is to bring treats. Depending on the size of the cast, everyone usually brings treats three times.

Finish reading the play and discuss it. Answer any questions the students have. Referring to your Character Analysis/Costume Cards from Chapter 4, give your actors some information about their characters. You have given them a snack for their tummies. Now you are giving them a little "food for thought" before their next rehearsal.

Reminders

I always want the scripts back in good condition, so I announce that all scripts must be covered with good, stiff covering. A paper grocery sack works well. I also want my actors to attach a pencil to the script with string. The next rehearsals deal with blocking or stage movement and the students need to write everything down. Remembering to bring pencils to rehearsals is difficult. Having it attached to the script helps tremendously.

Remind your actors that they can use rehearsal time for studying, especially if they do not have a large part. Using the time they are not on-stage constructively is another way of not wasting anyone's time. They, of course, could use this time — early in the rehearsal period — to learn their lines, but I always stress the importance of grades and keeping up with schoolwork. You never want a fellow teacher or parent complaining that students did not do their homework and are failing because they were at play practice! Believe me, actors will try to get away with murder if you let them. Again, remind them that you mean business with your off-book rehearsals.

If you are going to have a theatre contract, also remind them that you want it returned within the time limit you and the administration decided, and you mean business about this, too.

Final notes

It is imperative that you end this first rehearsal, as you will every rehearsal, with two types of comments to your actors: **congratulatory** and **constructive**. These are comments about the rehearsal in general combined with comments to specific actors. It is always easy to find fault or criticize actors because we are so caught up with wanting our plays to be as good as possible. We end up just being critical. We tend to be inflexible, often forgetting to say good things, even if it is a thank you for never being late or having memorized lines perfectly. When something is going well, you need to compliment your actors. Remember this is an extracurricular activity and your students are giving their time to be involved. They don't get credit or a grade or a paycheck. They need to be thanked, congratulated, and criticized.

Start these comments by asking for the actors' reaction to the rehearsal and what they learned from that rehearsal. This can be very valuable. Often they have great insight and provide a critical analysis of their performance, which leaves you only to praise them. Never underestimate your students.

These comments can also be called a "Praise Sandwich." You start with the good stuff, then you fill it with the constructive comments, and then top it off with more good stuff. These comments however, cannot be too long. Keeping your actors for thirty minutes after a rehearsal to hear your comments is a very quick way for them to lose interest.

Being too critical and only finding fault can be the biggest mistake most directors make. I did this, and paid for it dearly. I was not flexible, but inflexible. Do not make my mistake.

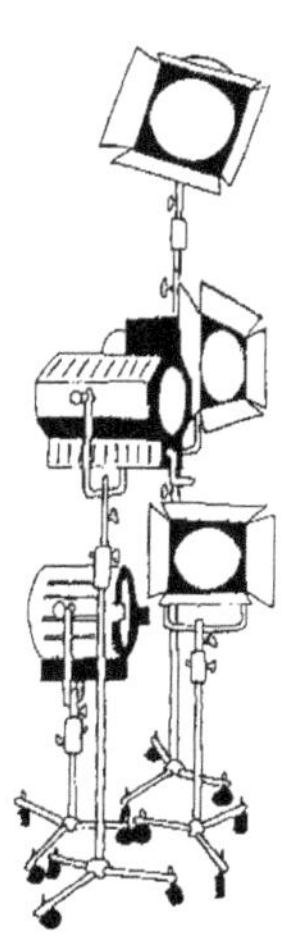

When I was student teaching, one of the few negative comments my professor gave me was, "Miss Friedl, you are too hard on your students. You must find something good to say to them about their speeches. Do not just criticize." Did I take his comments to heart? No.

After my third year of teaching, my students performed in June at the National Thespian Conference in Portland, Oregon. They received a standing ovation for their production of *Beauty and the Lonely Beast*, a musical by the Harders, and we all were recognized with an outstanding high school theatre award. We also were asked to attend the Florida State Thespian Convention the following December.

That fall, besides doing *The Sound of Music* with about 180 students and children, my eleven students, their parents, my husband, and I worked for two solid months raising the $3,500 for the trip.

We prepared *Annabelle Broom*, another Harder musical, for the convention and for performances in Washington, D.C. Our congressmen had been notified, and they set up three D.C. performances. By the time December sixth rolled by, we were all very tired but excited as we boarded Northwest Airlines in a snowstorm and ended up in Miami with sun, surf, and eighty-five degrees.

The show was a great hit. The headline in the *Miami Times* read, "BRAVO—'Annabelle Broom.'" But I felt the production was not the best my students could have done. After the show, when everyone was raving and before the paper came out, my students asked, "Wasn't the show great?"

I answered truthfully, "No. You were slow, the pacing was off, and it lacked energy!" There was dead silence in the station wagon, stuffed not only with all thirteen of us, but our set including a cast iron cauldron, too.

That night at the hotel, the entire group came storming into our room, threw the charm they had gotten for me on the bed, and said, "We have worked hard for this trip. All you ever do is criticize, criticize, and criticize. You never say 'Thank You' or 'Good job.' All you wanted from this trip was something to put on your resumé to look good." I sat there with my mouth open, not saying a word. I was shocked. "And furthermore, when you asked me," one of the boys continued, "to go out to the airport to check on the set pieces, you never expressed thanks or anything!" and they stomped out of our room.

My husband and I just sat stunned. We had worked as hard as any of them. True, I did criticize, but I wanted them to be perfect. I did not want any swelled heads, and I had been right, the show was not as good as it could have been. And true, I did not say thank you. I just expected them to do their jobs, as I was doing mine. But it was not true that I was doing it to put on my resumé. It was an honor, yes, but for them as much as me. Needless to say, the rest of the trip was uncomfortable.

Do not make my mistake. It is not necessary. Always find something good to say; sometimes a simple "Thank you" is enough.

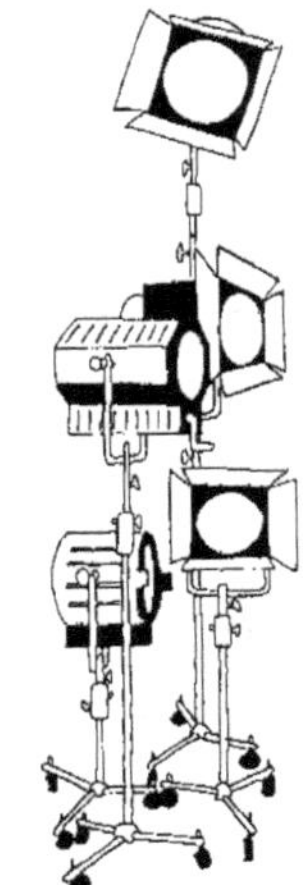

January 11th, 1999

Dear Mr. and Mrs. Sousa,

The Drama Department of Sentinel High School is thrilled to have Ted in their upcoming production of *A Midsummer Night's Dream* on March 5th. As Bottom, he will be involved two nights a week, every Monday and Thursday. This will start tonight, January 11th. The rehearsals are from 7-9 PM in the Sentinel Little Theatre. When he is not on-stage, he is welcome to bring his studies and work on them.

Starting February 22nd, he will have to be at all rehearsals. The time will vary, but generally you should expect him home by 9:45 PM. We have included a complete rehearsal schedule with Ted's commitments highlighted.

Would you *and* Ted please sign the top copy of this letter, keep it for your records, and return the other two copies to the Drama Department? This means:

- Both you *and* Ted understand the commitment he has made to our production; and
- He will be at all of his rehearsals.

Thank you very much.

Sincerely,

Margaret F. Johnson, Theatre Director

Brittany Court, Student Assistant

Parent Signature_________________________ Date _____________

Student Signature_________________________ Date _____________

Example 12: Sentinel High School's Theatre Contract

Chapter 8

Blocking Rehearsals

Blocking gives your actors action to fit their words. This action or movement is what makes a play a play. It means directing or telling each character in the play, very specifically, who they are, where they should move, what they should do during the scene, and why they do it.

Theatre terms you need to know

First you need to know more lingo. The list below is very general.

Ad-lib: The presence of mind by an actor to improvise when:

- another actor fails to enter on cue;
- the normal progress of the play is disturbed (scenery falls down, props are not in place); and/or
- lines are forgotten;
- it may also be a bad habit by some actors who think they do not have to memorize the lines given in a play but say what they "think" is better.

Blank: Mental fade-out causing lines or business to be forgotten.

Build: To bring a scene to a climax by increasing volume, emphasis, pace, or intensity.

Clear stage: Command to leave stage.

Close in: Move closer together.

Come down: Approach part of stage nearer audience.

Counter: Balancing move in opposite direction to make all the actors seen. See **counter-cross** on page 88.

Cover: To attempt to hide mistakes in lines or action. Also, to block another character from the audience's view.

Curtain call: At the end of a performance, the acknowledgment of applause by audience for the actors; the bows.

Fake: To seem to be doing something without doing it.

Focus: To center attention on something or someone.

Give stage: Move to less important position.

Grouping: Arranging characters for meaningful and emotional interest in the play.

Hold: Keep position without moving.

Improvisation: Short bit with lines and action created by actor. Often used as rehearsal exercise.

Open up: Turn more toward audience.

Pace: Timing of lines and action.

Pick up cues: To begin speaking immediately on the last word of the previous speaker for rapid speech, or attach your line to the former speech, no space between.

Position: Actor's place on-stage as set by director.

Run-through: To rehearse play without stopping.

Stage whisper: Giving the illusion of whispering but speaking loud enough for audience to hear.

Steal a scene: To call attention to yourself when it should be elsewhere.

Strike: Call given to stage crew to remove scenery or dismantle the set, remove it from the stage, and put everything — not just the set but costumes, lighting, sounds, and props — back where it belongs.

Tableau: Living picture posed by players who are frozen in place.

Take a call: Bow before audience.

Take stage: Move into stronger stage position.

Topping cues: Pitching voice higher or louder than cues.

Turn in, turn out: Turn your body toward or away from others.

Upstaging: Moving Upstage to gain audience's attention, thus compelling cast to turn toward that actor, and away from the audience. This is something an actor must never do.

The terms listed below have to do with actors, their parts, and the type of plays they would be in.

Dramatis personae: Latin, meaning persons in the play.

Bit part: Role with very few lines and little action.

Character part: Role depicting an unusual individual.

Ensemble: An acting group. Normally used to describe actors who work well together, with no one outperforming the others.

Featured: Billing secondary only to the star role.

Ham: Someone who overplays his or her part with voice, body, and facial expressions — but thinks he or she is good. Also referred to as *chewing the scenery.*

Headliner: Star or leading player.

Juvenile: Player of youthful roles.

Lead: Actor playing the most prominent or important part.

Quick study: One who can memorize a part quickly.

Repertory: Collection of plays that are familiar to a group of actors and may be readily performed.

Revue: Musical comedy without plot.

Stock company: Performing a new play every week.

Trouper: Seasoned actor who always works for play's best interest.

Understudy: Actor capable of playing another's role in an emergency.

Walk-on: A small acting role with no lines. Also known as a "spear carrier."

The terms discussed in detail below deal with directing and are used for telling actors where to go when they are on the stage. The directions are the actors' right and left as they are facing the audience. Upstage is always the furthest from the audience. Downstage is always closest to the audience. Prior to the 1900s when these terms came into use, all stages were sloped toward the audience, higher in the rear than in the front. The purpose was to make the action at the rear more visible to the audience and to help with the illusion of perspective.

Using this shorthand takes less time than writing out the entire blocking:

- ✓ L – Stage Left
- ✓ R – Stage Right
- ✓ U – Upstage
- ✓ D – Downstage
- ✓ C – Center Stage
- ✓ X – Cross (x to door, x to Sally, etc.)
- ✓ DR – Down Right
- ✓ DL – Down Left
- ✓ UR – Up Right
- ✓ UL – Up Left
- ✓ UC – Up Center
- ✓ DC – Down Center

The four body positions are:

1. Full-front position — body and head directly face the audience.
2. Quarter position — three-quarters of body facing out to the audience; halfway to profile.
3. Profile position — side of the body and head toward audience.
4. Full-back position — back directly to the audience.

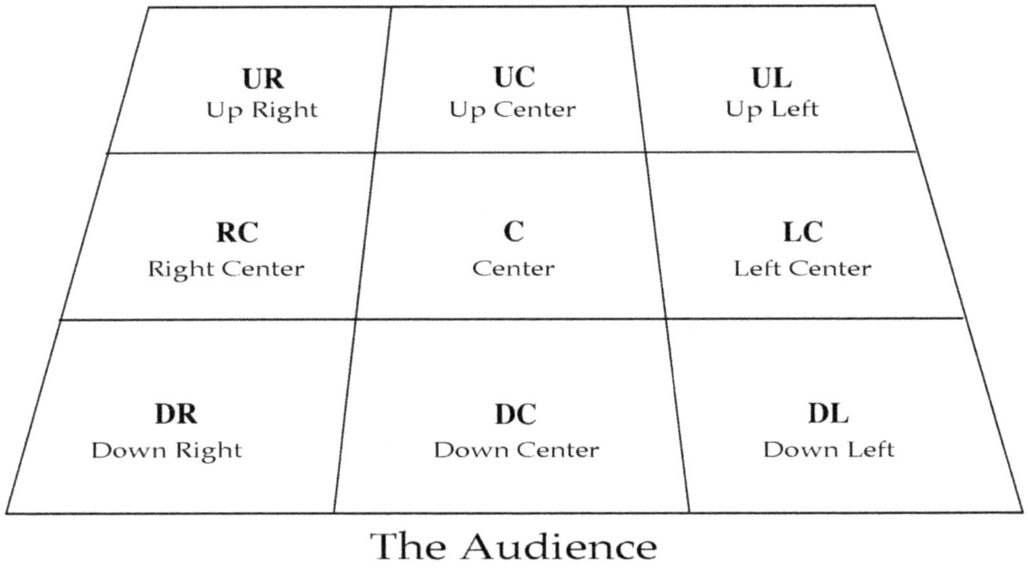

UR Up Right	**UC** Up Center	**UL** Up Left
RC Right Center	**C** Center	**LC** Left Center
DR Down Right	**DC** Down Center	**DL** Down Left

The Audience

Stage Diagram

Blocking Essentials

Blocking is a planned procedure for most of the action in the play. Blocking includes such movement as crossing the stage, taking steps, entering, exiting, backing away, and going into and out of groups.

Before you start blocking, envision what the show needs to say, what action each scene or act needs to build to, and what each character is required to do to get to the climax of the scene or act. Think about motivation. Why do the characters do what they do in the play? Every movement, reaction, line, and facial expression has a reason for happening. If you cannot identify that reason, the action on-stage will be forced and look unnatural.

When considering blocking for the first time, you will need some uninterrupted time to mark your script using the shorthand discussed above and your floor plan (see Chapter 4). You will be moving your characters, giving them life. Each character comes from somewhere, does something, and goes somewhere.

You must also concern yourself with the reason for each character's movement, based on what his or her character does in the play. Refresh your memory for each segment you are blocking by checking each character's Character Analysis/Costume Cards (see Chapter 4).

Now ask yourself the following two questions:

✓ **What do people do in real life?** Besides the principles of movement, what do people do every day? If the phone rings, who answers it? Is it the person closest to the phone or the maid or the owner of the house? What motivates each character should answer the question easily. Much of what directors do is create pictures of relationships. If people like each other, then have them close together. If they do not like each other, then you certainly do not want them sitting on the couch together. Just imagine what happens in real life.

✓ **Can the action be put into questions?** Another way to look at blocking is to put the general action into sentences, then ask questions. These questions and how you answer them become your action; hence your blocking.

Scene one of *A Midsummer Night's Dream* starts with a static scene between the Duke and his betrothed. Then a father comes in with his disobedient daughter. (The scene is no longer static.) He wants the Duke to do something about her. She has disobeyed him. He also has brought along the man he wants his daughter to marry. The other young man, whom the girl loves, is coming in, too, to help support her pleas. Both boys "love" the girl. She does not want or love her father's choice. The two boys get into a heated argument; the boys argue with the father, the girl argues with the father and is finally given an ultimatum. Then the adults leave, allowing the young people to decide to run away. As they are planning their elopement, the girl's best friend comes in. The two lovers leave, promising to meet the following night and the girlfriend is left alone on-stage. Here are a few questions to ask about the scene:

✗ Does the father drag the daughter in?

✗ Does the daughter want to be there?

✗ Why does the father pick one boy over the other?

✗ Where is the Duke's mind — on his upcoming marriage?

✗ Does the Duke really care what happens to this family?

✗ How do young men argue?

✗ Is there anything physical about it?

✗ Why do the adults leave the young people alone?

✗ What causes the girl to run away?

✗ Where has the other girl come from?

✗ What does she want?

Next, consider the various attributes of movement: its purposes, do's and don'ts, principles, groupings, and balance.

Six purposes of movement:

✓ To set the mood;

✓ To open space for others;

✓ To show characterization;

✓ To reveal feelings such as anxiety, nervousness, sorrow, and delight;

✓ To show relationships; and/or

✓ To give focus to the key person or speaker in the scene.

Do's and don'ts of character movement:

Do:

Speak and move in character.

Use full playing space of stage.

Group in twos, threes, fours, fives.

Have consistent relationships with others.

Don't:

Stand in a semi-circle.

Stand in a straight line.

Stand equal distance apart.

Bunch.

Principles of movement

The following principles of movement have been developed through stage experience. They are not rules — acting in the theatre defies rules. The following principles of movement need to be modified at times to fit the needs of you and your actors. Usually, characters:

✓ Cross toward the objective point. If grace and beauty in the scene are desired, then cross in a curved line.

✓ Cross on their lines.

✓ Break up their speeches while they cross behind others.

✓ When crossing with another character, the speaker walks Upstage and slightly ahead of the other, turning his or her head Downstage to speak.

✓ When entering with a group, the speaker enters first.

✓ Move smoothly when opening an area for another important character. They do not want to call attention to the movement.

✓ Counter-cross. When a character Upstage Left crosses to an area Stage Right, a character at Right may counter-cross to the same area Upstage Left to retain good balance.

✗ *Example:* Joe and Tom are at a table Stage Left, playing chess. Sam moves from his easy chair at Stage Right to watch their game. Then Ron comes down from Upstage Left to pick up a magazine and lounge in the easy chair vacated by Sam. This is a counter-cross which Ron motivated by picking up the magazine.

✓ May address a part of their speech to a character across the stage, then walk toward that character as he or she finishes his or her speech.

✓ Make room for new characters to enter by clearing a path for them. Have the on-stage characters move prior to offstage characters' entrance so they will not have to walk around someone.

✓ Are close together for heated arguments, fierce disapproval, and conflict as well as bright, happy scenes and secretive dialog. Minor differences or major dislikes may be played by keeping characters across the stage from each other. How you group your characters indicates their relationships.

✓ Usually turn toward rather than away from the audience, unless this involves a wide, awkward turn. If so, turn the easiest way.

✓ Back up a step or two toward an exit just before leaving; this shortens the distance to walk. Characters may speak, turn, walk to the door, and then finish their speech.

Effective grouping

Grouping is another way of arranging your actors. Effective grouping gives visual pleasure to the audience. Just as a painting works for pleasing line, balance, color, and light and dark contrasts, so you work to give aesthetic pleasure through stage arrangements. You must understand stage balance.

The set is designed in an open triangle allowing the majority of the audience to see the action and the actors. You never want set pieces or actors in straight lines even if you have three or more characters on-stage at the same time. It is very uninteresting and unnatural. People do not stand in straight lines. All mass, including stage setting, furniture, and characters, contributes to stage balance.

You are trying to create real life on-stage, so straight lines may be eliminated by:

✓ Using triangles or some less rigid grouping; the use of triangles is pleasing to the human eye.

✓ Creating depth through building visual layers and making use of different levels. Some actors might be seated, others standing, and still others reclining against some furniture.

Become conscious of grouping, always watching to keep the arrangements interesting and using the triangle as the basis for many pictorial effects.

Stage balance

Drama is action, so stage balance is constantly changing because it includes characters who move. Balance of characters really means balance of interest. One dominant character on one side of the stage can balance a dozen minor characters on the other (who are not standing in a straight line). Effective groupings often involve counter-crossing, which is only a shifting of positions. Your characters are motivated to move. Use the areas you have designated by your furniture. After you have given your basic blocking, you can encourage actors to move about in a playing area you assign them to if it does not interfere with other actors.

Sometimes there is blocking already written in the script. These directions indicate either how the writer saw the play or how the first director directed the show. They certainly are concerned with balance. This blocking will work best if you duplicate the set described in the script. As a first-year director you will find this helpful. Sometimes these stage directions will work, even if your set is different from the one in the book. A rule of thumb is to try them. If they do not work, you will just devise your own blocking and/or movement.

One final reminder: *No movement without a purpose.* Now you are ready to block the show. Nothing is going to stop you!

Marking scripts

Teach your cast how to mark their scripts. You will have to familiarize those who have not been in a play before with the stage directions you have just learned — Up, Down, Left, and Right. The actors are to write their blocking with pencil in the special shorthand, just like you did. Marking their blocking in the script with pencils makes changes easy to erase. Yes, there will be changes (see the end of this chapter).

You also want the scripts back in good condition if they are to be used with English classes or if you keep them for drama class or another production down the road. Before the marking is done, hand out a small diagram of the set. The actors will then know where to go and can mark their scripts. Each of us has our own method but these are the most common.

Blocking rehearsals

Before your blocking rehearsals start, refresh your memory about the segment designated on the rehearsal schedule for each night. Visualize your blocking! Begin by:

- ✓ Starting the rehearsals on time;
- ✓ Making sure each actor has a sharpened pencil attached to the script;
- ✓ Doing five to ten minutes of warm-ups. Play the games you did at the first rehearsal or new ones;
- ✓ Being energetic.

Then get down to business. Be sure that each actor understands the floor plan and where everything is. You and your student assistant will have gotten some chairs or benches to be your furniture and placed them where the actual set pieces will be. Your student assistant has taped off the set on the floor so everyone knows where the entrances, exits, and walls are (be sure to use easily-removable tape). This is like the athletic field where games are played: it is the map of the territory actors must enter into and explore.

As you give directions, be sure that your actors are writing them down. Stop the actors whenever something looks awkward or does not seem real. Ask them why you have blocked them specifically that way. Do they understand what you want? You might need to discuss the scene or the motivation behind the action or change the blocking.

While giving your directions, allow enough time for your actors to write down all their blocking.

Sit on the side or at the front of the acting area, close to your actors. It allows you to side coach and/or get up and demonstrate. Remember: enthusiasm. Let your actors see you up and active while giving them their blocking. Let them hear your enthusiastic instructions. Not only do you not have to shout but also you establish closeness to your actors. Just sitting out front and telling them what to do is not being active. You have to be up and *doing*!

Review blocking

Be sure that you have enough time to review all the blocking done on each segment before the actors go home.

✓ The first time through, you have just given your actors places to go. The second time they can begin to motivate their lines with the action you have given them.

✓ You want to check to see if the actors have written everything down. For the next rehearsal of that segment (off-book rehearsals), the actors must memorize all their lines as well as their blocking. You do not want them to just memorize their lines because then you will have to re-block the show. Actions and words go hand in hand. In fact, the blocking can help with the memorization. Not reviewing the blocking can cause aggravation.

✓ You want to see if the blocking makes sense.

Your student assistant has written everything down in his or her prompt script. As the actors review their blocking, they say out loud where they are going or what they are doing as they say their lines so your student assistant can check to see if they have indeed written everything down.

Each night, as the review process goes on, you need to sit in the middle of the audience area or as far away from the action as possible to see what your blocking looks like. Answer the following questions and write down things you need to change.

- ✓ Are the actors speaking out towards the audience? Is everyone facing three-quarters of their body out to the audience? It is hard to hear if everyone is speaking Upstage or away from the audience. You do not want the actors' backs to the audience; they cannot be heard.
- ✓ Check to see if their heads are up. Often students tend to keep their heads down, making it equally difficult to hear. Yes, they are reading, but remind them to hold their scripts up.
- ✓ Is anyone standing in front of anyone else?
- ✓ Is the entire action taking place on only one side of the stage?
- ✓ Is the action static? Does something need to be done about it?
- ✓ Is there only one major action taking place at one time? Two things can happen simultaneously, but the audience can only watch one. Where is the audience to focus?

If you need to change any of the blocking, do so. Don't ever be afraid to change. Here is another place to be flexible. If the show is not working — the story is not being told — it needs to be changed. Some of it is due to what you see. You may have visualized something in your head that just did not translate to the stage. You also did your preliminary blocking alone, with only the script, your floor plan, and your vision, not realizing that your actors can have input as well.

Do not be afraid of your actors' input. Often they have an impulse to move or do an action that will make the character come alive. Sometimes allowing your actors to block themselves after you have given them the general movement works well. Whether or not you take their ideas or impulses, consider them. Their suggestions and/or actions should be explored. You then decide whether or not to add them.

Blocking may also change as you work with characterization later on in the rehearsal period (working rehearsals). Change is not a sign of weakness, but of brilliance. Make sure that both the actors and your student assistant make the changes.

Included in the rehearsal schedule is one night to catch up blocking pages you have not gotten to or that need further work. End each blocking rehearsal with a discussion concerning what the actors have learned about their specific characters.

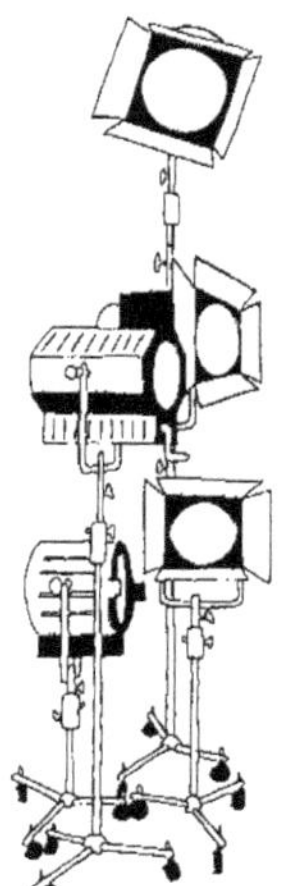

> I recently did *The Taming of the Shrew* for the third time. It was not going well. Two weeks before we opened I happened to watch the San Francisco Repertory's version and totally changed what I wanted from the minor roles. They were to be on-stage for most of the show, Down Left and Right cheering whenever "Padua" was spoken, and playing their drums, horns, and tambourines to accentuate the action of the story. We changed the whole show for the better.

Chapter 9

Off-Book Rehearsals

The rehearsals marked "off-book" are just that. These rehearsals ensure that your actors have memorized their lines and blocking. Remember you have reminded your actors to memorize their blocking as well as their lines. Having movement connected to lines makes the job of memorizing much easier. The key to these rehearsals is for you to remain calm. Primarily you will be sitting in the theatre area, watching. These rehearsals are for the actors. They need to be able to make mistakes, practice their lines, and not worry about anything else. You can take notes, but first and foremost these rehearsals are for your actors.

Three things to get you started

- ✓ Begin with a warm-up.
- ✓ Then give your actors five to ten minutes to review their lines before you start. Everyone will be nervous, so this takes down the anxiety level a bit.
- ✓ Tell the actors they may be cued. Your student assistant is invaluable during these rehearsals. This means that if they need help with a line, they say, "Line please." Your student assistant will give the needed lines to them. The actors are not to drop character but ask for their line as the character would ask for it. It is a rare person who has every line and every word memorized perfectly the first night off-book. Be understanding but firm.

Why no scripts?

You cannot have a quality production if your students are not off-book early in the rehearsal process. In order to create believable characters, actors must use their whole bodies. Having an actor's hands tied up with a script is not acting; it is reading. It becomes a crutch. You need to start working on character development, and you cannot do that if the actors have scripts in their hands.

You are not going to win a popularity contest. Be a dictator if that's what it takes. You cannot let your actors be lazy. Give them an extra day to memorize, but *no scripts on-stage.* Actors will use any excuse for not having memorized their lines. They will use their scripts forever if you do not take them away!

"Why must I be so mean?" you sigh. Because the rest of the rehearsal periods will not be productive otherwise. Actors cannot concentrate, use their whole body, or communicate with others if they have books in their hands. Where are the connections that the characters must make with the other characters in the play if their head is buried in a script? Others cannot rely on them, either, and what is theatre but everyone working together?

Where to put scripts

Actors must not be on-stage or directly offstage with their scripts. Have all the scripts put in the front of the acting area after the warm-ups so they are easily accessible when actors are not on-stage but in your full view when they are on-stage. The actors can ask for them back when they are not on-stage and can work on their lines. They, however, are not to work backstage. If they have not learned their lines very well, just let them struggle. Do not get mad or upset. Remain calm. Simply sit back and let them stumble.

No paraphrasing

If any actors have memorized their basic thought process but have not memorized their lines, word for word, be sure to tell them that they must be ninety percent accurate. Paraphrasing is a no-no! The lines were written in the play for the following three reasons:

- ✓ To convey the author's plot, characterization, and theme;
- ✓ To cue other actors so they can say their lines; and
- ✓ To help the crew working lights and sound who are going to follow the script. Words that aren't there will cause both actors and crew members to miss important cues.

Get those lines memorized correctly.

Stop at the end of the segment

If no one stops and asks for cues, even if the actors are not saying the right lines, do not interrupt your actors the first time they go through the script off-book. Break after the first run-through and have the student assistant tell them where they were wrong so the next time through they will be aware of where their mistakes were and try to correct them.

Final notes

Remember to end your rehearsals with your final notes. Of course, these comments will relate to the individual actors and be helpful in the development of their characters.

You will notice that there is one night in the off-book rehearsals for memorization time. On that night you will want to review one of the segments your actors have already memorized or run the segment that is not memorized (making it easier for your actors to memorize that segment). Four straight days of memorization is difficult. Remember your actors have homework, chores, etc., as well as lines to memorize. They cannot give up everything for the play. Allowing actors an extra night to get their lines memorized on one segment is good common sense.

Act III:

Working Rehearsals

Chapter 10

Working Rehearsals

Now comes the time for fun! All that hard work you did earlier on your various readings of the script will now pay off big time! Working rehearsals are primarily character-development rehearsals. You know all about the characters, and now you will be working with your actors, helping them write analyses, playing games, adding stage business both for the individual characters and the plot, and picking up cues.

Checking memorization

Allow your student assistant to cue your actors for one more run-through of each segment. The actors are then on their own. If they still do not remember what they are to do or to say, that is OK. Let them continue to struggle through it. Just remain patient — be calm. They will learn! The other actors will not tolerate laziness. Peer pressure is an amazing thing. As a final resort, tell them they will be replaced if they still do not have their lines memorized by the thirteenth rehearsal. This is an arbitrary number, but you need them to be free of their script by that time. (This might be a good thing for you to cover in your expectations at tryouts and/or your discussion at the first rehearsal.) You cannot have one or two slackers ruin your production. You have the two options suggested in Chapter 6 — your student assistant can replace them, or you can go to your tryout sheets and/or cards and find new actor(s) you did not cast originally — and there are two more options to consider:

✓ Someone else in the cast with a smaller part can step in.

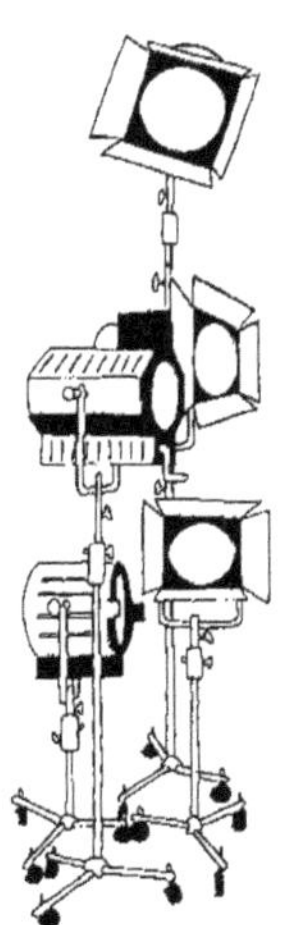

While doing *Hotel Paradiso,* I cast a freshman boy as the Furniture Mover and a sophomore in a little larger role, the Bellhop. The sophomore got himself in big trouble and was forced to drop the play. I had cast all the men's roles with every boy who tried out; I had only one choice: the freshman had to play both roles. He did. He had all his lines memorized the very next day. (Incidentally he is now in Hollywood, doing TV and movies. His first major role was also that of a bellhop in *Radio Land Murders*!)

- ✓ As a last resort, you play the part. I have. Again — I repeat — this is a last resort.

The point is: no one is so good that they cannot be replaced!

After lines are learned, each person on-stage must be in character at all times. "How do I get my actors to build their characters and begin to react to each other and events? Are they going to know how? I have some ideas, but actors need to discover their characters for themselves." Read on ...

Ways of assessing your character

Analyses

Your actors must come to understand their characters inside and out. Being a good actor is like being a good detective. They must ask themselves every possible question. Discovering how and why a character reacts in a certain way begins with a written analysis. Give each actor a character analysis form (see Additional Resources section) and allow them a week to fill it out. This is best done early in the working rehearsal period and not before, when it was more important to memorize lines and blocking.

The hardest thing for an inexperienced actor to do is use his or her imagination when filling out his or her analysis. The most common comment is: "It doesn't say anything about that in the script." Your answer is simple:

"From what your character does and says in the play, what do you think? There is no right or wrong answer, just be able to justify it." Pick any of the forms and/or questions provided and feel free to add some of your own.

The major concern in doing these analyses is to get to the heart of each character. What makes the character do what he or she does in the play? The answer is **the character's goal** or **the character's want**. What does the character want more than anything else in the world? What will he or she do to get it? Does he or she have a goal in life? If so, how is he or she going to attain it?

Before the analysis is turned in, have your actors share one interesting thing they have written about their character at the beginning of one of the working rehearsals. This shows everyone that his or her work on the analyses is important.

Autobiographies

After the character analysis forms are filled out and turned in, you and your student assistant read them, comment on them, and give them back. Then have your actors write an autobiography of the characters they play based on the information they wrote on their analysis. There is no specific form. The only directions you give are that it should be:

- ✓ Written in first person;
- ✓ Double-spaced; and
- ✓ On one side of one sheet of paper.

Have your actors turn this in the last week of working rehearsals. See Examples 13 and 14 (pages 113).

Drawings

Try an artistic approach to understanding characters. During a break or at the beginning of a working rehearsal, give your actors paper and pencil. Have them go away from fellow actors and draw either a picture of their character or a picture of what their character thinks of the play or another character in the show. Tell them you want it to be abstract — no literal faces or walls, etc. Do not look at the finished product, but have your student assistant pick them up.

After the rehearsal is over and you have given your final notes, display the drawings and have the actors try to figure out who did what. This allows more sharing, and everyone can see what other characters in the play are thinking. Posting these pictures in a display case with the names of each character underneath can pique interest for your prospective audience. Adding autobiographies to these pictures makes an even better display.

Collages

Another exercise for character development is to have each actor create a collage based on his or her character and what he or she does in the show. A collage is an artistic composition. It is the art of making pictures by sticking cloth, pieces of paper, photographs, and other objects onto a surface to make one unified picture. These objects all relate to the actor's character. By looking at the picture, anyone can get a real feeling of the character. These may be shared at your first complete run-through rehearsal. These also make great exhibits before you open. Below are directions I have used:

A facial picture of your character (at least 3" X 5") mounted on an 8-1/2" X 11" piece of cardboard. The picture cannot be a drawing.

Surround the picture with the following which represents your character:

✓ Color — painted or a swatch

✓ Object — cut out (not drawn)

✓ Key line or phrase your character speaks in the production

✓ Animal/bird

✓ Food

✓ Character's secret

✓ Flower

✓ Famous person in history

Include with this collage a separate sheet of paper with the list of items you chose and their justification.

Rehearsal activities

Below are various activities you can do at rehearsals to help your actors develop their characters.

Playing games/exercises

A great way to engage actors is to play games. Most actors have not been exposed to this kind of rehearsing. These exercises often do not get great results at first, so give them some time.

To help develop characters

While the actors are working at home on their analyses, at rehearsals you are helping them find answers to the questions posed in the analyses by teaching them what acting is. Acting means action. For an actor, it means using his or her whole body and voice while reacting to either something that happens or something that someone says. It is the way we humans deal with other people.

Example: You say, "Good morning, Sarah." How does Sarah react? Does she smile and say, "Good morning to you, too," or just growl and trudge away; or yell, "You pervert!" and slap your face? She has reacted to you and what you said. The next step is how you react back to her.

Ninety percent of acting is reacting. How your actors play the games or react in the exercises is what you want. The key word is *reaction*. It's all right if one of the games doesn't work. That in itself is important because you and your actors then will know what not to do. Pick only one game and/or exercise per rehearsal. You might only want to do a total of four games and/or exercises during all of your working rehearsals.

These activities are meant to be used only at the beginnings of rehearsals. You do not want a whole night of these activities but allow time for your actors to explore their characters in new situations. Do not run them longer than twenty to thirty minutes. After you have called a halt to these activities, be sure to take time to share what everyone has learned from the experience and what they can use for their character. The following are activities I have used successfully (I did not do all of them on every show; I picked those that would help the cast for a specific show).

Animals

One of the best ways for actors to discover their characters is to have them come to a rehearsal as an animal. The actors have to pick an animal that best exemplifies their character as they did on their written analysis. A prime example would be Cassias from Shakespeare's *Julius Caesar*. He has a "lean and hungry look." What animal best represents this? A snake is one possibility.

For this rehearsal, your actors are not to tell anyone their animal but are to move and sound like that animal. The actor playing Cassias could slither around on the floor and hiss.

When everyone has had the chance to play his or her animal, stop the rehearsal. Have them share what they were and why. This should be a fun, exciting, eye-opening rehearsal. If the actors have done their job, their animal should help them not only with voice but also with movement.

> *Example:* When I was directing *Inherit the Wind*, our opening scene before Brady entered was awful. It had no excitement. Nothing was working. As these people in the play were farmers, I told my actors they were each to be farm animals. My, did that scene come alive! When Brady entered, he played a rooster. When we stopped this exercise, he continued, not crowing, but speaking and walking with authority, much like his rooster.

Object

Another helpful game is for the actors to decide what object their character is. Ask them to bring the object to the rehearsal and give it to the student assistant, who puts it in a paper bag (so no one else can see it). When the rehearsal begins each actor is the object. They must walk, talk, and move as their object.

When everyone has had an opportunity to be his or her object, take time for sharing. Again, the actors must explain or justify what they were and why. You might not agree, but if they can justify it, you accept it.

> *Example:* In *Our Town,* Mrs. Soames, the one who cried at the wedding, came as an eggbeater! She turned and turned, fast and then slow. When she was moving fast she talked high and screechy. When she slowed up, she lowered her voice, almost slurring her words.

Food

A different game is for the actors to come as a food their character might be. Again, this is a question that could be asked on the written analysis. They are to dress, talk, and walk as they envision that food would look, sound, and move. Of course after the exercise, they must justify why.

> *Example:* When directing *A-Haunting We Will Go*, I cast our principal as a utilities operator who comes in at the beginning and end of the show. He memorized all his lines but had no energy. He just walked on-stage, said his lines, and left. The night we played "Food," he decided that his character was popcorn. Well, he started jumping around the stage, as if he had ants in his pants. The kids loved it, and he was never static again.

Touching

Often a script calls for the characters to be a caring family. This requires trust and touching, which are often very difficult for inexperienced actors. An exercise that works well is to have the actors (as their characters) touch the person to whom they are talking. It does not have to be in a romantic way. It may be just a tap or a cuff or a little shove — no one is to hurt anyone! Then the next actor, as his or her character, touches whomever he or she is speaking to, and so on. The object of this activity is to have the actors make physical contact every time they speak. There are two things they must do:

✓ Know the person to whom they are speaking.

✓ Touch them the way their character really feels.

If they are talking to the entire group, they must touch everyone. Feelings play a big part in how this contact is made. If the part calls for someone to be happy, they will touch people that way; if they are sad, the touch would be very different. Actors having difficulty with this exercise may need some prodding from you. Side coach gently, and soon your actors will get the hang of it.

> *Example:* While directing *I Remember Mama,* I was having great difficulty getting the actors to feel like a loving family, so I tried this game. Many of the touches turned into hugs. They began, within an hour, to feel like a family, and I never had to work on that aspect of the show again.

Pick an important line

Have the actors pick the character's most important line. They are not to tell anyone what it is. When it comes time for the line to be delivered, they are to stop the show and sing and dance it! They then have to tell everyone why it is their most important line. Justifying the line often causes actors to look at a character or the show in a whole new way.

> *Example:* This was one of the hardest exercises I ever tried. Often actors would forget to do it and just before their character was to exit, remember it and just pick any line. I was a large part of the problem. I needed to constantly remind them about their important line. When this activity worked, it truly was an eye-opener for everyone.

Wants

Have the characters play their wants. This means that before each line is said, each actor says, with conviction, "I want _____" and then says his or her line. If a character's want is to get a book from the shelf to read to his niece, it will be said quite differently from the character whose want is to get the job no matter who is in the way, and the book is his way of getting that job. The want can change from scene to scene or even within a scene, depending on the relationship between the characters.

Each and every person must say his or her want before each of their lines. This rehearsal, although longer than many of the other games, will determine if the actors know their characters. Even lines like "Hi there!" or "Good-bye," represent a want. Does the character want to be friendly, or does the character want to be the center of attention? These two phrases would be delivered quite differently, depending on the want of the character. Every line must make sense; therefore, every want must make sense. If it does not, stop and discuss the play or the characters. It is possible that a character has the same want throughout the entire play and it never changes.

The big why and what

Once your actors know their lines, they need to discover why they are on-stage, what they have to do when they are there, and why they leave. They also need to explore what goes on with their characters on a twenty-four-hour basis.

> *Example:* When directing *Arsenic and Old Lace* for the second time, we spent an entire rehearsal (I had given myself enough time in the rehearsal period to try several different and prolonged exercises) with each character telling me exactly what he or she was doing when not on-stage while the actors on-stage tried to carry on with the play! I found out the reason why the little ladies did not come down when Elaine was pushed into the cellar:
>
> ✗ Abby did not come down because she was in the middle of reading a romance novel.
>
> ✗ Martha was hard of hearing so missed out on all the excitement.
>
> This was a very chaotic evening, and I would not suggest it unless you are up to two hours of disorder and noise! But it is well worth the effort!

To help with energy, voice, and movement

If your play needs energy and your actors are not giving their all, stop the rehearsal and try one of the following. These exercises will get the juices flowing and add that much needed energy and movement. They do not necessarily fit with the production you are doing, but they make a great break in the rehearsal, get your actors *doing*, and besides that, they love it. You might even do many of the suggestions given below in one rehearsal.

From where you sit, just shout out, "Sing the lines as an opera." Then, about three minutes later, shout, "You are all gunslingers at the OK Corral!" followed by, "This is a soap opera and everyone is going on a cruise," and then "You are all in an insane asylum." You get the idea. It makes your rehearsals come alive as your actors improvise on the spot as you chuckle. Energy happens. Your actors have to use their voices and movement to create the new world you have suggested for them, even for two minutes. (This is truly one of the joys of directing — you are not laughing at your actors but with them.)

Many of these exercises will not give your actors specific things they can use but, more importantly, they will get your actors to use their voices and bodies. The five exercises listed below are the ones that I found to be most helpful.

The little why and what

Actors who meander around stage or who cannot stand still or stay where you have blocked them need a special kind of exercise. Often actors have not even thought of what their characters are doing before their entrances or what their characters are going to do after they exit. Before the actors enter the stage, they announce to you and your student assistant where they have been and why they are entering the stage. They must be very specific and be able to justify it. Before they leave stage, they must also announce why they are leaving the stage and where they are going. If you do not agree with them, stop the rehearsal, discuss their answers, come to an agreement, and pick up where you left off. Why does this help meandering actors? Knowing why they are entering and exiting makes their movement purposeful.

Singing

Having your actors sing their lines, not paying any attention to their character's wants or motivation, gives great freedom. The type of singing is up to you, but I found singing the scenes several ways and then getting down to work helped tremendously. Your actors were then not afraid of trying something because they had just sung as a group. The various types of singing can be:

- ✓ Opera
- ✓ Western
- ✓ Rap
- ✓ Hard rock

Pretending they are inhabitants of an insane asylum

Visualizing inmates in an insane asylum gives students many ideas. They can have any mental disease they want, but they are definitely not to be sane. Of course, the lines and blocking stay the same, but the locale has changed. You will have energy.

Behaving like young children

It's as simple as it sounds: have everyone play the scene as if they are young children.

> *Example:* Everything was getting boring while I was in the middle of rehearsing *David and Lisa,* so I decided to have everyone play their characters as little children. It really livened things up and great relationships developed, especially between the students.

Playing other people's roles

Early in the rehearsal period have your actors take on the personalities of other characters in the play. They say their own lines but the attitude, voice, and movement is that of one of the other characters in the play. This not only adds energy but it also adds wonderful insight into what your actors are thinking about:

- ✓ The other characters in the play;
- ✓ The relationships of the characters; and
- ✓ The plot.

Playing these games at rehearsals allows us to do, say, and see things that we would not ordinarily do, say, and see. It gives the actors a new perspective on their roles and relationships with others.

Bonding

An added reason for all of these exercises is bonding. Every play you produce creates a feeling of family. The actors start to care about the other people in the play. They look forward to seeing one another every night. This is one of the intangibles of play directing. No amount of money can create this feeling of warmth.

Adding business

Actors must do things other than just what you tell them to do in the blocking. You are turning your actors into real people. Each character in your play is unique, just as each of us is unique. You and your actors have started exploring what makes each character a unique individual by playing the games mentioned above and working on the analyses. Your actors have started developing how their characters:

- ✓ Say specific lines;
- ✓ Sit;
- ✓ React;
- ✓ Talk;
- ✓ Move; and
- ✓ Feel about other characters in the show.

Now you need to take this character development one step further by adding business. The following suggestions help actors discover that singular thing that makes their characters special and different.

Rehearsal clothes

The first working rehearsal is the time to begin thinking about the types of clothes each of the characters will be wearing. Your actors have to know how to sit, walk, and use their costumes. If it is a modern play and the characters are young, costuming is not much of a problem. If, however, some are playing fathers, mothers, or older folks, it is imperative to get them into appropriate clothes as early as possible. Vests, aprons, hats, and/or gloves give young actors an immediate feeling they are not themselves. Also, greasing down boys' hair or tying girls' hair back adds another dimension to their characters and makes them feel different.

If you are doing a period piece with girls in long dresses, get them in long skirts so they learn how to work in them. Two yards of inexpensive cotton material gathered at the waist with a tie works very well for rehearsal purposes.

Walks

Many directors wait until the end of the rehearsal period to costume their actors, including their shoes. Do not wait for the shoes. You want your actors to do the best job possible, and shoes help them start their characterization. Begin working with the actors' walks on your first working rehearsal.

Most of us today wear soft, casual sneakers. If your actors are playing an older person, wearing character shoes is the best way to start the transition. This means that you will need to get old orthopedic or "sensible" shoes for your girls and oxfords or lace-up leather shoes for your boys. It is absolutely amazing what happens to actors' movements when they are wearing shoes other than their regular sneakers. If they are playing someone close to their own age, then talk about how this character moves differently than they do. You never want actors playing themselves — that is not acting. You are not creating a clone, but a completely new and distinct person.

After everyone is outfitted with their shoes, take a few minutes at this first working rehearsal and just practice walks. Parading actors around the acting area and having them justify why they are moving in a specific way starts the analysis process.

If any of your actors cannot come up with a walk, help them. Try different things! Most of the time things you try will work, but if they do not, you can always throw them out. But what have you learned? A particular character does not walk like that. Doing something that does not fit your character often teaches you even more about your character.

> *Example:* During *The Prime of Miss Jean Brodie,* I decided to try giving each of my actors something to use with their hands. I gave Lowther, the Scottish man infatuated with Jean, a handkerchief.
>
> I have seldom seen an actor try as hard as he did to use the prop. It just did not work. When the game was over he apologized profusely. I said, "Well, what did you learn? Your character is not nervous. He does not play with his hands. He also is not one to be overly demonstrative either. You have learned a great deal."

Habits

One thing that makes us unique is our little habits. Sometimes it is an overused gesture or phrase, or we may habitually make a specific sound. Every actor has to find his or her character's habit. Shifting and rolling eyes, drumming fingers, chewing fingernails, tapping feet, clearing the throat, sniveling, sniffing, twirling hair, and bouncing knees are all habits we have done or been around every day of our lives. They indicate things about us as human beings. Do characters in plays have some of the same habits we do in real life? Of course.

If you are doing a comedy, a habit can often be exaggerated for a laugh. Consider:

✓ Twitching or a similar tick that gets bigger and bigger;

✓ Limping that is so obvious it does not hurt or even switching legs every time the character enters, (or switching a hump as Igor did in the movie *Young Frankenstein*);

✓ Being farsighted and refusing to wear glasses (the actor talks to tables and chairs!); and/or

✓ Waving a scarf in everyone's face.

Anything is fair game.

For a serious play, many of the same habits will work, but they are played quite differently. They are not exaggerated.

✓ The tick might not be noticed until the character is pushed into a situation he or she cannot control. It then becomes menacing or sad.

✓ The limp is done so everyone feels the pain the character is feeling.

✓ The glasses truly are needed for the character to see.

✓ The scarf is used with the hands to show nervousness or suffering or to cover a scar.

Avoid the stereotypical habits such as wringing of hands when nervous, leaning over and holding an imaginary crick in your back when one is old, or rubbing your arms when cold. You need to help your actors discover other ways of portraying nervousness, old age, and cold.

Ways of speaking

After your actors have their walks, habits, and rehearsal togs, the next thing you need to do is work with their voices. Can you hear them? Get as far away from your actors as you can and listen to them. Be sure that you can hear the ends of their sentences. Many inexperienced actors start their lines strong and loud but lose volume by the time they get to the end of their speech.

Another thing inexperienced actors do is speak too fast, which makes them extremely difficult to understand. Putting a pencil in the mouth, lengthwise, biting down on it, and then speaking can help with enunciation. It makes the tongue work. It is absolutely amazing how your actors' diction improves after working with the pencil. Another way of helping with diction is to tell your actors to pretend they are projecting from the top of a mountain. This does not slow the speech down, but it makes the speech easier to understand.

If they are talking fast, can you understand what they are saying or is it a jumble of words strung together with breaths? Most often I could be heard saying, "Slow down — we're not on a fast train to Paris!" You will need to slow the speech down. Try doubling the time. Time a two-minute sequence. Then ask the actors to do the scene in four minutes.

Next, check believability. Do you believe what they say? Is the tone they are using what normal people would use when saying these words? If you do not believe them, why not? Is it because of the way they're saying their lines? Remind them that emotion is the vowels and meaning is in the consonants (especially in Shakespeare).

Do any actors have speech patterns? This means that everything they say starts and ends the same, or they have no variety in tone and emphasis. Monotone falls into this category, too. Often we do not recognize these problems in our own speech. If we are made aware of it, we start correcting ourselves.

The best way to help actors correct their specific speech problem is to videotape the rehearsals. Actors often do not believe our comments, but when they see themselves and their "problems" on the screen, they cannot escape the fact. If the school does not have video recorders, one of the actors' parents may have one and when asked — using your best diplomatic tone — would be most happy to come and tape a rehearsal or let you borrow it.

Your job

What are you doing while the games are going on and afterwards? When playing the games, you must make sure that your actors are following the rules. The only way the games work is to be sure that the actors know the goal(s) of the game and play them with the best of their ability. You are either on the side of the acting area or right out front. You do not want to shout. You are enthusiastic! Don't forget to side coach the actors if they are having trouble playing the games. This assistance gives actors focus during the activities and often leads to new and exciting discoveries about the play and their characters. Your assistant, as hard as it may be, is keeping track of the lines and blocking to the very best of his or her ability!

As soon as the games are over and you are ready to put what they have learned to work, you and your assistant go out into the house. Your student assistant has a notebook and a pen or pencil. As the segment is progressing, you see things that your actors need to change. Don't interrupt the flow of the action with instructions. Relay these changes to your student assistant who quietly writes them down. Don't speak loudly and disturb your actors. Always keep your focus on the play. Another way of taking notes is to speak into a tape recorder and play it back after the first run-through of each segment.

When the segment is done, read or play the notes you have taken. The assistant can read them, but it is much easier if you do the reading — you are the director. The assistant can clarify if you don't remember what was written down or what it meant.

Final working rehearsals

There are two things you need to be concerned about during your final working rehearsals: **focus** and **picking up cues**.

Determining focus

So far, your actors have been concentrating on their individual characters, but now it is time to go back to the play as a whole. What is the story about? Which characters help tell the story and which are there to listen or create atmosphere? Focus has to do with what you want the audience to pay attention to. Many lines are just said to give character insight or tell us the general "stuff" about the play. But when something happens that is very important to the story, all the characters on-stage must pay attention to it. This may mean that everyone looks at the character who is speaking or the item or set piece that is being referred to. No one is to "do his or her own thing." A good rule of thumb is for each actor to truly listen to the character who is speaking and react to them as his or her character would react. Then they are doing what all good actors do — listening and reacting. Remember, ninety percent of acting is reacting. If their focus is where it needs to be, the audience's focus will be there, too.

Refresh your memory on why you blocked the show as you did (go back to Chapter 8). You grouped your actors to the way your furniture was arranged because it dealt with focus. Be sure your actors have not lost sight of your original intent.

Picking up cues

The tempo of the play also needs to be considered. By working on characterization, you have started building interest in the play, which eventually leads to pacing. If actors are playing their wants, then your play automatically builds to the climax, with no stumbling along the way. The play gets more and more exciting.

On the other hand, if the actors are saying their lines but there seems to be little enthusiasm or purpose, everything in the show becomes static. There also might be long pauses between one character's line and the next character's answer. If these things are happening, you have a problem with pacing.

Speed-through rehearsals

There is one very simple way of correcting this. It is called a **speed-through rehearsal**. All this means is that your actors say and do all that they have been working on at rehearsal very quickly. It is like fast-forwarding a movie. There is no time to think. The actors are to just say their lines, do their blocking, and react. Don't let your actors stop — keep them going. If they have to stop, make them go back a page and pick it up again.

When the actors stop or stumble on any section, mark it in your script. It means that:

- ✓ An actor does not know what to do and needs to be prodded;
- ✓ All of your actors are having trouble remembering their lines and there are long pauses; and/or
- ✓ Someone was loosing focus.

These pauses are called **slow cue pickups**. For good pacing we generally want fast cue pickups, not long pauses. In real life we do not wait very long to answer many questions directed to us. Often, because the lines of a play are memorized, actors have to stop and think of the answer before they can give it. This raises havoc with any pacing we might want to accomplish in a play. (Another reason for having your actors off-book early in the rehearsal process!) There are times, however, that a pause is necessary. One of these is when there is movement. Crossing either before or after a line emphasizes it.

Example: Harry may say, "Pete, this time I really am leaving!" then turn and walk briskly out. Or Harry may walk to the door, pick up his briefcase, turn, speak his line, and go out. If he should speak while walking, the line would lose its force.

Running a speed-through of the night's rehearsal segment at the beginning of the rehearsal period lets you see what you should work on for the rest of that rehearsal.

Word of Caution:
This might also be a good time to let actors share as a group; however, *you* are the director. Don't let the actors take over your job. There are always those in your cast who "know everything" and will give their comments to all. Helpful hints are welcome, but you must remain in control.

Final notes

Be sure that you share with your actors things you have learned after every rehearsal. You and your student assistant have taken notes as you watched the play progress. As you know, directors have to see the action taking place on the stage in order to see what the audience will see.

Remember your final notes. If new ideas pop into your head, tell your actors these changes and then get to work on them. I repeat, never be afraid to change blocking or focus. Be flexible. Also, if something is very wrong you need to state it, too. Remember, actors need both compliments and criticism, in equal amounts. Do not forget the "praise sandwich." (And don't forget *your* praise sandwich — you know what needs to be done, but look what you have accomplished. You have gone on this journey, and you are almost at the end.)

Concentrating your comments on actors who are not doing well and never saying anything good to those who are doing fine is also a no-no. Everyone needs to hear from you. It is very frustrating to be overlooked.

Never end any rehearsal without having made personal contact with each actor. It can simply be a pat on the back, a "See you tomorrow," or the notes read at the end of the rehearsal period.

Finally, opening night is approaching — only about six rehearsals left. Are you ready?

Miss Casewell

I am twenty-four years old, although I look much older. I was born in England. I never knew my father, and my mother was an alcoholic. I had two brothers, Jimmy and Georgie, and I had to be a mother to both of them. I loved them both dearly. The Cheesemans, who lived on a farm, later adopted us. They were cruel, and my little brother Jimmy died.

I was then adopted by a very rich family, but was separated from Georgie. I was hurt but tried to put the past behind me. But Georgie was always there. My new parents seemed to realize my need to travel and find my brother and, therefore, financed my search. They were very loving and caring, but I never let them close enough to really express this love they had for me. I was so afraid of being hurt again.

I am very independent because of my situation and past life. It is in my quest for Georgie that I arrived at Monkswell Manor where a young school teacher (Mollie) is residing. She played a part in my past. The rest may be discovered in the contents of *The Mousetrap* .

Example 13: Character analysis: Miss Casewell

Mrs. Rogers

My name is Ethel Rogers. I've been married to Tom Rogers for twenty-two years. My maiden name was McClooney. I was born in Devonshire, England, on March 17th, 1898, which makes me forty-two since the year is 1940. I have one sister, Ellen, that I haven't seen since I married Tom after he stepped on my foot on a trolley car, and we got to talking. We were both eighteen.

We've been traveling about the countryside going from one job to the next.

The best and longest job we had was with Jennifer Brady. She had heart palpitations and had to have nitroglycerine tablets for it. One night when it was raining, she was having problems. Tom went to fetch a doctor. I couldn't find the nitro tables anywhere. By the time Tom returned, she was dead. I didn't want her to die; I almost loved her. I was looking for something under Tom's coat after he returned that night and when I lifted it up, the bottle of pills fell out. I told him I was gong to go to the police and turn him in. He said he'd tell them I was in on the plan, so I had to keep quiet. I haven't liked him ever since, and I try to find ways to be mean to him. I'm almost looking forward to death. I might finally have some peace. From *And Then There Were None.*

Example 14: Character analysis: Mrs. Rogers

Chapter 11

Final Rehearsals

You have almost completed your journey, but you are not performing the play for the public just yet. Everything you do from now on is in performance conditions. Final rehearsals include all the technical aspects of the play, backstage etiquette, and the curtain call. *No one* can miss these rehearsals. The key words are **concentration** and **complete**.

First run-through rehearsal

Technical jobs

So far your rehearsals stressed character development and were divided into segments. You have not worried about adding lights, props, costumes, or makeup, although you have been working on these technical areas outside of rehearsals (see Chapters 14-19). Now is the time for you to add your **running crews** to the show. These are the students who will not only be at the final rehearsals but the performances as well. Your light and sound crews have already made their cue sheets and been at rehearsal for at least a week.

First you need to have a meeting with these students. You have given them their jobs for rehearsals, but now you may need to add things for the performance conditions. Talk them through the show during the first run-through rehearsal because during the following rehearsals everything starts to work together. Most of their jobs do not change from rehearsal conditions. Two jobs that do change are the video and house manager.

Video

Night(s) of dress rehearsal
(Because of copyright laws, it is often illegal to videotape performances.)

✓ Get the best tape of the entire show.

House Manager
Night(s) of show

✓ Collect cash box from your drama teacher.

✓ Collect all actors' and crews' ticket envelopes (see Chapter 13) and tabulate.

✓ Get table and two chairs and put them out front of the theatre doors. Sell tickets at the door — have all tickets counted beforehand so you can figure how many tickets you sell at the door.

After the show

✓ Turn in all money to your drama teacher.

✓ Turn in completed list of all people who received tickets and how many each sold. Include how many tickets you sold at the door.

What lies ahead is organization for your crew and anticipation for your actors.

Backstage etiquette

This is also the time to discuss with your actors what goes on backstage during a run-through and/or performance. When your actors are offstage, they should always strive to help the play go smoothly by trying to be quiet, listening to what is going on, and being ready for their next entrance.

Sometimes a number of characters are waiting in the wings. The temptation is to talk to one another rather than pay any attention to the lines of the play because they have heard them many times before. They may speak using an undertone of their natural tone of voice. You need to explain that this tone carries, even when the volume is low. Members of the audience are sure to hear these tones, which draws their attention away from the play. If the actors have to talk, tell them to use a voiceless whisper. Explain that actors reveal their lack of courtesy — not just for the play but the actors performing on-stage — by speaking backstage during a play.

Between scenes actors should hurry off to dressing rooms or other available space so that they do not get in the way of the stage crews who have important jobs to do in a short time.

This discipline needs to start now and continue through the performances. If after several rehearsals you have too much noise backstage, tell your actors, "If I must tell you to be quiet one more time, we will start the rehearsal all over again," and mean it. No talking backstage — just like no books on-stage!

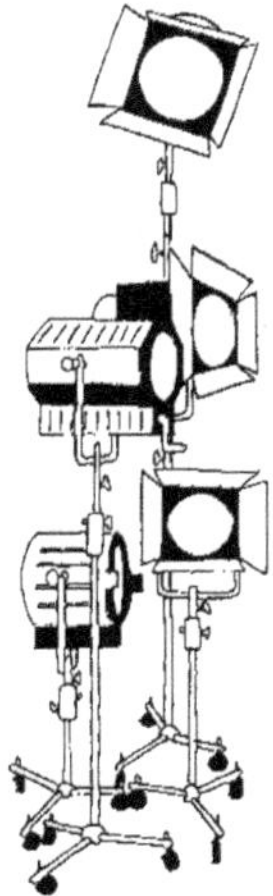

> One young director could not get her students to be quiet, so she told them that she would contact their parents and make out a schedule so that each night of final rehearsals and performances there would be parents backstage baby sitting! She meant business. Just the threat was enough. No parents were needed.

Go through the entire show without stopping

The goal of this rehearsal is to get through the entire show. Be sure that you have allowed enough time. Shoot for two-and-a-half hours; if you have chosen a major musical, however, the first time through can take as long as four hours! You really have no idea how long it is going to last. You need to see how all the pieces fit together. This is also the time to check how all of your segments work. If you find a scene that needs improvement, make a note of it so it can be worked on during the act run-throughs.

Act run-throughs

In act run-through rehearsals (your next four rehearsals), you will be running your play, one act each night. Take time at the beginning of each of the act run-through rehearsals to work scenes that you found needed improving or changing. The theatre games are over. You need to get down to serious business. Everyone is working together to create the play — crews and actors. Everyone is equally important. You are adding ensemble to your production. These rehearsals generally last two-and-a-half to three hours.

Run the act once, give notes, take time for treats, and run it again. All the crews are doing their respective jobs (pre-show music, sound effects, open and/or close curtain, run lights, scene and/or costume changes), too. The important thing is to build or increase the excitement of the story to the end of each act with no stops.

Before you begin, give your actors three helpful hints. Tell them:

- ✓ Before you go on, remember to stay far enough backstage so you are seen only when you should be seen. If you can see the audience, the audience can see you.
- ✓ Let me see what you want out of the scene in your eyes and face as well as your body.
- ✓ Simplify your character's thoughts.

Pacing

Train your actors to begin speaking immediately on the last word of the previous speaker to add to the excitement. You started working on this towards the end of the working rehearsals with cue pickups. Another technique to help with pacing is topping of lines. Instead of coming right in after the last line is spoken, have your actors start their line as the last word is spoken by the other character. Also, point out the spots where a dramatic pause is needed. Everything that an actor does in the play is important, whether speaking or not. Not only must an actor speak, he must also listen and react.

If you are doing a comedy, you need to remind your actors that the audience will laugh and the actors will need to hold for laughs. The show is funny, and you want your audience to feel free to enjoy the performance. If your actors do not hold, the audience will stop laughing. After a funny line is delivered, the character who is to speak next holds — everyone essentially freezes until the laughter has died down (under no circumstances do your actors laugh or break character). When it is fairly quiet — you don't want to wait until it is absolutely dead silent (you will lose your pacing) — the next person to speak says his or her line loudly, and the action continues.

Focus

Remind your actors of focus — again! You have worked hard with your blocking to help each character direct his or her attention to what is important. Remember, you started working on this at the end of the working rehearsals. Focus takes solid concentration. Nothing must distract your actors. Prompt your actors with a saying coined by James Cagney, "You plant your feet, you look the other guy in the eyes, and you tell the truth."

You and your student assistant are sitting out in the house with your notebook, pen or pencil, and a flashlight (remember, the lights are now on the actors, not the audience). As the act progresses you see things that your actors need to change. You relay the changes to your assistant who writes them down. Do not interrupt the flow of the action in the act. I repeat, always keep your focus on the play. Answer the following questions:

- ✓ Are the characters the same in Act I and Act II? (In Act I Sally is skipping, playing with her hair, and slouching on furniture. For no reason in Act II she stops playing with her hair and slouching.)
- ✓ Are the actors entering and exiting from the right place? Has an actor exited Stage Right and re-entered Stage Left for no reason?

"Come on, I know better than that!" you say. I know you do, but believe me, these things do happen. You are now after a total product.

Dealing with technical problems

You need to be concerned with the technical aspects of your play as well. If problems arise with the set, lights, sound, etc. you must deal with them. Let your student assistant take notes on the play while you work out the technical problem. Yes, sometimes you have to leave the rehearsal for a short time. After the problem is solved, get right back to viewing the play. Don't leave your student assistant alone for any extended time. Your assistant is not to critique fellow students for the run of the entire act. Students criticizing students is never good. Friction happens! It's not fair for your actors or your student assistant. Certainly when you are taking care of a technical problem they can look at a ten-minute segment, but giving notes is your job. You need to be there.

Read aloud the notes you and your assistant have written down to actors and technical staff after the first run-though of the act is complete. Work on any rough scenes or technical aspects that need it. Take a break for treats and then run the act a second time, non-stop. Again, take notes to determine if the changes you gave during the note session are being executed. Remember, change can be good!

Complete run-throughs

Your final rehearsals are complete run-throughs. You run the entire show, from start to finish, without stopping. Do not stop! Even if your walls fall down, your actors forget to come on, a dress comes undone, or some other technical thing is not correct. You want performance conditions.

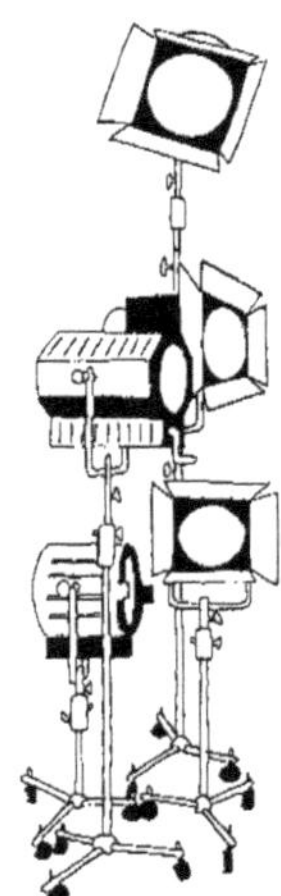

> The following three incidents did indeed happen at our final rehearsals:
>
> Annabelle, the lead character in *Annabelle Broome*, sings a song very early in the play: "Pink Is My Color, I Think?" She is dressed in an ugly gray witch outfit. As she was singing, the snap at the back of her dress gave way. At the end of the song she tried to hold the neck up but it wouldn't stay. She valiantly kept on. The nosey witch, who had been spying on her but was not to make her appearance just yet, came on-stage in character with a safety pin and pinned up her dress, saying, "You shouldn't wish for things you will never have. You must take care of what you do own!"
>
> In *Gold Fever*, Rob Roy's medicine wagon goes through a flood. It is to stay intact. We were using an old wagon given to us by the University when they did *Fiddler on the Roof*. As Rob came out after the flood saying things were going to get better, his wagon started to deteriorate in front of him. It took five minutes, but it totally fell apart, piece by piece (almost like slow motion). Luckily, after the rehearsal we were able to get the janitor to weld it back together.
>
> In *Catch Me If You Can,* the policeman gets a very important phone call toward the end of the show. The phone rang; the policeman answered it, acknowledged himself, listened, reacted, and then hung up. Another character asked, "Who just called you?"
>
> The policeman, with a straight face said, "I don't know!" He had blanked out his line and could not remember. I began laughing so hard — not out loud — I don't remember how the actors got themselves out of the predicament, but they did.

Remember, your actors must be allowed to develop the story of the play through their characters as they will during the performance. In addition, your technical staff must create the atmosphere that gives the play life. No excuses. Everyone must give their all. Concentrate! No doing homework, no carrying on, no nothing except total focus on the play. If there are problems, some may be solved on the spot with ad-libbing. Others need to be solved *after* your complete run-through.

Curtain call

At the beginning of your first complete run-through, block your curtain call. This gives all your actors a chance to be acknowledged for all their hard work. It will take time, but it's well worth the effort. You want your curtain call to be as professional as the total production. Blocking it before you have started the complete run-through lets your complete run-through be complete!

After the last line of the play, the lights go out. The actors who are left on-stage at the end will exit during the blackout. Count to three and bring up the brightest lights you have. As soon as the actors can see the lights, they come on in the order you dictate. They take their bows Down Center.

Then have them move somewhere on the set. When the curtain call is over, you have created either a picture on the stage or a straight line, with everyone Stage Left to Stage Right.

Usually the actors with the fewest lines take the first bows and then build to the leads. They can also take bows as a group — if three actors have about the same amount of lines or importance to the plot, then they can bow together. Not everybody has to have a separate bow. Always, when individual bows are done, be sure your actors take a company bow after everyone is on-stage. This is where everybody bows together. If the play is one where everyone has the same amount of lines or the characters are equally important, then just take a company bow.

The trick with curtain calls is to have your actors smile and move quickly. Actors need to hustle into place. The only exception would be if you were doing something very serious.

You might want to have the lights go down and wait longer than a count of three, then bring the lights up slowly, if possible. During the blackout the actors walk on-stage and take their places. This works well for dramatic plays like *The Diary of Anne Frank*.

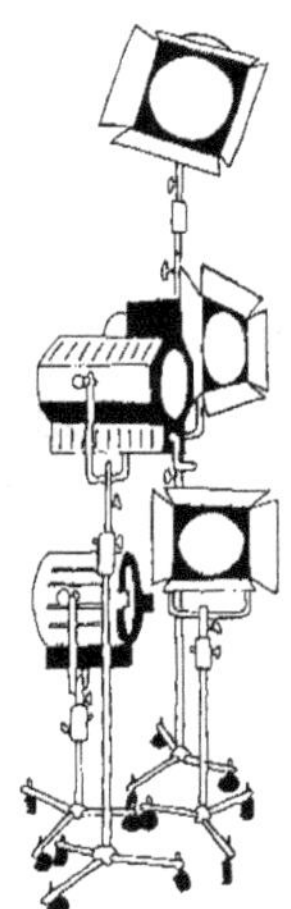

> The best curtain call I ever saw was for *Lend Me a Tenor*. In the two minutes the curtain call took, all the actors re-did the whole show — no speaking, just movement — in fast-forward time from beginning to end, doors slamming and all. It was wonderful.

If you are doing a comedy, you could bring up the lights, the actors could run around the stage like they don't know what they are doing, and after about twenty seconds get into place for a company bow. It is a bit chaotic but fun for the audience and the actors.

Three things not to forget

Cast picture

When your show is over, the stage area empty, your students returned to a normal routine, and you have had time to rest, you will want to have a picture of your production. Theatre is an ephemeral thing; it is there and then it is gone forever. Certainly we can take pictures and have our memories. I spent seven years of my career with just slides that my husband graciously took while watching the various productions, but there is something special about a cast picture. It is a constant reminder of not just the specific show but of all those students who worked on the production. It also was a great way to decorate my room! Years later students would look for their parents in pictures and their parent would want to share that specific experience with a husband or wife when they came to an open house or class reunions.

Contact a local photographer and ask if he or she would be willing to come and shoot a cast/crew picture for you. Then you can offer to have the students buy an eight-by-ten copy. Often, if photographers know that they can make a sale, they will come for no additional "sitting" charge. If they do charge, it should be nominal.

Gift for your student assistant

You have been working with your student assistant for the entire run of your show. He or she has given up many hours to help you create your production. When the curtain goes up on opening night, your assistant is not out in the spotlight. He or she needs to have some recognition about how much you valued the time and effort spent. Buying a little gift and presenting it to your assistant before the first performance allows everyone to acknowledge their appreciation. Flowers are nice, but you may want to make the gift a bit more tangible. Maybe it is the cast picture or something that relates to the play. It shouldn't be too much, but make it personal.

"Break a Leg" cake

On the final night of your complete run-throughs, after all your final notes are given, present your cast with a "Break a Leg" cake. You never wish anyone good luck in theatre; that is bad luck. (Some say the popular origin of this phrase derives from the 1865 assassination of Abraham Lincoln. John Wilkes Booth, the actor-turned-assassin, leapt to the stage of Ford's Theatre after the murder, breaking his leg in the process. The logical connection with good luck is none too clear, but such is folklore!)

Presenting the cast and crew with this cake becomes a tradition. The cake may not be great, but it's the idea that counts. It shows that you are part of this family and you care.

You are now ready to open! All the hours have been worth it. You are a family who has worked together and is now ready to perform a piece of theatre for an anxious, adoring audience. You have created a special magical world — even for one night — that all will remember.

Act IV:

Performing the Play

Chapter 12

Performance and Post Performance

Performance

The day you and your students have looked forward to is here. You have magically weaved the many threads of a high school production into an ensemble work of theatre art. Yes, indeed! As the curtain time approaches, excitement seems to attack your actors. Their minds keep darting from one aspect of the production to another; their emotions will not behave; their tummies are full of butterflies. They are starting to experience the beginnings of stage fright. So are you! This excitement grows as the hour for opening draws near. But you have things that must be done before the curtain rises.

Before 6 PM

(This schedule assumes the show begins at 7 PM.)

✓ Do not forget your sneak previews during the school day.

✓ Get an adult to help sell tickets and handle any problems with the audience or seating.

✓ Get money from the business office to provide change for selling tickets.

✓ Get yourself ready for opening. Either wear a spiffy outfit from your closet or, heaven forbid, buy yourself a new outfit! Opening night is very, very special, and dressing up for the occasion is another way of telling your actors that this night is special to you, too.

✓ The day of your final performance before you start the strike (the call to dismantle the entire production/take down the setting, lights, etc.), make a checklist of everything to be returned or put away. You, of course, have kept a list of things you and your students have borrowed. Divide the list into your various stage crews and note what each crew needs to do. Add a general category for miscellaneous details that might otherwise be forgotten. After school have a quick meeting with your crews and any adults who will be helping, and tell them what you expect.

  ✗ Keep this list simple and as straightforward as possible. You will want to use it for your future productions, too. Revise it as necessary. Be organized!

After 6 PM

- ✓ Be early (many of your actors will be ready to go hours before the first curtain).
- ✓ Open theatre doors if the janitors have not done so in advance.

Some of your actors' nervousness will disappear while they are getting into costume and makeup, but tension will increase in spite of their will to control it. Seasoned actors feel a similar feeling, to a lesser degree, but they know better how to control it.

Warm-ups

Be sure everyone is ready half an hour before curtain. Meet with the entire cast and crew in your room or a room very close to the theatre. To relieve tension try the following:

- ✓ Take a little trip down memory lane. Remind them about tryouts and where you all were at the beginning of this process.

Then get some feedback from each of your actors and crew. You might ask:

- ✓ What does your character want?
- ✓ What do you as an actress/actor/crew member want to do in this performance?
- ✓ What have you learned from this production?

Or you might like to have them do an exercise or two:

- ✓ Have actors close their eyes and visualize their performance. Go over everything their character does in the play — see it!
- ✓ Have actors think about their town or city, the weather, or another interest of theirs. Maybe they can picture themselves changing a tire on a car or making cookies.

With the activities above, you are keeping your actors' minds off their lines and doing things other than the play. You are trying to eliminate that old nemesis, stage fright!

Stage fright

Before your actors' first entrances, their hearts will beat a mile a minute. However, this nervous tension will slow down and almost disappear thirty seconds after they are on-stage, acting as their character. You want to make their nerves work for them. You do not want your actors' nervousness to disappear completely. They need to be nervous. Stimulated nerves help actors think faster and remain alert. It creates a brightness of eyes and alertness of facial and bodily muscles. A healthy, alert feeling of nervousness is desirable, but not nervousness to the extent of having stage fright.

Although **stage fright** refers to the fear that takes place when actors are on-stage, it is the same human process one has when he or she is about to solo a plane, go for a job interview, go out on an important date, or embark on a trip.

Stage fright in a wider sense is not unique to beginning actors; it is common to people from basketball players to musicians to well-established stage and screen actors. The audience rarely, if ever, recognizes these fears. They place great reliance on actors to execute a positive, confident, and poised performance.

The audience

The audience is the most valued member of theatre. Without an audience there is no performance. Every technique learned by actors, every curtain and part of the stage, every careful analysis, and every coordinated scene is for the enjoyment of the audience. They make the performance meaningful. Without an audience, all we have is a rehearsal.

The audience members want you to succeed and are generally supportive of the production. Remember that the total theatrical experience includes the audience as well as your actors and technicians. The immediate response when talking about the audience is to think of them as critics, sitting out there in the dark, judging. This feeling fosters stage fright; so many directors use the phrases, "Forget the audience!" and "Imagine the audience in their underwear!" as a means of helping students relax on-stage. But this attitude probably created the fourth wall (the imaginary wall between the audience and the actors in a play). Actors must not forget their audience any more than their lines, their props, or their fellow actors.

When the role of the audience is understood, actors begin to see the members of the audience as a group with whom they are sharing an experience. They are the final members of the cast. When it is understood that the audience is a natural part of the theatrical experience, students are immediately given a host's sense of responsibility toward them that eliminates stage fright. The fourth wall disappears, and the audience becomes part of the experience.

When the audience responds to the performance, even if quietly, their concern reaches the actors, helping them do their best. At times, somebody in the audience laughs heartily, and the contagion soon spreads over the whole audience. Your actors will find themselves growing to the limit of their performing power. However, the audience response need not be something your actors can hear. It is often an inner feeling; empathetic waves of emotion, whether fear, anger, sorrow, or sympathy, that reaches them. Prepare your actors for this differing audience response.

However, there are dangers from both audible and inaudible audience responses. If your actors cannot sense the appreciation of the audience, they may decide that the audience is not appreciative, that they seem to be disinterested. Some people are less demonstrative than others but enjoy a play more than those who respond noisily. The fact that one audience is less demonstrative than another does not mean that they appreciate the acting any less. Actors must not let the audience down, even if they think they are a bad audience. The audience has come to see a good show, and it is up to you and your actors to give them what they deserve.

Another danger appears when the audience is highly emotional. They laugh, clap, and seem to enjoy the play tremendously. Somebody in your cast may decide that this is the time to throw in unrehearsed actions. He or she begins to overact, even clown. This is bad acting. This actor thinks him- or herself a big hit and goes through ridiculous antics. Do not ever let your actors be guilty of such foolishness. Remember Shakespeare's teaching in *Hamlet*:

> Do not saw the air too much with your hand — thus: But use all gently, for in the very torrent, tempest and, as I may say whirlwind of your passion, you must acquire and beget a temperance that may give it smoothness. O, it offends me to the soul, to hear a robustious periwig-pated fellow tear a passion to tatters, to very rags, to split the ears of the ground-lings ...

Ten minutes before curtain

Ten minutes before the curtain excuse your crew and make sure all the cast and crew know that you want to see them after the show. Now get the actors up and:

- ✓ Do ten jumping jacks.
- ✓ Go up the scales singing.
- ✓ As a group, count from one to ten getting louder each time.
- ✓ As a group, count back from ten to one getting softer each time.
- ✓ If nothing else, practice a short tongue twister or two:
  - ✗ Literally literary — literally literary — literally literary
  - ✗ I can think of six thin things,
    Six thin things. Can you?
    Yes, I can think of six thin things,
    And of six thick things, too.
- ✓ Have actors fill the space around them by stretching horizontally as far as they can. Slowly, have them begin to relax their bodies by beginning with the fingers, then the arms, neck, shoulders, chest, abdomen. Their bodies will fall forward until the upper part is hanging limply, arms dragging on the floor. The only tension should be in the legs and thighs. Alternate between stretching toward the ceiling and the hanging position.
- ✓ Try to make your actors as "wide" as possible. Have them stretch from side to side.
- ✓ Try to make your actors as "thin" as possible. Concentrate on being narrow.
- ✓ Try to make your actors as "short" as possible. Concentrate on decreasing their vertical height.

Remind your actors that you will want to see them after the performance. Before you excuse them to take their places for the opening curtain, go over focus for the last time.

Focus again

Remind your actors again about the importance of continuing to act when they have no part in the dialog. Perhaps they are members of a background chorus in front of which four characters are talking. In most scenes, the chorus members are supposed to be listening. If they are, they should show some feeling for what is being said. It may be appropriate for some of them to comment to each other, their eyes indicating that their comments relate to the dialog taking place. It should be new to them, as if they are hearing it for the first time. Try to project this "illusion of the first time" to the audience.

Perhaps there are only four or five characters on-stage, two of them in conversation. If the other two characters are not speaking, it is necessary for them to listen carefully to the lines — to hear the conversation with their minds. They will then really be acting by responding with facial expressions, actions, or perhaps by the way they stand or sit. Remember again, ninety percent of acting is reacting! But your actors must be careful and guard against over-reacting so much that members of the audience notice them and not the important information being given by the actors with lines. This is called upstaging, and/or mugging. Remind them again that at times they are merely background. Don't forget Hamlet's point!

Just before you start your performance have each actor find a quiet space to become his or her character. It may be where they will make their first entrance or the makeup room or the classroom or the backstage area. From now on, your actors are their characters.

What about you?

Be prepared for any emergency — from helping with makeup and costumes to handling sick actors and malfunctioning electronic equipment.

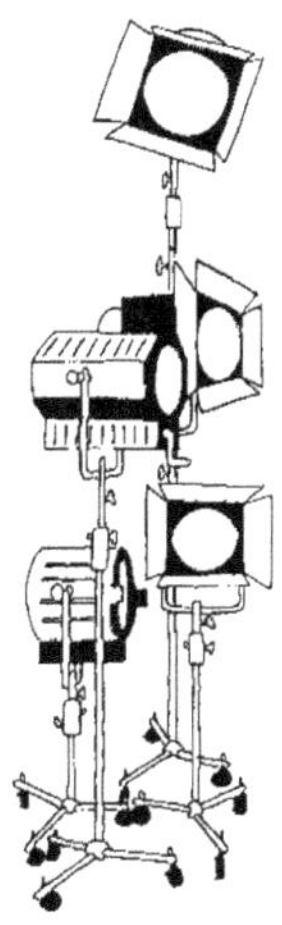

I have seen it all! During various performances, I have had a parent barge in the backdoor of our theatre, the light board blow all its fuses, the tape recorder expire during the first song of a full-length musical, leads break out in the hives, and a janitor walk across the stage to clean the heating ducts! Things happen, and you have to be ready to handle them.

. . . .

For most of my career I was out front, either sitting in the auditorium or up in the light booth. I wanted to take notes to make the next show better. Often I would even get a brainstorm and totally change a scene — not a great idea for inexperienced actors, but one that made the show better. However, I found quite late in my career that being backstage was much more comforting. I would find an out of the way place to sit (and pace) where I could listen to the show and sometimes see it. I still would make my comments after the show, but somehow I could not watch it any more.

So where are you during the performance? Probably out front watching your production. Be sure the crew knows where to find you in case of an emergency!

After the performance(s)

When the show is over, let your students go out into the audience to see their adoring fans and family. They need to be rewarded for all their hard work. They are what the audience came to see. Some directors also like to go out into the audience, meet parents and the audience in general, and spend time talking with them. That certainly is fine. The actors deserve recognition for their work. I usually stay backstage and help the crew put away props, electrical equipment, etc.

After the curtain call and the congratulations from the audience, meet with everyone as you promised before the show began. You need to tell them how good they were. If there are changes to be made or things that still need work, save those comments for your next performance. You all have worked so hard. Pats on the back are now what everyone needs. Thank them for their hard work, remind them to put all props back, and hang up costumes. Remind them they have school and/or homework to do and parents waiting for them.

The succeeding night/s, two things you talk about are:

✓ What really worked on your production

✓ What you need to work on for your next performance.

Ask the question, "You get to re-do last night's performance. What would you change to make it better?" Be sure to include your crew in this discussion. Continue as you did the night before and make arrangements for the meeting after the show. Before your final performance, you will talk about their final performance as well as the strike, which has been cleared with the actor's parents.

After final performance

Strike

When the curtain closes on the last performance, it is time to put everything you have used for your production back where it came from. It is time for the **strike**. This refers not only to the set and lights, but also costumes, props, and anything else you have used or borrowed for your production. The best thing to do is have your strike the same night as your final performance. You will have everyone there to help. You can have it the day after or on a Saturday, but sometimes not everyone can come, and cleaning up is left to the few who show up. The decision is yours.

You have talked with your crew heads and told them exactly what you expect, as well as adults who have helped. Each crew has an assignment. Add your actors to various crews. You will need to be the coordinator, going from crew to crew, answering questions and helping where needed, using your checklist to be sure everything gets done. Below are the general crews and what they do.

Set crew

Take down any walls and/or return furniture. If set pieces have been borrowed from parents, make arrangements early so they can be picked up that night. Have a designated area to store anything else (hardware, lumber, etc.) and be sure that the items are stored there. Clean up spare screws, staples, and sweep the stage area so it is ready for the next activity. Throw out anything you know you will not be using again.

Costume crew

Collect all costumes that are not from the actors' personal closets and hang/fold them up. Yes, they will need to either be dry-cleaned or washed, but you can do that at a later date. Sending them home to be cleaned by your crew can be a disaster — they may wash dry-clean-only costumes and/or not return them. Having all drama department costumes returned, even dirty ones, is preferable to not having them. Again have a designated area where you want them stored and be sure that they are there.

Those costumes brought by the students should be sent home that night. Students are forgetful and often leave things behind. Six months or a year later you do not want an angry parent traipsing up to your room demanding Pete or Janie's coat used in your production from last year! Yes, it has happened! Any clothes that have been borrowed from people other than your students should be cleaned and returned to the owners within one week of your production.

Light and sound crew

Store lights and cables in a designated area. Return microphones, cables, speakers, CDs, and amplifiers. Make sure that anything that was borrowed is returned promptly and is in working order before returning it. You may want to file any lighting or sound cue sheets for later use. Make a table of contents or a file card of your sound effects tapes and file them for future use.

Props crew

Store props in a designated area. Those that were borrowed should be returned promptly. Any that have been made specifically for the show should be boxed, labeled, and stored with other props.

House manager

Any unused tickets and programs must be returned along with an accounting for all tickets and money. These are turned over to you. (See Chapter 6.)

At the end of the chapter is a strike list the new drama teacher at Sentinel made for *Lost in Yonkers* (see Example 15 on page 133). She typed it up and posted it all around backstage so the cast and crew knew what they were to do. Everyone in the show had a job. What a great idea. Wish I had thought of it.

Your final job

When the dust has cleared and you are somewhat recovered, a nice way to end your journey is to write a short note home to all the parents of your students who worked on the show, crew and actors. With a computer it does not take too long, and the goodwill is immeasurable. Make it your goal to do this every time. See Example 16: Letter to Parents (page 134).

Final note

Well, you did it. You put on a school play. During your journey you experienced frustration and laughter and joy. Together with your students you all created a special, magical world that each will remember always. You accomplished many things. You are tired. You are happy. You are feeling what I felt for so many years. Enjoy the time off. Take care of yourself. Rest. Remember, you probably will have another show to do soon! And again, congratulations!

Strike List for *Lost in Yonkers*

SET

All the guys

1. Take furniture offstage. Put the sofa in drama storage, take old black couch out of the drama storage, and stick it out back.
2. Chair is Katie Ireland's. Take it back to her house at end of night. Call her first.
3. The radio is Erin Biondich's. Take it back to her house. Call her first.
4. Put the bookcases in the room stage right.
5. Take the pictures off the wall. They go back in the Upstage black box. Take the screws gently out of the wall.
6. Take the chair rail trim off of the flats and the baseboards off of the flats.
7. Take down the flats.
8. Put them gently in the flat racks.

PROPS

Kylie (head of crew), Jessica, Katie, Bethany

1. Take the books off of the bookshelf and put them neatly in makeup room on shelf.
2. Put all of the props away where they belong. The prop table should be totally clear. Throw anything away that needs to be thrown away: soup, soup cans, etc.
3. Please take personal props home. Thanks for lending them to us!

COSTUMES

Adrienne, Whitney, Ashley, Elisabeth, Nora, Alicia, Hilary

1. Make a pile of costumes that need to be laundered.
2. Make a pile of costumes that need to be dry-cleaned. (Remember, we are cheap!)
3. Put costumes neatly where they go.
4. This is a great time to purge the drama storage room. If it looks like garbage, it is. Throw it out! (Thanks.)

LIGHTS

Ashley, Kristen

1. Turn everything off. Make sure the light booth is clean and locked.
2. Take down the window special. You will need a ladder and a wrench. Put them in the room where the lights are stored.
3. Put the bar holding the window special away.
4. Remove the gels in the window specials and put them in the correct drawer.

SOUND

Ashley P.

1. Make sure all of the CDs are in the cabinet in 155 where the sound equipment is.
2. Put floor mics away.
3. Make sure sound booth is cleaned.

Example 15: Strike List for *Lost in Yonkers*

March 22, 1999

Dear parents of my *Midsummer* cast and crew,

In these past weeks, I've been privileged to work with your children. My, oh my, what a thrill it was to witness *A Midsummer Night's Dream*. They created a sumptuous production, from the costuming and lighting to the dancing and glitter! All their hours of hard work paid off.

I should have known that the show would be special when they asked for two extra rehearsals making the difference between a good show and a great show. This was one of the best shows I've ever directed. I just wanted to take a moment and let you know how impressed and proud I am with everyone in *A Midsummer Night's Dream*.

Thank you very much.

Margaret F. Johnson

Example 16: Letter to Parents

Chapter 13

Publicity

Way back in Chapter 1 when you were figuring your costs of production, you outlined your costs of publicity. You know that if you can use the school's paper and/or machines your publicity costs you nothing! Or do you have to get the printing done outside? Either way, it is now time to be very specific about the four things that will concern you: **poster, program, tickets,** and **PSAs**.

Poster

What is the purpose of a poster? To advertise your play at a glance. It must include five items:

✓ Title

✓ Date

✓ Time

✓ Place

✓ Price

The lettering must be legible and in black ink while the background can be white or a myriad of colors that work well with black print. Remember, a person only reads seven words as they are walking. You will want them to stop and read the particulars, so choose your design carefully. A poster designed on an 8-1/2" x 11" sheet of paper allows you to copy it or have it printed at an instant copy place inexpensively and easily. Just remember that:

✓ You must have a one-half- to one-inch border all the way around the paper. All printers must have a margin. A one-inch border works with any process you will be using, whether it be a computer, a photocopier, or a printing firm.

✓ Your design cannot use too much black. Large amounts of black ink can be difficult to print..

Using the computer will give you good black and white copies and you do not have to worry about the lettering. There are several computer programs that have templates for posters. They are a good starting place. If you do not have a computer, and/or no one is a good calligrapher, invest in some rub-off letters which can be purchased at any office supply, hobby, or scrapbook store. They come in a variety of styles and are easy to use. All you do is draw the line you want to print on in light blue pencil (this is not seen by the copy machine) and rub the letter on the line with a regular pencil.

I have said nothing about designing a poster. If there is an artist who can draw at your disposal, let him or her try to add a design, but you do not want a cluttered poster. The key to good poster design is simplicity. Poster art is a whole design art all its own and is difficult to do. See Example 17 (page 142) for an example of a well-designed poster.

When and where do you put these "works of art"? The *when* is two to three weeks before opening night. The *where* is all around town. Map out the town dividing it into the areas where most people would see the poster (a great job for one of your crews). Have a poster day, right after school or on Saturday, and send the students out. Assign your students to go to each area in groups of two. In a matter of an hour, your town should be covered.

Arm your students with tape and remind them not to hang posters on telephone poles and to ask permission before affixing them anywhere. Also have them make arrangements to have the posters taken down after the performance — a great way for students to keep a poster of their show. Keep about fifty in reserve. You will want to hang them up at school, use them as yard signs, and file several for posterity.

Program

The program is the first thing that an audience sees when they come to the play. It is very important that it be neat, attractive, and correct. Start with a sheet of 8-1/2" x 11" white paper. Fold it in half. Now you have four pages. Put the name of the play on the front. If you have a design that you used on the poster, reduce it and use it as your cover. The important thing is that the name of the play and the author appear on the cover.

Inside the program list the cast of characters, usually in order of appearance. Then you need to place information about the play's setting, acts, and scenes. On the third page (the one directly facing the cast of characters), list the director, student assistants, and crew heads. Then list all those who worked on the crews. At the bottom of this sheet or on the back page, acknowledge those who helped you as well as the company that gave you permission to perform the play. On the back you can also write anything you would like to say and/or list other upcoming arts events at your school and your next play.

Inserts

If you have time and want to create an even more personal program, you can include inserts about the actors. An insert is usually a half-page, front and back, that slips into the fold of your program. First, have your actors fill out a short question/answer form from which your program crew will pick several remarks. See the questions we asked for *A Midsummer Night's Dream* in Example 18 (page 143). Several general forms can be found in the Additional Resources section. My student assistant did most of this work. We also had the use of a digital camera so we were able to not only include what each actor said, but his or her picture as well, making the program truly a keepsake.

Tickets

Many schools do not print tickets but rely on door sales. Some have used old roll tickets and several haven't used tickets at all but rather stamped everyone's hand. I always made tickets. It allows the students to sell to friends and re-enforces the fact that theatre does cost money! Tickets for your production can be made on a computer. You will need all the pertinent information:

✓ Show Name

✓ Date

✓ Place

✓ Time

✓ Price

Everything must be accurate. Generally you can get eight to ten tickets on one sheet of paper, leaving plenty of room (one-half inch on each side) for cutting apart. This is one thing you will want to print on card stock. You do not want them crumpled up. Your print shop or local copy shop can do this quite easily. Having eight to ten tickets on a sheet also saves paper.

Use one master ticket for each night you are running your show, selecting a different color for each night. Do not combine the nights on one ticket. You will not know how many are coming each night and you do not want to return money if there are no seats. See Example 19: Sample Ticket (page 143).

Run more tickets than you need for each night. Set at least fifty tickets aside for each night of the performance. You may want to have some seats called **House Seats** for invited guests, administration, teachers, family, and theatre friends. You do not want to oversell the show, and invariably someone will lose his or her tickets. These extra tickets can solve the lost ticket problem and allow you to sell tickets at the door, if all the tickets haven't already been sold in advance. After the production, students often want a copy of the ticket for their scrapbook, so those extras do come in handy.

Your trusted student, the house manager, (see Chapters 6 and 11), is in charge of this part of the technical crew. He or she has made up a cast and crew list (yes, the crew should sell tickets too), and numbered all the tickets. Giving five tickets to each member of the cast and crew for each night works well. They can, of course, come back and get more if they need to. Explain that those five to ten tickets are worth money, and if they lose them they will have to pay for them.

The house manager, who keeps a master list of names and ticket numbers, checks out specific tickets to each student using white envelopes. On the front of each envelope put:

✓ The actor's and/or crew member's name.

✓ The night(s) for which they have tickets.

✓ The number of tickets and their corresponding ticket numbers.

On the night of the performance, the house manager collects all the envelopes that the actors and/or crew members have sealed with the money collected and any tickets they did not sell. If anyone has forgotten their tickets at home, have them call their folks and have the tickets brought down to the theatre. You cannot sell one night's tickets another night. Be inflexible. If the tickets are not there, the student has bought them at full price.

You can decide if you want to give complimentary tickets out and how many. Generally, the faculty, staff, and administration are given two free tickets each. It is good public relations to give these out, but only you can be the judge. You know how much you have spent on the show and how much you can afford to give away.

Recently, several high schools have decided not to have tickets or advanced sales. They use a stamp instead. The "tickets" are sold at the door, your hand is stamped, and you then get your program. Not printing tickets or having to keep track of them is certainly easier and much less of a hassle. Decide which method works better for you.

Free advertising

Public Service Announcement (PSA)

Publicity also includes the written word. Free publicity can be obtained through the school newspaper, the school's daily announcements, and articles in the town newspaper. The key time frame for this free advertising is three weeks. You want to give everyone enough time to make room in their schedule to include your play information. One way of obtaining this free publicity is through calendars. First, you must write what is called a **PSA**. This is the type of announcement that you hear on the radio and see on television. Each broadcasting station is required by the FCC to do a certain number of PSAs. Generally they are thirty seconds long and include:

✓ Name of the play

✓ Production dates

✓ Location

✓ Time

✓ Cost

✓ Brief summary of the play

Write out all the particulars of your play and make at least ten copies. Now send the PSAs to the various calendars and/or current events offices of the daily/weekly newspaper and local radio and television stations.

By sending this PSA early, the newspaper, which usually has a society or education writer, might do a feature article. If there is only one newspaper, they might even do more. Your radio and/or TV stations sometimes have short interview programs dealing with community events and you and/or your students might be interviewed. They are generally very good about advertising student events. You will also want to notify your school paper. Hopefully, they have been keeping track of your progress throughout the rehearsal period, but it never hurts to keep them informed. See Example 20: *Midsummer PSA* (page 144).

Yard signs

Remember, you have saved fifty posters. It is now time to take out twenty-five of them (or more if you have lots of extras). Have each of your cast members find or borrow yard signs used for political campaigns or find and/or make stakes used for campaigns. Attach a poster to each stake and wrap it in plastic, cover it with clear wrapping tape, or use a plastic baggie and put it in each of their yards. As people drive/walk by, the posters will catch their eye and hopefully they will come to your production. Do check with the local authorities about any local ordinances.

School advertising

About one week before your show opens, it is time to hit the school.

✓ Haul out twenty-three of the posters you have kept in reserve, put them up all around the school, and start your daily bulletin barrage.

✓ If your school has a PA system, do three well-written, thirty-second PSAs. For the rest of the week write up something new and exciting about the upcoming event to appear in the daily bulletin. (Of course, you must clear the PA announcement with the administration!)

✓ If there is a school assembly any time within two weeks of your production, ask to get on the program and act out a little something to pique the interest of the student body.

✓ During lunch in the cafeteria, do a scene or create something to appeal to students while they are eating.

Either the day before or the day of opening, perform a five- to eight-minute "sneak preview" for all the English classes during the last ten minutes of class. Do this every period of the day that you have English classes and try to pick three different segments so you will not be doing the same scene every period. This variety not only gives the audience something different to see but it also gives more of your actors a chance to perform.

Have your entire cast, even if they are not in the sneak preview, wear their costumes and makeup all day. (Of course, this must be cleared by the administration.) Begin each preview with the student assistant or you introducing the play, the dates it will play, and the cost. Characters first introduce themselves and then perform the scene. The entire time should be about ten minutes.

Word of Caution:
Be sure that whoever is speaking at the sneak preview or assembly is very careful of what they say. It's a good idea to have them write down what they plan to say so you can approve/edit it if necessary.

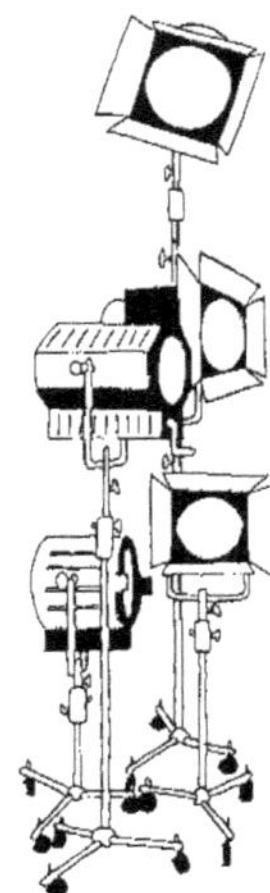

During my first year, we did a melodrama along with the one-act play we had presented at the state play festival. As the president of the student body was in the melodrama, I told him to talk about the show during his final assembly, which was the day we opened. Well, he spoke off the top of his head. As he was the hero in the melodrama, he told the entire student body to come to see him, the play, and throw peanuts!

That evening over 350 students arrived with, yes you guessed it, peanuts, tomatoes, cereal, hard candy, peas and pea shooters, apples, oranges, bananas, popcorn (popped and un-popped), and dead fish. Before the end of the first scene, the entire cast has been pelted, and the stage was a sea of bits and pieces of food, smashed tomatoes, and smelly fish. When one of the students went out to sweep the stage floor, after he had made one pass across the stage, it was literally covered again — you could not see where he had swept. One of my students who was to sing in the first oleo act came to me and said, "Miss Friedl, I am too scared to go out there!" I have always been of the opinion that, no matter what, the show would go on. This was an exception. No student of mine was ever going to be afraid to go on-stage.

I marched out on to the stage and addressed the audience. I said, "Ladies and Gentlemen — if I may call you that!" and ended with," ... and furthermore, if you are going to throw anything, you throw it at me. I am the director!" Dead silence. Not a word was said, no items were thrown, and then there was applause.

There were at least fifty adults in the audience, but not one of them did anything to stop the barrage of food. I found out later that even the superintendent of schools was among those adults and before I came out, he and his wife had sneaked out of the dark theatre.

I never allowed any students to speak "off the cuff" again to advertise a show!

You know that all the parents will come and everyone has at least two friends who will come, but that does not fill your theatre space. By involving your school you have tapped into the best audience for which you could ask. A student audience is great. It not only costs nothing to get them curious, but also, by working with your English department, it might be possible for the staff to allow bonus credit to students for coming to the play. There is nothing like a good grade to get students out! What you want is to get interest started in the drama department. By having a strong participation of your student body at your productions, you are making life-long playgoers out of your students. They begin to realize that seeing a play is just as much fun as seeing an athletic event or a movie.

Paid advertising

Newspaper ads

If money is no object, you should put an ad in you local paper at least a week in advance. The other alternative is to have someone's parents or business underwrite an ad.

Postcards

Purchase two to four postcards per cast and crew member. Take time during one of your last working rehearsals and have the students and crew write notes to people they want to attend the play — not their parents or anyone who they know will attend the show, but folks they would like to see at their production who might not attend if they didn't get this little reminder. You could even create a design on the computer and run these postcards through the printer. Be sure that they are all returned to you, and don't forget to mail them!

Two final reminders

All the advertising you do is viewed and judged by the audience before the show has even started. You want to impress them, not turn them off with tacky publicity.

Be sure that all your original copies are typed or drawn on one side of the paper in black ink with a one-half- to one-inch border all the way around. A quick rule of thumb is to use bright colors with black ink; heavy stock or light cardboard for tickets (eight to ten tickets can be put on one sheet) and posters; and regular paper for programs.

All written information should be done *three weeks in advance.*

The Encore Theater
PRESENTS

William Shakespeare's
A Midsummer Night's Dream

Friday, March 5th
8 PM

Sentinel Little Theater

$5 Adults **$4 Students**

Example 17: *Midsummer* Poster

Insert Form
A Midsummer Night's Dream

Name ____

Character ____

What are your plans for the future?

Are you a dog person or a cat person?

Are you like your character?

Do you have any faults?

What was your first theatre experience?

What era would you go back to if you could?

Example 18: Insert form — *A Midsummer Night's Dream*

Sentinel High School Presents A Midsummer Night's Dream by William Shakespeare Friday, March 5th, 8 PM	**Admit One** **$5.00** **Adult**

Example 19: Sample ticket

To: Whom It May Concern
From: Margaret Johnson, Director (Phone No.)
Joe Smith, Thespian Troupe 483 Corresponding Secretary
(Phone No.)
Sentinel Drama Dept.
Re: A Play: *A Midsummer Night's Dream*

On Friday, March 5th, *A Midsummer Night's Dream* will be playing at Sentinel High School at 8:00 PM in the Little Theatre. Tickets will be $5 for adults and $4 for students.

A Midsummer Night's Dream is one of Shakespeare's most high-spirited plays. It focuses on three different worlds: that of the law and order adults, the dull workmen, and the mystical woodland creatures. Love is a major theme and after much confusion, everything is put right. At the end of the play, Bottom the Weaver and his group of very unimaginative workmen present the play (within a play) of "Pyramus and Thisbe," a farce of *Romeo and Juliet.* This playlet is one of the funniest ever written. Many students have been involved with this production, not only as the actors but also as directors, choreographers, costumers, and technicians.

Example 20: *Midsummer* PSA

Curtain Call:

Technical Aspects

Chapter 14

Introduction to Technical Aspects

I know. You have been fretting and stewing about the technical aspects of your show; the set, lighting, costumes ... the list goes on and on. "Not only am I new to this theatre business, but I am not a designer of anything! I can't do that!" Take a deep breath and relax.

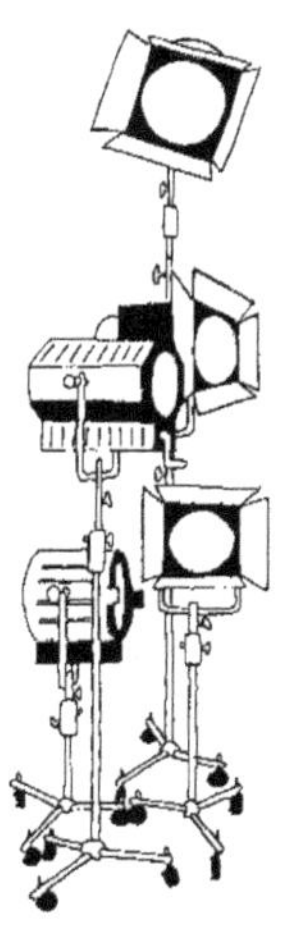

My students were asked to perform on the main stage at the International Thespian Conference in Muncie, Indiana, in 1984 at Ball State University in a three-thousand-seat theatre! First of all, after the euphoria and the honor wore off, we had to get down to the essentials: the money for all of us to go, the decision on what hour-long play we would perform, and the technical aspects.

Six students were able to go, so that limited what play we could do. We also knew that a complete set with fancy lighting was out. Not only did we not have the money to build and transport it three-quarters of the way across the United States, we only had fifteen minutes to set up whatever we were going to do and no rehearsal time. We had to spend our money on travel expenses and registration for the conference. Technically it left us an empty stage with general area lighting.

We chose *Elizabeth I*, a show allowing the students to play several roles — the characters were a group of actors put under a spell by a witch. I had done the play before and had kept the scripts. We knew we could ask for the royalty to be waived because it was being performed for the conference. Now we needed to look around our theatre and costume storage for things we could use for the set and props.

True, I had been teaching for over twenty years and had accumulated a great deal of "stuff" in addition to knowing two former students — Tom Valach [an outstanding theatre designer for high schools, community theatres, and colleges in and around the Twin Cities area] and John Shaffner [currently an Art Director for television with five Emmys] — who were theatre designers. I enlisted their help. In fact, throughout this book you will see their influences — especially Tom's, as he designed many of our productions — not just in costumes and set but in lighting as well.

For the set, I consulted John. He asked me if I had fabric. Yes, I had at least thirty yards in various lengths of red polyester that Tom had gotten cheap in Minneapolis. John also asked if we could use four-foot by eight-foot platforms from the theatre in Muncie. I said yes. Thus a design was drawn using the fabric draped over the theatre's existing light bars while adding platforms Stage Right and Left.

Next, I enlisted Tom's help for costumes. The play was loosely-based on the life of Queen Elizabeth I, so we needed to look like a troupe of players who go back to the Elizabethan era. We also knew that we could not design true Elizabethan costumes. With the minimal setting, Tom decided to do unrealistic costumes as well. After scrounging around we came up with very simplistic costumes. I had only two girls, one was Elizabeth and the other Mary, Queen of Scots. All wore leotards I had on hand, the boys wore sweatpants and running shorts, and the girls wore muslin rehearsal skirts. For Elizabeth, we used a child's inner tube to add fullness to the skirt, a cut off sweatshirt for her top, and a paper crown we had gotten for our production of *Cinderella*. The others wore children's folded newspaper hats, made after we arrived. We added various items, from a fifties gathered slip for capes to lacy curtains for over-drapes, capes, and doublets.

All of these fit into two brown plastic milk crates, which we loaded, wrapped, and used as luggage. When they were empty, they served as seating for the show. The thirty yards of fabric we put in a military duffel bag and used it, too, as luggage.

The show was a huge success. Based on their performance, all the students were offered scholarships at Miami University. Using our imaginations, abstract technical aspects, and creating a variety of unique characters, we produced an interesting production.

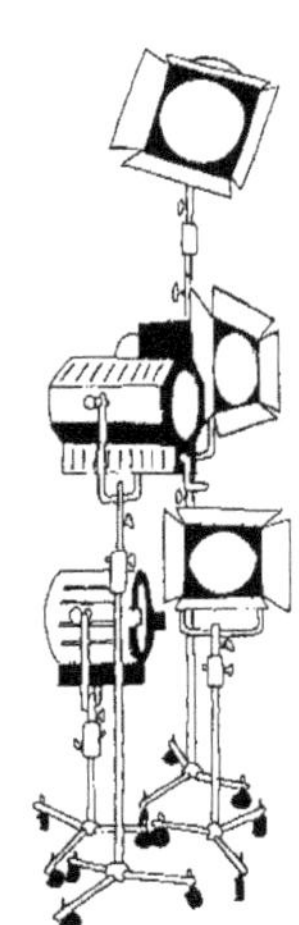

Technical theatre is not as daunting a task as it sounds. Never forget your imagination! Before you begin to get specific, however, ask yourself the following question, "What do I really need for my technical aspects?" The answer is:

✓ A place to perform.

✓ Actors who are dressed appropriately for their characters — costumes.

✓ Props to help create real action.

✓ Lights so that everyone can be seen.

✓ Basic makeup to make the actors' faces visible to the audience.

✓ Something for your actors to sit on.

Remember, a play is about people telling a story, and you have already worked very hard to create believable characters who do just that. You can tell their story with very limited sets or even a blank stage. The following plays can easily be done with things every school has including an acting area with some lighting and curtains.

12 Angry Jurors
David and Lisa
Inherit the Wind
Murder on Center Stage
The Prime of Miss Jean Brodie
Sorry, Wrong Number
Class Action
Here and Now
Love, Death, and the Prom
Our Town
The Importance of Being Earnest
Under Milk Wood

Works in Progress
Old time melodramas
Plays by Craig Sodaro

Rememberin' Stuff
Plays by Tim Kelly

Add one or a combination of the following to create your setting:

✓ Band platforms/risers
✓ Chairs
✓ Couches
✓ Desks
✓ Ladders
✓ Tables

The band platforms give you levels. The risers can be steps. The rest gives you what the specifics of the set require such as tables and chairs, etc. Keep it simple.

Next you need to tackle costumes, makeup, and props.

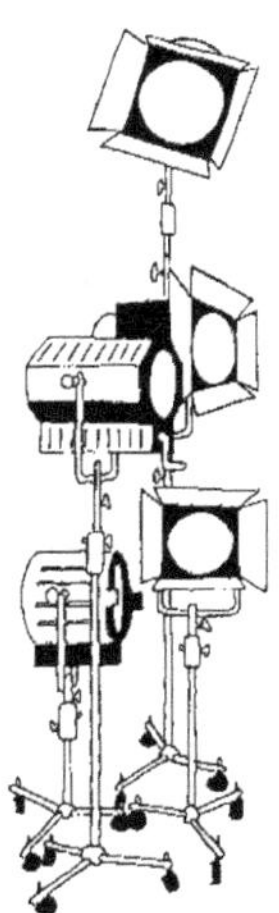

Do not do what one director did in a recent production of *Macbeth*:

They built a simplified set, painting the walls to look like a medieval castle. The stones looked like a committee painted them — very inconsistent. The set was never used or needed. The lighting was either too bright or too dark, the fog machine literally hissed every time it was turned on so the entire audience heard it rather than saw it, and the costumes were not convincing.

Half of the actors were in white tops, the others in brown or purple. MacDuff was the only one in plaid, not even his wife and child. Of the ten men in the production, six wore black sweat pants, three were in either black tights or slim-fit pants, and one was in jeans. The eleventh man was a woman who dressed totally in leather. On their feet were black boots, firemen boots, slippers, and/or tennis shoes. The ladies wore blouses that were too big, vests that were either too big or too small, and skirts that were so long that each actress tripped on her skirt at least once.

Their technical aspects were poorly executed, and the audience spent most of their time being distracted. Instead of paying attention to the story about a man obsessed with power, the director chose to spend time on aspects that assaulted the audience: visually with a conglomeration of clothing and set; and aurally with fog. No one understood the story.

You do need to become familiar with some basics of technical theatre. You want your audience involved with the characters and the story they have to tell, not in technical aspects that are poorly done. Don't forget the Internet. Do not be afraid to search the Web for what you are interested in. It can save you many hours of research.

The following chapters will give you some suggestions for costumes, props, lighting, and set, but they are only meant to get you started. Again, begin with something simple and do it well. The ideas in each chapter are intended to get you through your first plays with a minimum of expertise, expense, and time. They are meant for those who are not experienced craftsmen, as I am neither an electrician nor a craftsman. The suggestions given in the following chapters will spark your imagination.

The first most important technical aspect is **costuming**. As has been stated over and over, a play is about people, so what your actors wear is extremely important. Next, you always need **props** to help tell the story, then you have to be able to **light** your acting area so the actors can be seen. **Hair and makeup** are next, and they are almost always necessary. The final chapter ends with some ideas that make **set building** easy.

Dramatic sets, makeup, props, and lighting are wonderful, but they do not make or break a show. Four things are required:

✓ Expertise;

✓ Money;

✓ Construction areas; and

✓ Adequate time for building and/or painting.

Discussions about how to build extensive sets and props as well as create elaborate costumes, lighting, and makeup are not included in this book. All of that information is covered very well in the books listed in the Further Reading section. If you have the four requirements mentioned above, get those books and go for it.

Do not forget to take time and visit museums. Their works of art are not only glorious to enjoy, but the information you can glean from them is phenomenal. You can see hair, makeup, costumes, buildings, colors, props, and more.

As you become more familiar with your facility and gain some theatre knowledge from your first experiences with drama, you will decide what you need and want for your technical aspects. Read on, and good luck.

Chapter 15

Costuming

Costuming is an integral part of the play and is always needed. Remember, anything worn by actors is considered a costume. Their clothes not only explain who and what their characters are and something about the play, but they also create interest in the production.

Five purposes of costumes

✓ **To clothe the actors.** Parents frown on students acting in the "all together"!

✓ **To help establish the time period, year, and/or day.** Each play is different. One might stress a time in history like that of Shakespeare or Moliére while others need to tell us about the weather or the occupation of the characters as in *Inherit the Wind*. The important thing is that you must decide which time period is the most important for your production. Recently Shakespeare has been set in the streets of Los Angles as well as in the era of Hitler. It depends on your concept and how you see the play.

✓ **To help distinguish one actor from another.** Each character's costume should say something special about that character and tell us something about the play itself. In *Annabelle Broome*, one of the evil witches, Esther, is not too bright, so she was costumed in orange with patches sewn on her clothes, her wig cut in uneven lengths, her pointed hat bent up, and her makeup a mess. She was immediately recognized as a witch, but certainly not the typical evil sort of witch.

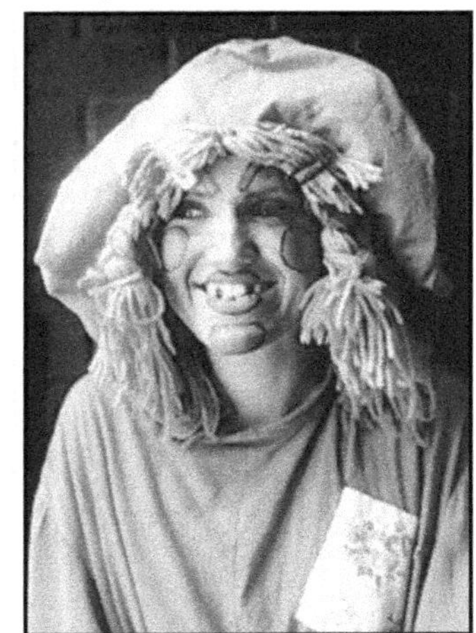
Esther from *Annabelle Broome*

✓ **To communicate the play.** Costumes can tell us the mood of the play instantly by use of color and fabrics. Again, *Annabelle* is a great example. Because we chose to put all the witches in colors, the mood was not dark and dreary but light and fun, something children love.

✓ **To give the actors the physical feel of their characters (psychological effect on the actor).** Students act very differently when they are in a costume rather than jeans and tennis shoes. They move differently, and their posture changes. They do not feel like themselves, which makes them less inhibited.

The costumes must reflect the show's concept. How can they do that? The trick is to translate the concept into costumes by making a statement.

Your costume statement — three questions to answer

Review your character cards. You not only have done a quick analysis of each character but you have also created his or her costume plot. You already know:

- ✓ The time period;
- ✓ What the author thought you should have for a costume;
- ✓ Your character's age, occupation, and gender;
- ✓ The amount of time each character is on-stage in the play; and
- ✓ The character's activity and personality.

Now, answer the following questions:

- ✓ **Should your concept be a color?** There are some common assumptions about color and costumes. Comedies, farces, and fantasies are frequently costumed in bright, light fabrics and colors; serious plays usually are costumed in subdued colors and heavy fabrics. Begin by thinking of your show in a color, even if it is not your concept.

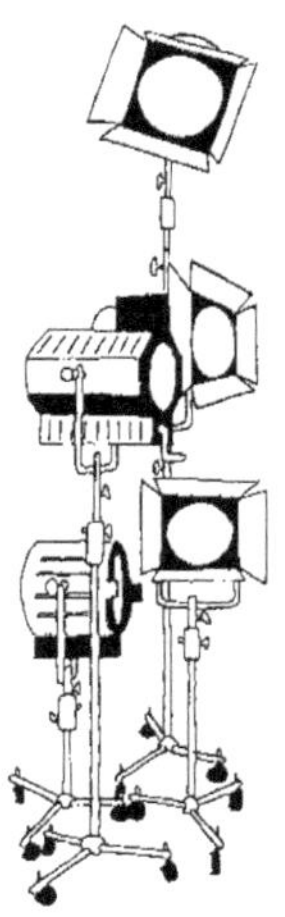

Tom Valach and I decided that the concept for *Inherit the Wind* was an old photograph, so we selected only one color — brown. Rather than having all the costumes just one shade of brown, we decided to use various shades. The lightest tone was sepia and the darkest a black-brown. The aprons and men's shirts were all sepia while Col. Brady's suit was black-brown. All the other folks were put into families, ranging from reddish to yellowish brown. Painters' overalls were used for the men and simple muslin dresses for the women. Dyeing was done in the Consumer Science's washing machine, doing each family together, starting with the lightest brown. More dye was added, then another family's costumes were dyed, and so forth until the last family was as dark as possible. A final cycle in the machine was run with soap and Purex and/or Clorox (a strong clothes-washing bleach) so the machine was ready for anyone to use the next time.

Below are five shows and the colors that could accompany them.

- ✗ *Web of Murder*: Steel gray
- ✗ *Arsenic and Old Lace*: Ecru and deep purple
- ✗ *Hotel Paradiso*: Garish Purple
- ✗ *The Unsinkable Molly Brown*: Red
- ✗ *The Trojan Women*: Aged earth tones

Remember that the color of the background, whether it be drapes or a set, must be considered part of the color scheme. If the drapes are your walls, keep their color in mind. It will be difficult to costume the students in the drape color because their bodies will fade into the background unless they are very well lit. They will look like floating heads. When a complete set is used, there will be more flexibility in use of color as the drapes will not be as important; however, care must be taken when selecting the wall color.

✓ **Should you stress the style or line of the period?** A period play is generally costumed to conform to the fashion, line, and material used in the specific period.

✓ **Should each character be instantly recognized for his or her profession, status, age, or relationship to the other characters in the play?** Look at the types of unique characters telling the story. No doubt they would dress in a variety of colors. If it is a modern play with teenagers telling the story, let your students design their own costumes from their closets, attics, or borrowed from friends. Give them guidance, but let them do the work. They are living with these characters every day and have some very definite ideas about them.

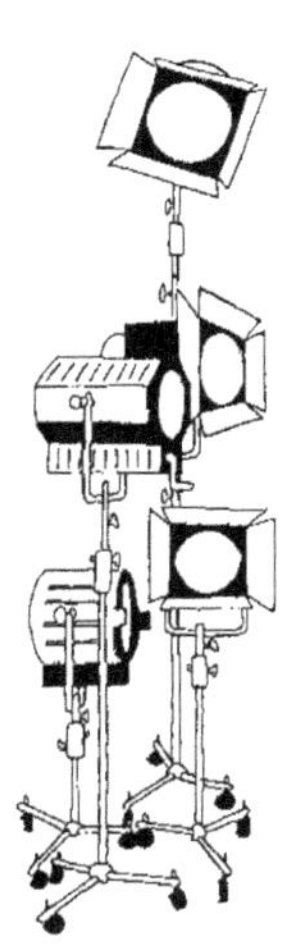

When doing *Tom Jones,* I wanted to set it in the Revolutionary period using the leotards and tights I had been given earlier as well as those I had purchased for *The Trojan Women*. When Tom Valach designed the costumes for *Once Upon America* (see the pictures on pages 167), there were several things I could use. I did not want to use heavy velvets or brocades because of the lightness of the show, so I chose to add pieces of costumes made of polished cotton and chintz. These fabrics became my concept. What I needed to do next was incorporate the new softer costumes with the leotards and tights as Tom had done earlier.

Using the Revolutionary patterns we bought for *Once Upon America* (I never threw anything out), we created new brighter skirts, shawls, and dust caps while using the aprons and hats from *Once Upon America* for the women; and the bloomer pants, long, sleeveless vests and tri-corn hats made of heavy felt for the men with several bright coats and matching bloomer pants and neck ruffles. The beauty of these costumes was that they would fit most any body type, were easy to move in, were not embarrassing for the students because the added pieces covered their bodies quite well, and they could and would be used for other productions, not just another version of *Tom Jones*, but also *Imaginary Invalid* and *Much Ado About Nothing*.

. . . .

For *The Curious Savage,* I costumed all the characters in the late 1950s to make it a period piece, but I felt it was even more important to have each of the characters, within the 1950s framework, be individual. Mrs. Patty (the painter) was in smocks and slacks, Mrs. Savage (the lady with a great deal of money — eccentric rather than insane) in good older ladies' clothes, and Fairy Mae (a ditzy sprite) in very floaty, frilly frocks!

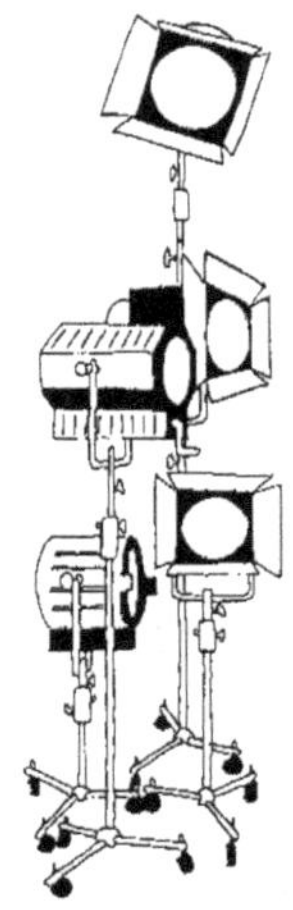

> When doing *2nd Class,* I decided to have all the students in jeans and two different colors of short-sleeved T-shirts. They then added coats, hats, sweaters, etc., to make each character unique.
>
> We chose modern clothes for the characters in *David and Lisa,* stressing their individual characters. I posed the question, "If the students in the play were going to Sentinel High School, what would they wear?" David dressed as a yuppie, looking extremely clean and neat with dress pants, shirts with ties, and either sweaters or sport coats. Lisa dressed in messy, rather young-looking clothes. I put her in short skirts and blouses as well as flesh-colored tights so she could play with her dresses as young children do and not have any fear of revealing anything to the audience.

By answering these three questions you have decided on your costume statement. So where do you find these costumes?

Six ways of locating costumes

✓ **Students providing their own** is obviously the cheapest way to costume a show but can be disastrous if you have not done your homework.

When doing another production of *Macbeth,* the director left the job of costuming totally up to the individual students and their parents. There was no thought towards any production statement. As a result, Lady Macbeth was dressed in white satin and her husband in cheap brown cotton!

How can a disaster like this be avoided? By having a Costume Coordinator. This person's job is described later in this chapter.

✓ **Pulling costumes from stock** is another low-cost way to get costumes. Stock means that these are costumes you inherited when you began as the new drama teacher. They are then pulled (out of storage) for a show. Give your costume crew ideas to work with, send them to the library, and then let them pull what they think is important. You are dealing with style and period for this concept, rather than color. This is a great, inexpensive way to costume period shows if you have stock costumes.

✓ **Going to rummage sales** offers a wide variety of costume options. Period dresses, suits, hats, purses, and other accessories can be picked up relatively inexpensively. A cotton dress of the sixties should not be more than the cost of a soda or a candy bar. Period floor-length formals and men's suits can also be adapted to many different periods with additions of new sleeves and trimmings. Wedding gowns, bridesmaid's dresses, graduation gowns, and nightgowns are also useful. You also can find great fabrics — drapes, bedspreads, etc. — to use when making costumes. If you are lucky enough to have the Salvation Army, Goodwill, or a church bazaar, they often offer even better deals and have large selections from which to choose.

✓ **Borrowing** is another economical way to locate costumes. If this is your choice, check first with your local community theatre and/or university. Start by putting a notice in the school bulletin and the teacher's boxes for what you need. This will generate:

✗ Things you can use.

✗ Interest in your next production.

Don't forget to check the school's lost and found. Service clubs, local merchants, and cleaners are other places to look. Motels, doctors' offices, restaurants, National Guard, or the VFW can provide various uniforms.

Word of Caution:
Garments borrowed must be handled with care, as you never want to return them damaged.

Putting the borrower's name on a tag and sewing the tag in the costume ensures that it will be returned to the right owner. At the conclusion of the show, return these borrowed items within a week, preferably cleaned and in better condition than they were in when borrowed.

If you are borrowing anything, give the people who loaned you the items complimentary tickets to the show, acknowledge them in the program, and write a thank you note. This insures more cooperation in the future. It also presents you and your theatre department in the way you want to be regarded; appreciative and professional.

✓ **Renting** is the most expensive way of locating costumes. Sometimes it has to be done. If you're doing a show where a character must be costumed in a specific way and all other options do not work, you'll need to rent. The question you must ask yourself is, "How important is that costume to the character and the show?" If you are doing *Peter Pan*, for example, you need to have the crocodile.

✓ **Making costumes** is the final option. Often directors think of it first and then just as quickly, it is forgotten. Why? Because of one of the following:

✗ Too expensive;

✗ No one to do it; and/or

✗ I cannot sew.

Well, do not throw the baby out with the bath water. Read on. Whatever you decide to do, when your show is over, keep your costumes (unless they have been rented or borrowed). You will be starting a costume collection from which to pull for your future productions. The one thing to remember is that you need to find a place to store these costumes in a cool, dry area away from insects and animals.

Costume coordinator

The next major decision needs to be made: Who is going to supervise your costumes? The answer is the **costume coordinator** — a person outside the department — a parent, a fellow teacher (possibly the consumer science instructor), a student, or a combination of any of the above. No matter which of the six options for locating costumes you choose, you need someone there to help. Any option needs a supervisor to eliminate the *Macbeth* disaster mentioned earlier. The costume coordinator makes all costumes unified, as well as making your costume statement. His/her qualifications are:

✓ Knowledge about sewing;

✓ Organizational skills;

✓ A knack for getting along with students;

✓ The ability to take direction from you; and

✓ An understanding of the various costume periods (or where to go to get that information).

Believe it or not there are quite a few seamstresses and taylors out there. The trick is to find them. Check with your local fabric and/or quilting shops.

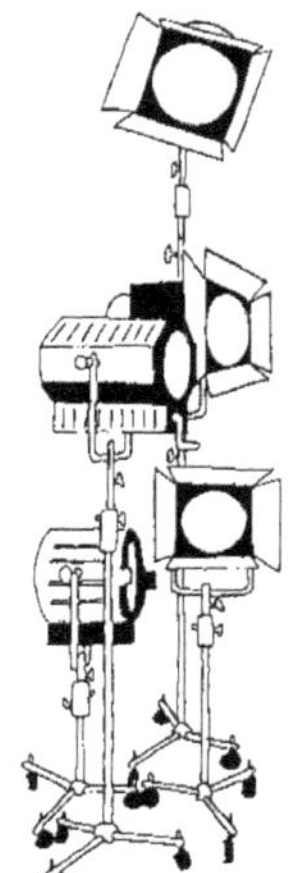

I was very lucky to have a student interested in costumes during her years in the Sentinel Drama Department. She designed and made all the flapper dresses for *No, No, Nanette* and then became my costumer when she and her family moved back to Missoula. If I had a student interested in costumes, Susan would help, which left more time for me to direct. As she is a full-time costumer at Missoula Children's Theatre, I have had the privilege of wearing many of her creations — even if she is not the designer, she finds something she can add to any costume I wear.

After you have found your costume coordinator, give him or her a copy of the script to read, then sit down and discuss the show, including your concept for the show and your costume statement. It is possible that this person can give you new ways of looking at the show and your ideas may change. Always be open to suggestions — be flexible.

Costume crew

Your next job is to recruit your crew to help your coordinator. Advertising your costume crew along with your tryouts can help immeasurably. Before the prospective folks sign up, give them a general list of what is required of the crew (see Chapter 6).

After your crew is chosen, be sure they understand that they will be working with the coordinator and following his or her directions. You need to be sure the coordinator follows through with his or her job, as well. Constant checking is necessary to eliminate any problems or misunderstandings. This also demonstrates that you care what is happening with this aspect of the production.

The remainder of this chapter will deal with three approaches to costuming a production. Helpful books on costumes are available from Meriwether Publishing Ltd. They include: *Elegantly Frugal Costumes* by Shirley Dearing and *Costuming Made Easy*, and *Costumes, Accessories, Props, and Stage Illusions Made Easy* by Barb Rogers. These books stress innovation while keeping the cost down.

Making complete costumes

Making complete costumes has three advantages:

✓ These costumes are made for a specific production, thus fitting the actors;

✓ These costumes can and should be reused with small additions for other productions; and

✓ You have started a great costume collection that can be used for years.

There is an initial expense, but the fact that the costumes can be used over and over again far outweighs the cost. Yes, it does take time and require sewing expertise, but believe me it is worth the effort. Again, the secret is to have a good coordinator. With the decision made to make the costumes, you need to consider:

✓ Selecting patterns and fabric (remember to pre-wash all washable fabric before starting construction);

✓ Making detailed instructions of how to construct the costume; and

✓ Sewing the costume.

Make a habit of checking current pattern books, especially the lingerie, craft, accessories, and costumes sections, as well as contacting the Consumer Science teacher (we used to call them Home Economics teachers) for creative and inexpensive suggestions. Often patterns can be altered with the help of these teachers or your costume coordinator to serve your needs.

If students and/or parents are making costumes, the coordinator will need to make the directions clear and simple, going step by step. Do not assume anything!! If possible include the fabric. If not, include on the directions where to get the fabric, the yardage needed, and the cost. This limits how much students can spend on their costumes. (See Example 21 on page 174 for my coordinator's costume directions on how to make a kilt for our production of *Brigadoon*. We provided the fabric — flannel plaid. Our coordinator was a parent who loved to sew.)

Another way for students to make costumes is to work on them in school while they are rehearsing. You and the coordinator will both be there to supervise. When the students are not on-stage they can be working on their costumes, along with the costume crew. This way, the costume crew feels like they are a part of the total production, the actors know what goes into costuming, and you and/or your coordinator are there if a problem arises.

Next, you need to be aware of the various historic costume periods. Following are hints on how to create period costumes.

Period costumes

Before constructing any period costumes, research the specific period. There are many places that can be very helpful, such as:

✓ Costume books;

✓ Encyclopedias;

✓ *National Geographic*;

✓ Movies;

✓ Old photographs;

✓ Paintings;

✓ Pattern catalogs;

✓ The Internet;

✓ Old *Life* magazines; and

✓ Old movie magazines.

The key to good costuming is to create the idea and/or illusion of the period while not spending a fortune in time and money. The following ideas give the general feeling of each period. I have also included several plays appropriate to the respective period.

✓ **Greek and/or Roman:** This period deals with all the plays written by Sophocles, *Antigone, Oedipus Rex*, and Aeschylus's *The Trojan Women*. The costumes are relatively easy to create. They can be made of fairly inexpensive materials, such as old curtains, old sheets, blankets, toweling and/or terry cloth, and washed, unbleached muslin. You need a length of cloth one-and-a-half times the actor's height — approximately three yards for an average adult because it is generous and can be draped around most anyone's body in many ways. It is usually caught at the shoulders with brooches, clasps, or ties.

✓ **Medieval 1:** This period features most children's fairy tales — *Cinderella, The Nearsighted Knight and The Farsighted Dragon, Beauty and the Lonely Beast*, and such plays as *Gammer Gurton's Needle, Ralph Roister Doister*, and *Good Grief, a Griffin*. The same materials that work for the Greek costumes work well here, too, because they need to be draped. The basic costumes for both men and women are large tunics that reach anywhere from the knees to the floor, generally belted with rope or rough material. It can be plain or colored pajama tops that are lengthened, making sure that the sleeves are full length and have elastic at the wrist. (Most everything was covered: arms, legs, and heads.) The legs, if showing, can be covered with loose and baggy sweat pants or dyed long underwear. A sweater, long sleeved T-shirt, or sweatshirt can be used to cover the arms with the tunic pulled over.

This was Mabel, the head witch in *Annabelle Broome*. Tom Valach added the lightning bolts because her big trick was to say, "Silence," and there would be a loud clap of thunder. She was costumed all in red.

The vest or jerkin worn over the tunic can be made from an old jacket with the sleeves removed or even the zip-out lining from an old coat. All heads were covered with scarves. Remember, this is the period of habits and cassocks worn by nuns and priests of the Catholic Church.

✓ **Medieval 2:** Another way of costuming this period and the best way to create Fairy Tales is to check your local pattern book. To create a tunic, find the choir robe pattern and lengthen the sleeves and skirt. As the neck is fairly low, a turtleneck will be needed underneath. Halloween witches as well as many other costumes can be found and used as well.

✓ **Shakespearean:** Costumes for most of Shakespeare's plays — *Romeo and Juliet, The Taming of the Shrew* — as well as *Elizabeth I* and *Arlecchino* fall into this period but are extremely difficult to sew. However, making them is the most cost-effective way to use your money because you will begin to build stock Elizabethan costumes. You can start with 1950-1960s lace/satin formals or wedding dresses. Your costume coordinator should be able to match the fabric and add sleeves and small pillows at the hips to create Elizabethan dresses. Be sure that the bodice is tight and the skirt is very full. Using tunics from **Medieval 1** and substituting richer fabrics would work for the men.

This is Kate's wedding dress from *The Taming of the Shrew*. We started with a satin wedding gown. Upper puffed sleeves with a touch of red were added along with pillows at the hip.

If that is not possible, use your money to rent such costumes because the set, royalty, and scripts will not be as expensive.

Ruffs, the neckpieces worn by most people of this period, can be easily made with the soft plastic doilies found in notion stores. Cut three doilies into three-inch strips and fold them as you would when making a fan. String a shoelace through them and tie it around the neck.

✓ **Seventeenth and Eighteenth Century:** These two periods can be bunched together with some minor alterations. They fit into the plays by Moliére — *The Imaginary Invalid, The Doctor in Spite of Himself, Tartuffe*; Sheridan — *The School for Scandal, The Rivals*; and Goldsmith — *She Stoops to Conquer*; as well as plays dealing with the French and American Revolutions — *Once Upon America, Tom Jones*. These costumes can be created using today's clothing.

✗ For men: take a long-sleeved sweater, sweatshirt, or leotard and add cuffs, a collar, and a sleeveless, button-less, hip-length coat for the top; then take pants, cut them just below the knee, make a placket, and put elastic in it. Add long, dark socks and shoes with buckles.

✗ For women: take a long-sleeved sweater or leotard, then add cuffs and a collar made of muslin, cotton, lace, or the soft plastic doilies mentioned above. A simple pleated or gathered full-length skirt with an apron completes the outfit.

- Toward the end of this period, women's dresses changed slightly. The skirt became distended at the hips. To achieve this look, the skirt should be worn over two hip pads (small pillows) attached to a belt around the waist. The sweater/leotard, trimmed with flowers and/or bows, should fit tightly. Adding a cummerbund gives the hourglass look of the eighteenth century.

✓ **Nineteenth Century — Victorian Era:** I have lumped these two periods together as well. I directed only one show from the early period — *Nicholas Nickelby* — but you would need this period if you were doing *Jane Eyre* or *Pride and Prejudice*. This part of history saw the empire waist (hike the skirt to just below the bust, rather than the waist), and little puffed sleeves and bonnets for the women.

Longer breeches, along with the coats, vests, and shirts from the seventeenth century, will work fine for men.

The latter part of this period was one period I used a great deal. This is the setting for most melodramas — *He Done Her Wrong, Egad, What a Cad, The Great Western Melodrama*; mysteries — *Gaslight, Terror By Gaslight, The Spiral Staircase*; the standards — *I Remember Mama, Miracle Worker, Our Town, The Importance of Being Earnest, Under Milk Wood*; Fedeau Comedies — *A Flea in Her Ear, Hotel Paradiso*; any western plays; and musicals — *Fiddler on the Roof, The Music Man, Peter Pan, Phantom of the Opera, The Unsinkable Molly Brown, Brigadoon, Forty-Five Minutes from Broadway*.

✗ For men: start with a white shirt. Iron the collar flat. When it dries, fold the point down, towards the buttons and iron it. You are creating a stiff high collar. Add either a string tie (easily made with shoe laces) or a long thin tie from the 1960s. Then find a single-breasted suit with pants that are not tight (or sports coat and pants). To the coat

This was a character from *Terror by Gaslight.* He is wearing a vest from the 1940s and has his coat unbuttoned.

add an extra "button" at the top by sewing a snap on the lapels, about five inches from the chin and sewing a button on the front. (The audience will never know!). Add a vest. Remove the creases from the pants by ironing them with white vinegar. Add black or brown shoes and dark socks. Your gentleman should look a little crumpled from the waist down and quite stiff from the waist up.

✗ For women: start with a long-sleeved sweater or a high-necked, long-sleeved blouse (even a man's shirt can work). Sew tucks at the waist so the shirt blouses over the bust and gives the illusion of a corseted waist. Next add a full-length, gathered skirt. If possible, take some of the fullness out of the skirt and add it to the back. You want to give the feeling of a flat front and a train in the back. Use ribbon, lace, and/or ruffles for the cuffs of the sleeves and the neck, as well as the hemline, (or four inches above the hem). These gentle ladies must look prim, proper, and straight as an arrow. White or black hose with slipper-type shoes completes this outfit. Short capes and boleros were worn for outside apparel.

- There are other ways of creating women's costumes of this era, too. One is to adapt wedding dresses or formals from the 1950s by adding a full ruffle all the around the hem (petticoats must be worn underneath), or use a nightgown. Dyeing it the color needed and adding ribbon and a belt creates a summer dress for plays such as *Our Town* or *Meet Me in St. Louis*.

✓ **1920 — The Flapper:** This era deals with mobs or gangsters as well as the plays *Inherit the Wind, Cheaper by the Dozen, No, No Nanette, The Bat, The Sting,* and *Our Hearts Were Young and Gay.*

✗ For men: Use a single- or double-breasted suit; a pinstriped suit is even better. The look is boxy. The real key is the felt hat with a wide brim. Be sure that the suit has only two buttons down the front.

✗ For boys: Start with a shirt and a pullover sweater. Any kind will work, but the V-necked ones are the best. Next are knickers, so do the same with pants that you did for the seventeenth century costumes.

✗ For women: The look was also straight but long. A V-necked, hip length pullover blouse, with or without sleeves, works well. Add a fairly straight, short skirt with an elastic waistband. It should be no longer than just below the knee (unless the character is older). Your women need to give the illusion of having no chest or waist.

✗ For girls: It is just like the women; the look was straight with very short skirts. (See Example 22 on page 175 for instructions on making flapper costumes.)

When costuming the following periods, concentrate on the actors' hairstyles, the length of the women's skirts, their hose, and the men's suit coats. Be sure that boys wear dark socks when playing men. It was most ungentlemanly to wear white athletic socks or show any bare leg. Men never wore white socks except when wearing white shoes and a white summer suit. With each of the following eras I have listed not only plays from my list of productions (there are, of course, many plays that I did not direct that would fit each period), but also several movies that will show great examples of how people dressed during these periods.

✓ **1930s:** Plays: *Night of January 16th, Babes in Arms, The Man Who Came to Dinner, You Can't Take It with You, George Washington Slept Here, The Prime of Miss Jean Brodie, The Sound of Music*. Movies: *It Happened One Night, The Thin Man, Stage Door*.

✗ For men: Double-breasted suits, long white cotton dress shirts, and vests with wide ties.

✗ For women: Long, straight dresses (mid-calf). Use an eyebrow pencil to run a line down the back of the legs to suggest hose.

✓ **1940s:** Plays: *The Uninvited, Ten Little Indians, Arsenic and Old Lace, The Diary of Anne Frank, South Pacific, The Mousetrap*. Movies: *It's a Wonderful Life, Double Indemnity, To Be or Not To Be, Casablanca, You Can't Take It with You, The Third Man*.

✗ For men: Double-breasted suits, long white cotton dress shirts, and vests with wide ties or thin bow ties.

✗ For women: Shorter and fuller dresses for the early part of the decade (knee length); suits, longer straight skirts for the latter part of the decade (mid-calf).

✗ For teenagers (often called bobby soxers): Long circle skirts, sweaters, anklets for the girls; rolled-up jeans, patterned or white T-shirts, and oxford/saddle shoes/penny loafers for the boys.

The Diary of Anne Frank was successfully costumed from the 1950s-60s. Anne as the little girl in Act I was put in a child's dress that was very short. Flesh-colored tights were added so that she was completely covered. Having the other characters' clothes fit loosely, the length of the women's skirts long, and stressing correct hairstyles, the feeling of the 1940s was created.

✓ **1950s:** Plays: *12 Angry Jurors; The Curious Savage; The Girls in 509; A Tomb with a View; Harvey; Bye, Bye, Birdie.* Movies: *All About Eve, The Blob, Rebel Without a Cause, On the Waterfront, The Sweet Smell of Success, Tammy, Gidget.*

Dr. Emmett, the head of a loving home for mentally-disturbed people. He is running out of money. *The Curious Savage.*

- ✗ For men: Single-breasted suits with baggy pants and boxy coats. The early 1950s saw coats with one button at belly-button level, in the mid-1950s, another button was added at waist level, and by the end of the 1950s there were three buttons and a fairly tight-fitting coat. As suits became more fitted the ties became thinner and the legs of the pants tighter. A cardigan sweater could always be added, rather than a coat.
- ✗ For women: Cocktail-length dresses (lower mid-calf — the movie *All About Eve* is a prime example) with full skirts (many petticoats — the square dance outfits of today are very close to this period except they are too short), and shirt dresses (short-sleeved, full-skirted dresses that buttoned from the waist up) for the early part of the 1950s; the latter part saw straight skirts with a kick pleat either in the front or the back and sweaters that matched. Suits were also worn with an overjacket covering the waist. It was to look like the straight line of the 20s. All skirts were at least three to four inches below the knee.
- ✗ For teenagers:
  - Greased hair combed away from the face, white T-shirts with rolled sleeves (a cigarette pack sometimes in the roll), and low-rider, loose-fit jeans with a paper-thin belt. Every boy wanted the Elvis look! Be sure to check *Rebel Without a Cause* and *The Blob.*
  - The girls were much like their mothers. After *Tammy,* the ponytail and bangs were all the rage!

✓ **1960s:** Plays: *The Savage Dilemma, Catch Me if You Can.* Movies: *Cool Hand Luke, The Graduate, Charade, In the Heat of the Night, Midnight Cowboy, Psycho* (the original).

- ✗ For men: Single-breasted, tight-fitting coat (a great one to also use in the Victorian Era) with a thin tie and tight pants. For the first time men wore short-sleeved shirts. Do not forget the Nehru jackets (and chains) at the end of the 1960s.

  - ✗ For women: Boxy suits and shorter skirts started the decade and 1969 saw the introduction of the miniskirt — a skirt that was a foot long. This was the major reason we have pantyhose. No more garters belts, girdles, or pairs of hose!

- ✓ **1970s:** Plays: *MASH, Godspell.* Movies: *Annie Hall, Network, Being There, Close Encounters of the Third Kind, Saturday Night Fever, Urban Cowboy, Breaking Away, The French Connection.*
  - ✗ For men: Sports coats and turtlenecks were ushered in, as well as polyester jumpsuits, pants, and leisure suits.
  - ✗ For women: Pantsuits, long, granny-type dresses, vests (long and short), and polyester were the epitome of this era. Of course the era ended with Disco!
- ✓ **1980s and Beyond:** I am not covering these periods because they represent modern day. Most shows written during this time can be done in modern dress without hurting the integrity of the show. If you want to be totally accurate, look at the following movies: 1980s: *ET, Ordinary People, Flashdance, Desperately Seeking Susan, A Fish Called Wanda, My Body Guard.* 1990s: *The Sixth Sense; Fargo; Run, Lola, Run; Good Will Hunting; American Beauty; Ghost; Twister; Sleepless in Seattle; You've Got Mail.* 2000s: *The Princess Diaries, Bring It On, Bend It Like Beckham, Freaky Friday* (the remake with Lindsay Lohan).

Animal costumes

If a complete costume is needed for an animal, check the craft, accessories, and costumes section of a pattern book, as well as men's pajamas and/or clown patterns. If you use the pajamas pattern, sew it in one piece adding a long, front zipper. Make individual mittens and feet, and the actor can then move easily.

How to use a basic costume for several changes

Adding to a basic costume makes the job of costuming a character with many changes or a chorus easier. For a chorus or a large cast who are all related because of the locality or marriage:

- ✓ Run down the line and have each costume dyed a fraction of a shade darker so that when the chorus is lined up, you go from one color to another, like orange to red, with pink in the middle;
- ✓ Break the chorus into two to four color groups; or
- ✓ Dress each character in the same color but have women wear different colored bows in the back of the costume or in their hair. Have men in a different length tie or even a varying size tie so as they stand in line, the ties range from six inches long to two inches long.

We used a version of this costuming concept for *Best of Broadway.* As it was an ensemble piece it was easiest to costume all the students the same. We made wrap-around skirts for the girls with different colored leotards for the tops and jumpsuits for the boys. The fabric was light blue cotton twill, not unlike kettle cloth. We added hats and shawls, etc. to make each scene/character different. This picture shows the entire cast singing a song at the end.

For a character who has many changes, start with a plain, basic dress with a zipper down the back. To this dress add one or more of the following:

✓ Apron	✓ Sash	✓ Collar
✓ Overskirt	✓ Blouse	✓ Coat
✓ Hat	✓ Skirt	✓ Sweater; and/or Tie

Enlist the aid of your student actors. Start with one basic outfit per character, and then get your actors involved. Suggest to them how they can make changes by adding one of the above.

For *The Sound of Music,* Roberta Manis designed a white shirtwaist dress with puffy sleeves for the children. To this was added a colored sash for the wedding, a long bib — sort of like chest armor — for the party, a bib apron for the play clothes, and a black corduroy vest and flowered skirt were sewn together and put over the basic white dress for the singing contest. When we did *The Prime of Miss Jean Brodie,* we made skirts much like the kilts of *Brigadoon* and the tops like the placket front we used in *Sound of Music* as we had to cover the girl's chests. To show the girls had grown up, we added a bolero for the second act. We bought matching long-sleeved, beige polyester blouses at K-Mart for ten dollars apiece that worked beautifully. The play took place in the 1930s, so the skirts were long.

You have created the appearance of several different costumes. Now you and your students have not only accessorized the costume but have made each unique.

Costumes with leotards, tights, and/or sweat units

By starting with both leotards ("leos" for short) and tights for form-fitted costumes or sweatpants and sweatshirts ("sweats" for short) for a bulkier, baggier look, the following periods can be created. The initial investment in leos/sweats is very expensive: however, with care these items can be used for years. Long-sleeved turtleneck sweaters can substitute for the leotards. Tights do not last as long as sweatpants, but they should last three years with proper care. Buying men's tights, which are heavier, is a wise investment.

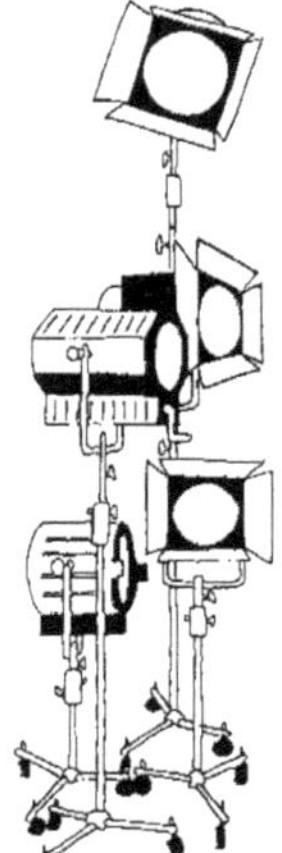

When doing *Love, Death, and the Prom*, I chose to costume all the students in the same color sweats. Everyone looked the same. As each of the actors played several roles, adding sweaters, scarves, hats, etc., they became a different persona in a matter of seconds.

Period costumes

✓ **Greek:** Use leos for both men and women. Dye to match gathered skirts and shawls (for the women) and a two-and-a-half- to three-foot piece of cloth wrapped around the body like a toga for the men.

My production of *Trojan Women* was designed by Tom Valach and executed by my students. The women were costumed in brown and deep red leotards with muslin skirts and shawls dyed to match. We did not hem them, as we needed the fabric to look worn/burned. Masks were worn during the Greek period, so we decided to create masks out of celastic (a material that can be molded using acetone and painted) — today you should find a better material to use. The mouths were not covered, so the actresses could be heard. The fabric pieces can be made of muslin, old sheets, light blankets, or drapes.

✓ **Medieval:** Add a long tunic to either leos or sweats and scarves for the heads and the look of peasants/serfs can be created. We used tights, leotards, and loose-fitting gowns, much like the witch's gowns found in the pattern catalogs. To make them look old we sewed patches on them.

This scene from *Good Grief, a Griffin* was towards the beginning when the townspeople are singing about the horrible griffin.

✓ **Shakespearean:** Use leos for the upper classes and sweats for the lower classes. Adding short puffy pants, a tunic, or vest for men and a full skirt with padding at each hip and a shawl for women can create the general feeling of the period. Making the ruffs explained on page 159 is a must.

✓ **Seventeenth Century:** Adding knickers, a shirt with full sleeves (if necessary), and a buttoned vest to leos creates a great costume for men. If the shirt is not necessary, add a collar and a vest or long coat. Add cuffs, wristbands, shawls, and a dust cap along with a gathered skirt for women. Later in the century the women's costumes became fancier. Bows, lace, and ribbons were added along with an overskirt. The following examples from the beginning of the century were taken from *Once Upon America*.

Our men's basic costumes for *Once Upon America* consisted of rust, dark green, and brown leotards, dark brown tights, tricorn hats made with very heavy hat wool, muslin shirts with a V-neck and gathered sleeves, cotton printed or plain vests (lined for sturdiness), and loose-fitting muslin "knickers" dyed to match the leotards — all worn over the leotards and tights.

Our pilgrims were very simple — boys in basic pants, leos, and tights, girls in leos and skirts. The collars and cuffs, made of white percale, were used for both men and women. The boys wore pilgrim hats, and the girls wore the hat pictured here.

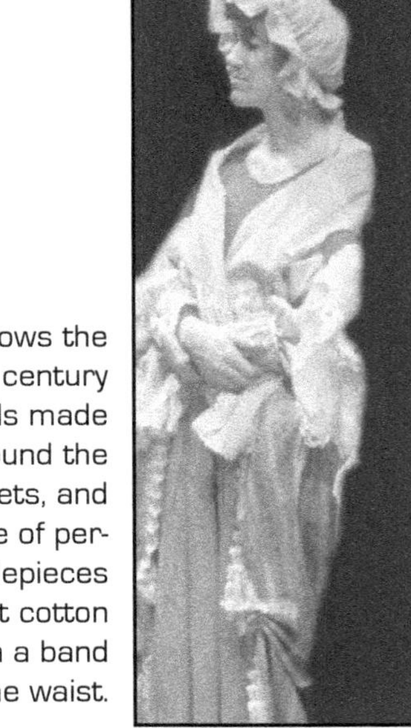

This picture shows the latter part of the century with frilly armbands made with elastic around the sleeve, dust bonnets, and frilly shawls all made of percale. The frilly sidepieces made out of a light cotton print were sewn on a band that went around the waist.

This costume was for the farmers. They are the same skirts and hats as pictured above. The dust bonnet in this picture was pulled down to cover most of the girl's hair.

These costumes, although made for *Once Upon America*, were used for all three of my productions of *Tom Jones*, *The Imaginary Invalid*, and *Much Ado About Nothing*. New skirts, shawls, and dust caps were made of chintz with lace/ribbons and bows added to give the show lightness and a feeling of richness.

Animals

Basic animal costumes can be easily done with sweats by adding mittens, tails, and a headpiece with ears. This allows actors to move around easily. As sweats are bulky, the human figure is not as obvious. Adding a knee-length, sleeveless tunic eliminates the human figure and works well for birds, ground hogs, and rabbits.

A sleeveless jumpsuit over a long sleeved T-shirt and tights works well, too.

Jersey wings can be added to a leo for butterflies; black plastic garbage sacks make wings for creepers and crawlers; felt military insignia and dark glasses are a great touch for ants. The makeup becomes a large part of these costumes.

Body suits

As leos cover the skin, they can either become the flesh or part of the outfit.

This was a bird in *Goldilocks and the Christmas Bears*. The tunic and hood were covered in feathers. We attached the feathers with hot glue, but she still molted!

This was the dragon in *Near-Sighted Dragon*. The tunic was covered in cloth scales that were sewn on. The tail and the body were stuffed with newspaper.

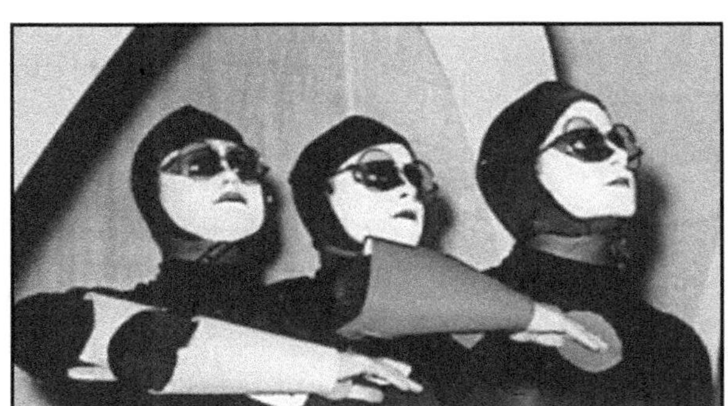

Ants from *And So Ad Infinitum*.

We borrowed some wonderful tops and skirts from Missoula Children's Theatre for our girls in our production of *Li'l Abner*, but they were cut rather low in the front. We put leos on each of the girls, and the tops worked fine. Notice the patches on Abner's overalls — they were cut in irregular shapes and outlined with a large black marker.

Masks

Do not forget that headpieces, masks, and fancy makeup are also part of costumes. If a mask must be used, make it a partial one and emphasize characterization. You want your actors to use their faces and the audience to see them, too.

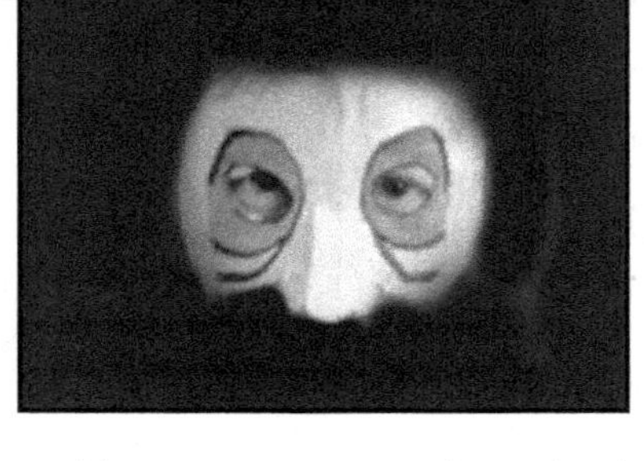

This is Andromache (wife of Hector) from *The Trojan Women*. Her son wore a mask made of heavy watercolor paper, as he had no speaking role. Her costume was a dark green leotard and tights. The muslin was dyed to match. She had a ragged skirt and shawl. As she had many lines, I did not put her in a mask, but rather created mask-like makeup for her (to match her son's mask) with green, brown, and white. We did not put a base on her face but just painted the lines on. The idea was from the book *The Mask of Reality*.

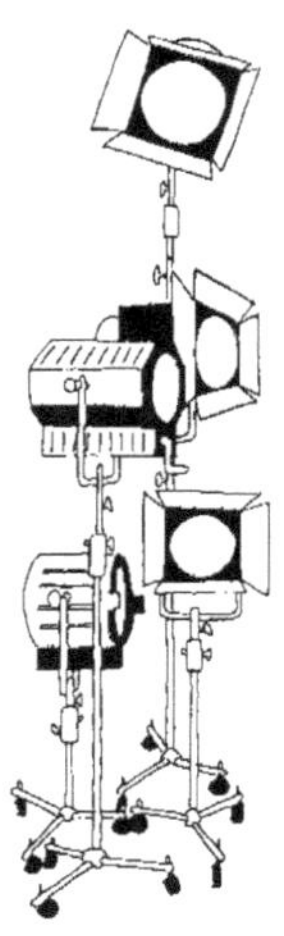

When I did the children's show, *Sacramento: 50 Miles*, a show loosely based on *The Bremen Town Musicians*, the lead characters were a dog and a donkey. I had wonderful students playing the roles. I wanted the donkey and the dog to look real, so I put full head masks on them. It completely destroyed their facial expressions. The head was later used successfully in *A Midsummer Night's Dream*.

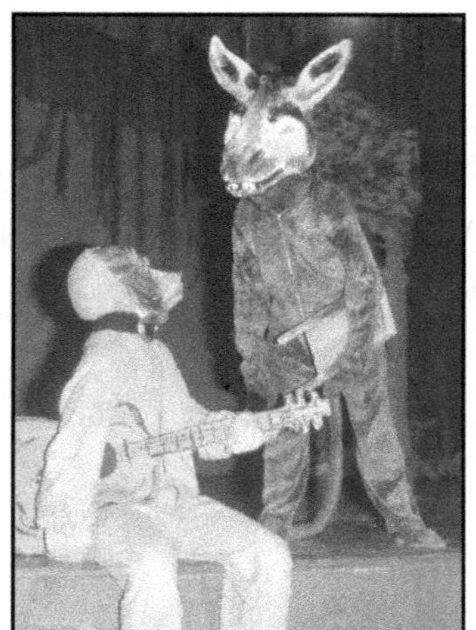

Although the donkey head is wonderful, you can see that it truly limited the actress's ability to use her face and voice. She had to do everything with just her body. Losing faces proved detrimental to my production. Her costume was a bodysuit made of velour that zipped up the front and had attachable mittens and feet.

Great substitute materials

Before you go out and buy new fabrics, look around at rummage sales. Old drapes or blankets can make great costumes. Velvet dresses and skirts can be cut up to make trim. Never forget your local motels and hotels. They often have old sheets they will donate to the drama department that you can dye and use (they make great linings for costumes). There are some fabrics, however, that you have to purchase because they give you the effect you want. Five are listed below.

- ✓ **Burlap:** For color and rough texture, burlap works very well. This fabric does not give and ravels so it must be lined.
- ✓ **Corduroy:** Corduroy looks much like velvet from a distance. It works well for any rich fabrics needed for a production. It is considerably more expensive than other fabrics mentioned, but it is about half the cost of velvet.
- ✓ **Flannel:** Flannel is a good substitute for wool plaid or fur. It works well for kilts and skirts. In *Peter Pan*, flannel fur was used to costume the little lost boys, Tarzan fashion. It drapes beautifully but can hold its shape if lined.
- ✓ **Muslin:** For making curtains, most costumes, lining, and building sets, unbleached muslin is the best. It is an inexpensive cotton fabric which comes in a variety of widths from thirty-nine to one-hundred-twenty inches. There are various weights, so be sure to check before you purchase it.
- ✓ **Terry cloth:** For any animal or rough texture effect that might be needed, heavy-duty terry cloth works perfectly. It is extremely durable, dyes well, and is easy to sew. It does ravel so lining with muslin and or sheeting is a must. Be sure that it has been preshrunk in hot water and dried in a hot dryer before cutting out any pattern.

Helpful hints

Aging fabric (Distressing)

Aging can be achieved by bleaching your fabric before cutting out your pattern or after it is made. There are six other ways to age fabric as well:

- ✓ Spraying the garments with a strong solution of instant coffee (one part coffee to two parts water);
- ✓ Spraying the fabric with a weak solution of colored dye (one part dye to five parts water);
- ✓ Dirt, either watered down and sprayed on the fabric or rubbed into the fabric dry;
- ✓ Regular paint (one part paint to three to five parts water, depending on the color) sprayed on the garment;
- ✓ A solution of one part bleach to three parts water sprayed on the fabric; or
- ✓ Shoe dye spray. It works well as it does not fade with repeated washings.

Another way to show age is to sew patches on the fabric. Be sure that they are big enough to be seen by the audience and either colorful if doing a comedy or subtle if doing realism. They can be sewn or ironed on with a fusible lining. After they are attached, be sure to run a black or dark brown permanent/laundry pen around the patches so they can be seen.

Duct tape

Recently, several newspapers and magazines, among them *The Wall Street Journal* (in an article printed on February 28, 2003), discussed making costumes out of duct tape. Essentially you cover muslin with the duct tape, then cut out the pattern and sew using carpet thread while being sure to keep the needle clean with solvent. It takes a long time to create these costumes, but the end product can be luxurious. It would make an outstanding Tin Man costume for *The Wizard of Oz*. Check the Internet for other great costume ideas.

Graying fabric

Pure white should not be worn on-stage because of the glare under the lights. It takes focus away from the play itself. The audience just sees white! Tea dyeing works beautifully. In a washing machine, use a tablespoon of instant tea per article of clothing. (Dilute tea in water before adding fabric.)

Lining

The more inexpensive the fabric chosen to make costumes, the more important it is to line the garment. A good lining material is unbleached muslin. Not only does it give body to the fabric, but it makes the costumes last much longer. It is well worth the extra cost and time spent. If a stiff look is needed, do not hesitate to line the costume with a fusible interfacing along with wire. Lining the waistband of a pair of pants with stiff wire makes clowns look great.

Prints

If prints are used, keep in mind that at a distance a small print will look like a texture or even disappear. The pattern must be large and have a wide expanse of background color between the designs.

Removing blood

To remove blood from fabric, use peroxide. It is the best thing going according to doctors.

Trims

All trims must be exaggerated. Start at three inches wide. Do not spend time and energy using small strips or decorative stitches on the sewing machine because the audience probably will not be able to see them. An excellent way to make trim is to take fabric remnants, cut them into three inch strips (or wider), cut iron-on interfacing the same size, and fuse the two together. This keeps raveling down to a minimum. Attach the trim with either double-faced interfacing or sewing.

Checking age of donated costumes

If you are lucky enough to have some old dresses donated to your drama department but are unfamiliar about their period of time, a good rule of thumb is to look at how they are fastened. If it is on the side and with snaps, you know that it likely comes from the 1930s or before; if it has a metal zipper down the side it probably comes from the 1940-50s. The older the zipper looks, the older the dress. Generally buttons were added to the front of the dress to give the illusion of a front opening. Back zippers as well as plastic ones started in the 1960s.

Costume tricks to help young actors become old

This was Drummond in *Inherit the Wind.*

Old men can be costumed easily by:

- ✓ Pants that are so big for them they have to wear suspenders that make them ride around their chest.
- ✓ Slippers or lace-up shoes too big for their feet causing them to shuffle.
- ✓ Combing the actor's hair back away from his face.
- ✓ Remind your actors that older men hike up their pants when they sit down and always try to keep their ankles covered with black socks. No gentleman wants any leg to show!

Old women can be costumed easily with:

- ✓ Skirts longer than the period.
- ✓ Heavy wrinkled hose.
- ✓ Orthopedic shoes or bedroom slippers too big for their feet causing them to shuffle. (Of course the noise from the shuffling must not disrupt your production!)
- ✓ Heavy hairnets over their hairdos.
- ✓ Remind your actresses that when they sit, they need to smooth the fabric on their posteriors before they sit — they do not want their dresses wrinkled.

Final note

A costumer's most prized possession is his/her imagination, which is developed by trying out ideas. Work with your coordinator, always keeping your costume statement in mind. Never think of costuming as a problem but rather as a challenge to the imagination.

Instructions for a Kilt

1. Cutting: The material is cut lengthwise instead of the usual crosswise direction. This eliminates side seams in the kilt and the necessity of matching plaids.

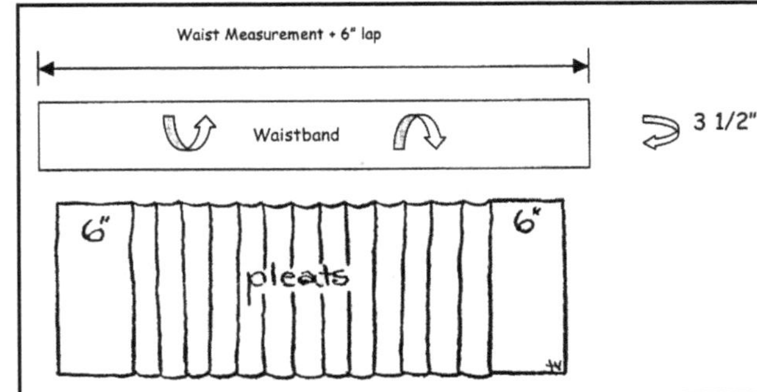

2. Waistband: Measure boy's waist and add six inches (for overlap). Use this measurement for waistband length times three-and-a-half inches wide. Cut waistband off one edge of fabric, across end.
3. Sewing Kilt:

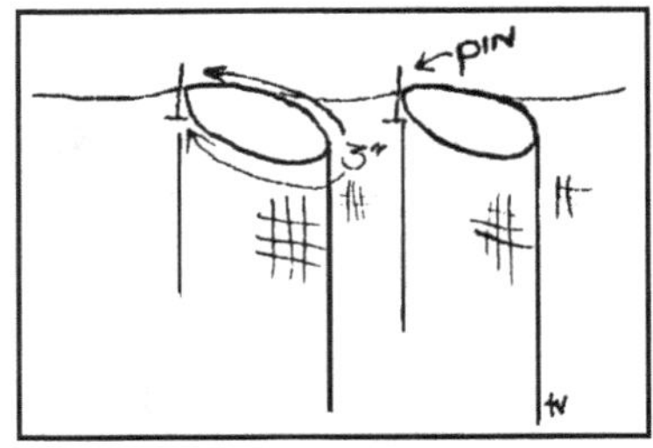

Using waistband as your guide, and leaving six inches on both ends unpleated (this will be the flat overlap in center front of kilt), divide remaining fabric in approximately fourteen to seventeen three-inch, evenly-spaced sections (when pressed they will be one-and-a-half-inch deep pleats) and hold with straight pins. Stitch waistband across top with wrong side of kilt, making sure all pleats lay flat and in the same direction. Turn waistband over to the correct side of kilt and top stitch.

4: Finishing: Finish both ends of kilt and waistband with narrow hem or fringe top edge of overlap, if desired.

Try on kilt, and hem bottom edge of kilt so it is knee-length. Adjust waistband and overlap so that it is comfortable, and sew on Velcro to fasten waistband. Sew on snaps and press pleats flat. (Note: pleats are not top-stitched.)

Example 21: Instructions for Kilt

Flapper Pattern

1. Top — measure:
    - Bust of the actress
    - Length from her armpit (arm relaxed at side) to her hip
    - Her hip measurement (the fullest place around the hips)

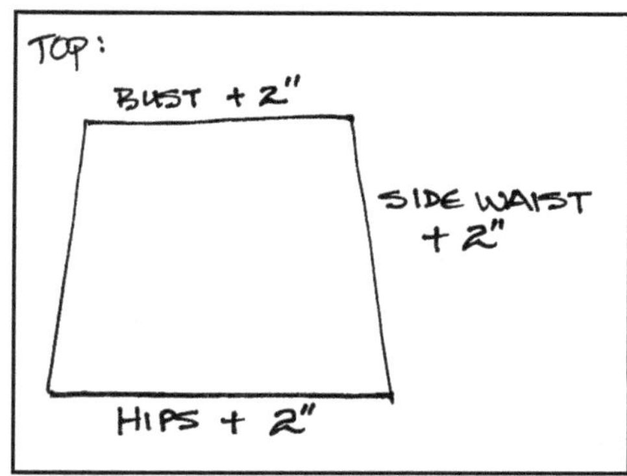

Add two inches to all measurements for the seam allowances.

Cut out two pieces this size (see diagram). Sew the two pieces wrong sides together (like a pillow slip), along the sides. Iron out the seams and turn right side out. You will have a tube with an opening at the top and bottom (the opening at the top will be smaller).

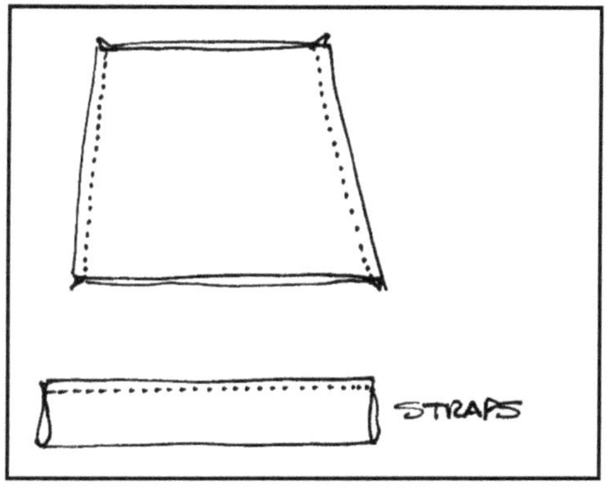

2. Skirt — measure:
    - Width: take the hip measurement with the added two inches and either double the width of the hips for a straight skirt or triple it for more flair.
    - Length: Twelve inches for a young girl; eighteen to twenty-four inches for an older lady.

Cut one piece of fabric this size. Sew the two ends together and press out the seams. Then gather or pleat this strip of cloth and sew it to the hip side of your tube. Iron out the seam. Put the dress on the actress, taking small tucks in the top over the bust if necessary, and sew these tucks down as you would a dart. Next, cut two strips of the fabric (one for each strap), two inches wide by fifteen inches long (longer for larger girls). Sew each piece lengthwise, allowing a half-inch seam, and press out the seam.

Attach the straps with safety pins and fit the dress to the individual actress. Stich the straps to the dress after fitting, leaving any extra length of the strap so the dress can be adjusted for another actress in the future. A scarf can be added to the hip line as needed.

Trim can then be added to the hemline, the hipline, or the top of the bust-line and/or the straps. Fabrics that drape work best — usually satin or jersey.

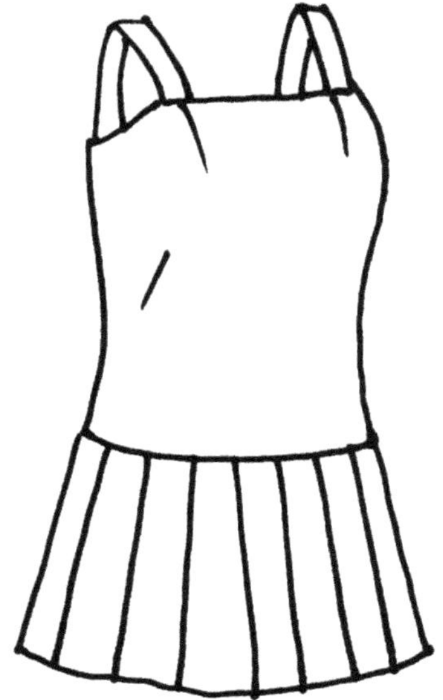

Example 22: Flapper Pattern

Chapter 16

Props

Who do you think of when a character walks on-stage with a/an:

- ✓ Hook for a hand?
- ✓ Glass slipper?
- ✓ Basket holding a little dog?
- ✓ Eye patch?
- ✓ Wand?

These things — either worn or held — are props. They help tell the story. A prop is anything actors handle or wear on-stage or that helps define their characters. Props can also be furniture and other items used to enhance the set.

Four types of props

There are four basic types of props:

- ✓ **Floor:** All the furniture normally used by the actors.
- ✓ **Decorative:** Furniture or set dressings and all items large and small which cannot be classified as scenery, lights, or costumes. These include objects like books in bookshelves, lamps on tables, pictures on walls or tables, and plants on plant stands or tables. They serve no practical purpose, but help to give ambiance to the setting.
- ✓ **Hand:** Small objects carried to or from the stage by the actors or handled by them while on-stage, such as glasses, books, dishes, or flowers, and/or a hand-carried object small enough to be lost by an actor thirty seconds before it is needed on-stage!
- ✓ **Costume/Personal:** Any part of a costume not worn, such as hats, purses, gloves, glasses, umbrellas, walking sticks, or a pipe.

So where do you start?

Prop lists

First check the back of your script for the master list of all items that could be considered props. Often these lists have things that you decide you don't need or things that have been forgotten or left out. If you have this list, compare it to the list your student assistant will be making, discussed below, and revise the printed list as needed.

If you don't have a list, your student assistant can help you. As you are blocking your show have your student assistant make a list of all the things the actors need to handle that help tell the story. When the blocking is done, have them check the list with the actors and you to complete the list. They then will make a final prop list for your production and give it to the prop crew. Tell your prop crew you need substitute props by your first working rehearsal. Substitute props are items that actors can use to "substitute" for the actual prop — a cardboard box for a Christmas present or a water pitcher for the coffee server.

Prop crew

Next you need to get your students involved. As you have done with the costume crew, advertise the need for a prop master (the person(s) in charge of getting the props to rehearsals and making sure they are in the right place for the actors) on your tryout sheets. Before the prospective crew members sign up, give them a general list of what is required (see Chapter 6).

Four places to locate props

Where do you find props? Almost anywhere. Before you start hunting for them keep one thing in mind; most props are meant to be seen from a distance. Up close they do not have to look or be real.

✓ **Check around your school.** Start with the theatre area. Possibly the former drama teacher has kept a prop shelf or box with various props in it. This is also a great time for you to become familiar with the school building and its contents. Check the teachers' lounge, the janitor's closet, basement, or other storage areas. Schools never throw anything out, and they just might have some floor or decorative props that you could use. If you are in a district that has several buildings, do not hesitate to check their sources, too.

✓ **Borrow them.** Start with your students. Who knows what someone has in his or her basement or attic? Furniture stores or second-hand stores might be willing to loan you furniture. Acknowledge them in the program and supply them with complimentary tickets. Returning the furniture in pristine condition and sending a thank you note will help insure borrowing in the future.

Word of Caution:
If you are borrowing anything, make sure that it is not a priceless antique or family heirloom. Accidents happen, and you do not want to make a call about the four-poster bed having been broken during a performance of *The Sound of Music* or that the antique frame of Grandma got dropped and splintered during a rehearsal of *Arsenic and Old Lace*.

✓ **Build what you cannot find.** There are two excellent books about making props: (1) *Theatre Props Handbook* by Thurston James and (2) *Costumes, Accessories, Props, and Stage Illusions Made Easy* by Barb Rogers. Also, the Internet can steer you to various good sites; www.halloween-magazine.com has a great link for blood and props! Cardboard refrigerator boxes can be a base for many things — coffins, caves, bookshelves, trees. Paper paint buckets also make great helmets. All that is needed, besides your imagination, are X-acto knives, hot glue guns, and paint.

✓ **Buy what cannot be borrowed or made.** Sometimes you need to investigate the local second-hand stores, antique malls, swap meets, thrift shops, and garage sales. One never knows what might be lurking in a dusty corner. A great catalog to own is "Theatre House." They have wigs and various fabrics plus the best selection of props — from balls and chains to umbrellas and plastic chickens.

Food

Food is also considered a prop. It can be divided into two types:

Food that is eaten

If people have to eat, then either the real food or a look-alike substitute that can be swallowed easily must be on-stage.

✓ Mashed potatoes work well for ice cream or anything requiring that kind of consistency. Just tint them the color you need.

✓ Angel food cake is easy to eat, can be colored and cut into shapes, and goes down easily, not causing anyone to choke.

✓ Slices of bread with a half of an apricot in the middle create fake fried eggs.

✓ Snack food:

 ✗ Cut-up carrots work great. Not only are they good for you but also they can be chewed and swallowed easily.

 ✗ Oven baked rice crackers will dissolve easily in the mouth.

✓ Drinks:

 ✗ Tea is a great substitute for alcohol or coffee. (If you are going to do a show where characters use alcohol be sure it has been cleared with your administration. Many districts have strict rules about seeing students drinking on-stage.)

- ✗ Teacups rattle in their saucers. If tea/coffee is being served put a small paper doily on the saucer. It will muffle the sound.
- ✗ Ginger ale works well for champagne. Or fill the champagne glass with tan/light brown netting and fake drink the liquid. It doesn't spill! Again, check the drinking with the administration — this is a must!
- ✗ Milk is another beverage that is easy to drink but can coat your throat. Watering it down will help. Taking the glass, painting the inside white, and faking it also works well.

✓ Spewing Food is needed if you are doing *The Miracle Worker*. Mashed potatoes work beautifully, as well as scrambled eggs and well-cooked bacon.

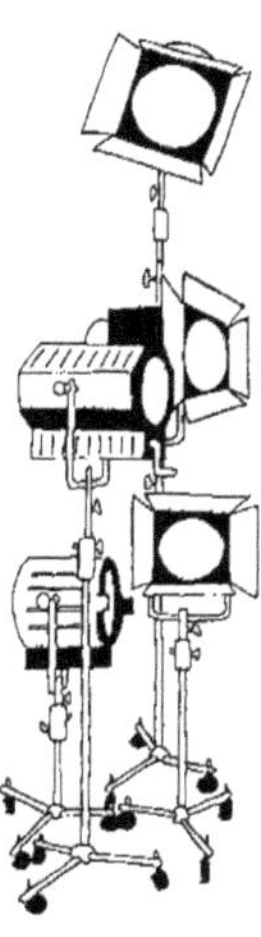

When I was doing *The Miracle Worker*, my prop boy had to supply fresh food every night at rehearsal so the actress could get used to spitting it up. As we did not have any stove backstage, he had to cook the food at home. One night he was late getting started and knew he had to have food at the theatre by seven o'clock. After preparing it he put it in the car and raced down to the theatre, but he didn't get far before he was picked up by the police. As he was being questioned for speeding — forty-five miles per hour in a fifteen-mile zone — the officer asked him why he was going so fast. He blurted out, "I am the prop master for *Miracle Worker* and I've got to get this food to rehearsal right now or the director is going to kill me!" The policeman immediately put his book away and said, "You'd better get there *now*, but I never want to see you speeding again, you hear? And be sure in the future to give yourself enough time to cook."

Recently I attended a professional production of *Driving Miss Daisy*. As I was walking up to the entrance, one of my former students ran past, out of breath. I asked, "You are running props, but why ten minutes till curtain are you running in the wrong direction?"

"The lead actress has to have a certain kind of pie for a scene in the play. She is allergic to most fillings and the pie, especially made for her, was eaten this afternoon! We are going to get the last one the store made right now," and off she went. Yes, she made it back and yes, food is tempting to anyone backstage, even with notes plastered all over it!

Food that is not eaten

There are four ways to create realistic-looking food:

✓ Desserts can be created using seven-minute boiled frosting. It works beautifully for cakes, meringue, and cookies. Here's how to make it:

Ingredients:

2 egg whites

1-1/2 cups sugar

1/3 cup cold water

1-1/2 teaspoons light corn syrup

Whisk the ingredients together in the top of a double boiler. Cook over boiling water, beating constantly with a hand-held electric mixer, for approximately seven minutes until it is satiny and fluffy and forming peaks.

Frost it over cardboard, Styrofoam, or whatever has the right shape. It does need to dry for several days, but it will last. The cake we made for a show in 1981 is still around!

- ✓ Baking a turkey without dressing and then covering it with Vaseline makes it look perfect. It can still be cut, and the audience will think it is ready to eat.
- ✓ Cut up foam rubber to resemble whatever food you want. Paint and then hot glue it to a plate. This works well from a distance.
- ✓ White Styrofoam (or bead board which comes in four-foot by eight-foot sheets) can be used. Cut it with an X-acto knife to the shape you want and file the rough edges with an emery board. Hot glue pieces together to form your food. When the glue is dry, cover with small cheesecloth strips dipped in a glue and water wash — two parts glue to one part water. This must be done at least twice. When it is dry, paint the food using acrylic paint and then spray to seal it with either a gloss or matte coat, depending on the look you are after.

Interesting props

Aging paper

When the show calls for an old map or a parchment document, take regular typing paper and spray it with a solution of one part tea to three parts water. After it is dry, write on it with black or brown magic marker, crumble it, and then fold it. Marking the creases with the marker works well, too.

Breaking window glass

When a show requires that glass in a window breaks, you can buy breakaway glass or make your own. Use the following recipe:

2 cups sugar

2/3 cup light Karo syrup

1 cup water

Mix and boil to hard-crack stage (300 degrees). Pour into a flat, parchment paper-lined pan that is a bit bigger than your pane of glass.

Tape the "window" in place with duct tape. The thinner the "glass," the easier it is to break.

Chopping a head off

Just in case you are doing a mystery or Halloween show, you may need to fake someone's head being chopped off. Here are two ways of doing it. Before the actual "chopping" begins, be sure that you block the "chopping" behind something as big as a couch.

✓ Drop a ten-pound sack of cement mix wrapped with duck tape (so it does not break open).

✓ Bring a knife blade down on a head of cabbage, slicing it as many times as you need. Of course the cabbage is held in place with hot glue on a board that will take the hacking. You do not want to damage your stage. Then pick up a Styrofoam wig head that resembles the "dead" person (which has been pre-set behind the couch). Done quickly it should get the idea across.

Smoking cigarettes

The fake "smoking cigarettes" you buy at variety stores do work and look real. The powder does, however get on your teeth. If the character needs to smoke, then this, too, must be cleared with the administration.

Paper clips

Paper clips did not come into use until the twentieth century. Before then, papers were put together with straight pins, pinned in the corner of the papers at a slant. I have several of my great grandfather's writings with the pins still intact.

Snow

As long as there is some distance between the action and the audience, cotton batting — used for quilts — works beautifully. TV shows use it exclusively for the snow banks covering rocks and snow that hangs on the mortar between bricks on a building (you are caulking the bricks with white). If you have a backdrop and you need to give it a snow effect, use white chalk where snow would fall. It does not damage the paint on the drop and can be easily erased. (Brown/red/gold chalk can be added to trees to give them the wonderful color of fall as well.)

Prop table

After all the props have been collected, they need a home — a place where they will live during the rehearsals and performances so the actors can collect them and return them when they are finished.

The easiest way to create this home is to have a table backstage covered with butcher paper. Place all the props on that table. Take a magic marker and outline each prop, as it lies on the table. Label the outline with the item's name. This makes it very easy for actors to find their props (and return them) and for the prop crew to check to see what has not been returned. Sometimes the props get left on-stage. When the rehearsal is over, your crew needs to collect all of the props and return them to the prop table.

Final note

Creating props relies on your students' and your ability to be good scroungers and use ingenuity and imagination. Again, do not forget to return those items you have borrowed as soon as your show is over, in excellent condition, with a thank-you note.

Chapter 17

Lighting

Your primary concern as a first-year director must be to make sure that your actors can be seen. Remember, the audience will accept any convention (even if it is just turning overhead or work lights on and off) as long as it is done in a professional manner. If you and your actors accept the convention, the audience will, too.

What do I do first?

Before you begin lighting your stage, be sure to check the Glossary for lighting terms you need to become familiar with. Next, a thorough investigation of the stage area is needed to see what lighting is available. Answer the following two questions:

✓ Do you only have overhead lighting or work lights?

✓ Or do you have special lighting consisting of stage instruments (along with work lights)?

If the answer to the first question is "yes," then you will be dealing with visibility lighting, making sure your actors can be seen. If your answer to the second question is "yes," then you need to be concerned with theatrical lighting, which uses stage lighting instruments and dimming equipment explained below.

Visibility lighting

When the stage facilities are less than adequate — with little or no lighting equipment — concern yourself with using the lights that are available. This is called **visibility lighting**. You are concerned with making sure your actors can be seen. The lights you will be using are generally called work lights. Find their wall switches and turn them on.

Do you need brighter lights? Working with the head janitor can be a great help. If he or she is unable to help you, possibly another teacher, parent, or community volunteer could help. First check the electrical outlets. Next, find out what and how much wattage is available. If there are enough outlets and wattage, three options are available:

✓ Additional lights called **clamp lights** can be purchased at any hardware store and are reasonably priced. They have a socket, a clamp that opens so it can be attached to a pipe, and a six-foot power cord. They just need to be plugged into an outlet. Some have a polished reflector. They can also be plugged into extension cords if you need more distance from the outlet. These extension cords must not be the household type, but rather the heavy-duty type generally used by the custodial department. When care is taken to return them promptly, custodians are usually quite willing to lend their extension cords.

✓ Lights can be wired to a household dimmer, which is then plugged into the outlet — with the help of an electrician, of course!

✓ Purchase plain, unfocused **reflector lights**. These are three- to five-hundred watt quartz floodlights available at any hardware store. They are inexpensive and put out light! They cost about the price of two movie tickets. They can be easily installed — the directions are in the box. They do need to be wired above your acting area, so an electrician is a must. Having the music people go into this investment with you can make an additional saving — if you use the same facility. They always need lights for their band, orchestra, and/or choral concerts.

For the power required to run one hair dryer, four of these quartz floodlights will light an area thirty feet wide and twenty feet deep with the touch of one switch! It is "general" lighting and rather harsh, but at least you have light.

Checking to make sure the janitorial department does not use the identical power source at the same time you are rehearsing or performing is important. You do not want to blow a fuse or flip a breaker!

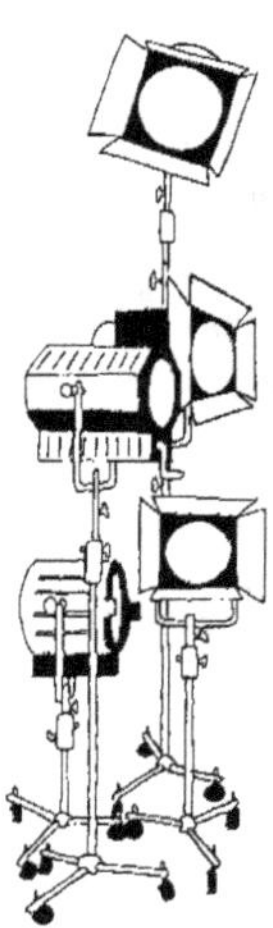

While doing *The Sound of Music* in our gym, I needed our two one-thousand-watt spotlights to cover the singers during their songs. We plugged them into outlets on the balcony on each side of the gym. Every time they were turned on they worked perfectly, until we got to the second act. Then we would have trouble every night. I just knew it was the students running the spots. It could not possibly have been anything else. Well, guess again, it was.

When we stared the second act, the janitors would be cleaning the second floor with their electric scrubbers and plugging them into the same circuit. The mystery was finally solved, and the janitors scrubbed at a much later time.

Theatrical lighting

Lighting basics

If you have stage lights you will be doing **theatrical lighting**. You need to concern yourself with learning to use the equipment. There are two categories of lighting instruments:

✓ Those that can be focused called lekos or fresnels which:

- ✗ Have lenses;
- ✗ Have shutters;
- ✗ Have bulbs that cannot be bought at the local hardware store; and
- ✗ Need to be plugged into a device that turns the lights on and off (the "power pack" or the big black box which has dimmers attached to it).
- ✗ There are two types of focused lighting instruments:
  - ✎ Those with a relatively long focal length for the longer distance between the pipe they are attached to and the stage; and
  - ✎ Those with a shorter focus that are attached to the pipe over the acting area.
- ✗ Each instrument is focused at a 45-degree angle to get the best lighting.

✓ Those that cannot be focused are called flood, PARS, or spots which have:

- ✗ No lenses;
- ✗ No shutters;
- ✗ Bulbs that can be bought locally; and
- ✗ Plugs that can either be plugged into an ordinary outlet or into the special box.
- ✗ They give either a **wash** — lighting that covers the whole stage producing a large spread of soft unfocused light — or a round circle of light.

Familiarize yourself with the available theatrical lighting

If you have a book that came with your lighting equipment, read it! If you have trouble understanding it, contact an electrician — possibly a parent — and have them explain it to you. I never took physics, but I do know if you have a circuit that can hold one-thousand watts and you plug fifteen-hundred watts of light into it, you will trip a breaker.

Next you need to familiarize yourself with your lighting instruments by:

✓ Asking the janitors — remember, they are your friends.

✓ Checking to see who ran the lights for the last year's performances and contacting them.

✓ Asking the local college for the name of a lighting person who could come and work with you.

✓ Contacting a parent who might know about your lighting.

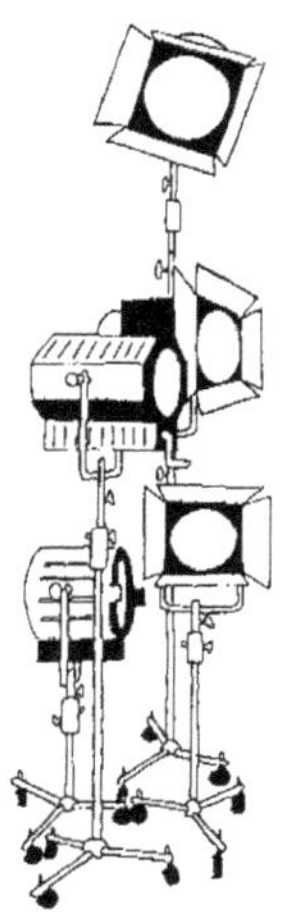

I always took the word of my students/janitors when it came to electricity. If they said they knew how to wire lights, I believed them. We needed very specific area lighting for *I Remember Mama* requiring lights we had not used for a long time. They needed to be rewired. One student said, "I know how to wire lights, Mrs. J. My dad taught me." As I had no adult handy, I assumed he knew what he was talking about. We discussed the fact that there were three leads — the hot, common, and ground. My last words to him were, "Now, you do understand they have to be wired correctly?"

"Yes," was his final remark. I went back to rehearsal.

An hour later all the lights went out. We were in total darkness. Nothing would come on. We tried every trick I knew. I sent the actors home, called my husband, got any janitors that were handy, and we spent another two hours trying to make something work. Nothing did!

As soon as I got to school the following morning I reported the situation to our head janitor and our principal and filled out a work order. (When something was broken or did not work, the district had another form to fill out. I knew something major had happened!) Luckily for me I had four days plus the weekend before the show opened! The administration contacted the electrical company in town who had purchased the dimmer board. They came and were able to make one dimmer pack work — one-half of my lights — but could not get the other dimmer pack to come on.

To make a very long and harrowing story short, the lights had been wired incorrectly and my student had blown both our dimmer packs! The company we purchased our dimmer from sent repair stuff, and the local electrician put the pack back in running order three hours before the opening curtain! The lighting system never worked very well after that. The cost was born by the school district but my guess is it was at least $1000, and that was a considerable amount in 1981.

Several years later I needed two lighting instruments wired to give us better general lighting. I didn't ask a student, I asked the janitor. He wired the lights but they never worked. I found out later that he "knew" each light had three wires but it did not matter how they were wired! Thank goodness he did not blow any circuit or cause a fire!

I finally learned my lesson! From then on I hired an electrician to do all my required wiring and a theatre-trained person to focus my lights. I never had another problem.

Basic focusing

When you feel confident to start focusing your lights, read the following description of **cross lighting**. (There are many ways of focusing lights covered in the books in the Further Reading section. Cross lighting is fundamental and covered in the books as well.) Cross lighting is a general plan of how to light the stage giving you good coverage and is relatively simple to do. It is the basic of stage lighting.

Word of Caution:
Once you start using your lighting equipment, you will want to do more and more. You will never have enough instruments! It can be addictive!

Divide your acting space into areas between six and eight feet, depending on the size of your stage. Generally you can do it in six areas — Up Left, Down Left, Up Center, Down Center, Up Right, and Down Right. Then divide your lighting instruments into those areas. In each acting space you need three lights for ideal coverage: two ellipsoidals and one fresnel. One of the ellipsoidals is focused from the right, one from the left, and the fresnel is focused in the center. This way of focusing eliminates any shadows and gives good, even coverage.

Always keep on researching and reading. Taking university classes on lighting is necessary to obtain additional information and knowledge of specific instruments.

Lighting crew

After you have determined which type of lighting you will be using, you need to involve your students. Again, advertise for your crew with your tryouts (see Chapter 6).

After your crew is selected, you will need to spend time — before they are needed for your rehearsals or performance — teaching them where switches are, how to run the dimmer board (if you have one), and explaining your lighting basics. Do not assume they know anything about electricity. Be sure to make clear to them that any liquid around your equipment is unacceptable! The last thing you need to have is your equipment shorting out.

Work towards good lighting

As your program grows, you need to work towards providing your stage with lighting equipment either from proceeds from plays or through the school administration. The three suggestions mentioned under visibility light are only stopgap measures. You know lighting will cost a great deal of money, so begin by contacting a professional lighting company or your local university and getting a cost estimate. Your theatre should have a minimum of nine five-hundred-watt fresnel spotlights for the lights directly above the acting area, nine five-hundred-watt ellipsoidal spotlights for the lighting placed in the audience to focus on the forward acting area, and a professional dimming system which will safely handle two lights per dimmer. (You of course are going to add more lights to this list when money becomes available). This will cost a minimum of four- to six-thousand dollars. If you are buying a package, with everything together, companies often make good reductions, so it is much cheaper than buying each piece individually. With the rapid changes in technology, buying used equipment may not be a good idea.

Lighting shows with blackouts

I recently attended a production that had many scenes consisting of flashbacks. I'm sure the blackouts were given in the script so the actors could prepare for the flashbacks or to tell the audience that they were being transported back in time. But as an audience member, every time the lights went out I was immediately taken out of the flow of the story.

When you are confronted with this dilemma or one that does not contain flashbacks but many short scenes separated by blackouts, try to avoid a complete blackout and come up with a common thread.

One suggestion would be to use music as the bridge between the present and the past. When I produced *I Remember Mama* I used that as my link between Katrina's talking to us and her memories.

Another suggestion is to use a change of light, if you are lucky enough to have sophisticated lighting facilities. Even if we have to see the characters add a costume or prop before the scene begins it indicates that we have another flashback or memory.

Yet another suggestion is to combine some of the scenes. Having one scene flow into another can eliminate many blackouts, *David and Lisa* is a prime example. Also, if you have a large stage, indicating one area for your memory or flashback can add to the flow of the show.

I guess what I am saying is use your imagination and always keep your audience's attention in mind. Anytime they are sitting in total darkness takes them away from the action and the story.

Final note

Do not apologize for inadequate lighting; do the best you can with what you have. Realistically, few schools have adequate lighting equipment, so stress the other aspects of technical theatre that you feel you can accomplish. Just be sure that your actors can be seen while you work towards better lighting equipment.

Chapter 18
Hair and Makeup

It is time for the actors to start the final step in creating their characters — working with their hair and makeup. There is something very wonderful about the makeup room, whether it is the band room, a restroom, or a classroom. Everyone is together and you are finally ready to perform the show for an audience.

Makeup

Basic makeup must be worn by everyone

There is only one hard and fast rule for makeup: everyone must have some. Base is not always needed. Using dry, brush-on rouge, eyeliner, mascara, eyebrow pencil (almost never use black — one of the very few rules in theatre — it is too stark), and lipstick may be needed for everyone. These makeup basics work extremely well for shows whose characters are teenagers or for those whose characters are no specific age. Age is always created with characterization. Costumes, basic makeup, and hairstyles do the rest. See Examples 23 and 24 (pages 194-199) for pictures of actors with basic makeup.

Teddy and Abby from *Arsenic and Old Lace*

Age makeup

The character comes from within; it is not painted on. The best thing for an inexperienced director to do when thinking about makeup is *don't*! Drama directors recognize that youthful faces are difficult to age. Essentially, the audience is not going to be fooled. They know that the father is their son or next-door neighbor. The primary concerns are that:

- ✓ Lighting does not wash out the actors' faces;
- ✓ Hairstyles are accurate for either time or age of characters; and
- ✓ Illusion of age is given by having the makeup become part of the total characterization.

You worked hard to create believable characters. If time is spent on hair and costumes, the audience will believe. Age lines put on young faces by inexperienced actors/directors can look like railroad tracks and totally destroy the hours of character study done at rehearsals. Less is better — much better. Do the basics discussed above and concentrate on hair, costumes, and characterizations. See Example 25 (page 200-201) for pictures of actors with age makeup.

If you must consider age makeup, you can either buy one of the makeup videos currently on the market or Richard Corson's book, *Stage Makeup* listed in the Further Reading section. Keep in mind that stage makeup is expensive. In order to be successful with full age makeup, you must purchase the makeup they require and follow their instructions to the letter. It will make the job of doing makeup much easier.

Check the Internet. I went into my favorite search engine and typed in "stage makeup." I found many helpful Web sites this way. The best Web sites will give you places to purchase makeup as well as some great ideas for makeup.

Setting makeup so it will not run

Every book/video will tell you that after the makeup is done it must be set with powder. If the makeup is not powdered, it can be smeared by hands and on costumes, and if you perspire it will run all over the face. You need to set it so it will stay in place. There is an additional way to ensure that the makeup will not run. After you have set the makeup with your powder, re-powder your face with baby powder, quite heavily. Then remove the baby powder carefully with cold water. This works extremely well if you are doing clowns and everyone's face is white or if you have someone who perspires heavily. I know this sounds strange, but it works!

Stylized makeup

Animal

If your production calls for animals, illustrated children's books are an excellent way to discover the animals' facial features. Under no circumstances do you want your actors to wear full-face masks (unless they are worn for a special effect — masquerade parties as in *Romeo and Juliet* or *Much Ado About Nothing* — and are worn for approximately four to five minutes and then they are removed.) Remember, masks cover expressions and can muffle the dialog. Irene Corey's book, *Mask of Reality* is a must. The idea is to keep the face as simple as possible, and yes, you may use black, but avoid using a great deal of it as it hides expression.

Clown

Clown makeup is very easy — all you need to do is exaggerate the eyes, mouth, and cheeks. Black can be used in moderation. You do not need any base; the tone of the flesh works very well and is so much cleaner. Outline the eyes and mouth with brown or black liner. Fill in the outline with colored eye shadow. Using rouge or lipstick, paint circles on the cheeks. Covering the face with white can also be used but with the kind of activity clowning takes, this technique is messy and often runs all over the face. See Example 26 (page 202-204) for pictures of actors with stylized makeup.

Hair

Hairstyles are an integral part of the stage picture. Hairdos give the wonderful illusion of age and period. The right hairstyle not only helps the total look of the production but also, more importantly, helps actors internally, giving them the feeling of their characters. By looking in a mirror, students instantly see they are not themselves but someone new. One major key is to get the students' hair off their faces if you need to create age.

Research

Research the play's specific time period for pictures of what people's hair looked like. I cannot stress this enough. If your play is set anywhere from the 1920s through modern times, the first place to check is the school annuals. Not only do you have pictures of teenagers but the teachers as well. Remember, too, that not everyone wore the same styles. Below are other places/people to check with, depending on the type of production you are doing:

- ✓ A beautician;
- ✓ Children's books;
- ✓ Grandparents;
- ✓ Neighbors;
- ✓ Parents;
- ✓ Photographs from home;
- ✓ Relatives;
- ✓ Secondhand bookstores;
- ✓ The school/town library; and/or
- ✓ *Life* Magazine

Reproductions of great paintings are also a good source for historical hairstyles. Bring any pictures you have to rehearsals so everyone can see them. This will start the actors thinking about what can be done with their hair. If you're doing a modern play, have your actors observe people at malls, restaurants, bus depots, or airports. Of course you also need to check the Internet. It has several wonderful hairstyles sites.

Once the style is chosen, allow time in rehearsal for experimentation. It is amazing how characterizations grow when students create their individual character's hairdos and work with them at rehearsal. Below are some techniques I have used. I was interested only in the impression of the specific period, not an authentic reproduction.

Techniques

Women

✓ **1890-1915; 1960:** Beehives — long hair was fashionable, so backcombing for body is necessary to get the bulk of the hair on top of the head. The general feeling of the early period is the pompadour. After being backcombed, the hair is swept up off the sides of the face and pulled off the forehead. The back of the hair is put in a French roll or swept up to join the sides and front. Curls can be made with the hair on top with some curled tendrils hanging down. During the 1960s there were many curls at the crown of the head ("Texas hair") used to create the bouffant look. Bangs could be added as well as a bun in back.

✓ **1920s:** This period's hairdos were short, very styled, and close to the head. It was the antithesis of the early 1900s — a modern streamlined look. Part the hair and create soft waves, called Marcel waves, around the face using hair clips (worn as hair decorations today) for the finger waves. Or set rows of pin curls alternating the direction of the curls clockwise and counter-clockwise. Your hair will fall naturally into deep waves when you comb it out. You can control the size of the waves by adjusting the number and size of the curls. Many smaller curls make deeper smaller waves; fewer larger curls make gentler waves.

✓ **1930-1950s:** The key to these years is to have a defined part. The 30s still kept the Marcel look of the 1920s, but pulled the hair (with no waves) to the nape of the neck in back forming a bun, or turned up the hair at the nape of the neck in tight little sausage rolls. The 40s lost the Marcel waves but kept the same treatment for the back of the hair from the 30s. However, the hair on the sides and forehead were pulled away from the face, again in sausage rolls or braids. If curly hair was needed, the curls were tight to the head, but as the 50s approached, hair hung loose with the curls turned under. In the 50s, bangs were curled under on the forehead. The styles did change during the mid 50s with the advent of *Tammy*, especially for teenagers. Wrap a small amount of hair by your cheek around your index finger and hold it in place with bobby pins or clips for spit curls. Pull the hair severely away from the face and wrap it with a scrunchie to create the ponytail or bun. Rubber bands also work but will break the hair and are sometimes very difficult to pull out.

Your first job is to become familiar with the period of your show by doing your research. With the use of curling irons, rag rolling, and/or hot rollers, most women's hairdo's can be achieved.

Men

✓ **1910s:** Part hair in the center and slick down. You might even have a wave on either side of the part.

✓ **1920s-1940s:** Part hair on the side and slick down. The hair should be fairly short.

✓ **1950s:** "Greasy" was the look with side hair combed back away from the face and a bit of a wave on the top.

✓ **Old age:** Comb hair straight back, away from the face, as mentioned under costumes. Water works well to experiment with, but it does not last. Hair setting gel or conditioner allows you to do many things in a short period of time. If you want body, comb it out. If you want a "greasy" look or a flat-to-the-head look, just don't comb it out. Leave it in until after the performance. Do not use Vaseline — it does not wash out easily.

Graying

One of the first things inexperienced drama directors do when having their young actors playing older people is to gray their hair. "Aren't all old people gray?" you ask. Yes, older people have gray hair, but it is not all gray. There are tones of black, brown, red, gray, and white — a hard combination to do on young people who want to look old! Gray must be used sparingly. Never cover the whole head with gray. Age comes from within, and putting white in one's hair does not make one old. Most of the time it will just look like a young person with white hair. If some gray is needed, use it at the temples. There are three ways to do this (all three wash out easily):

✓ **Sprays:** The most expensive and hardest to get are the white and silver sprays found at most big drug stores. They must be used sparingly. A combination of both colors of sprays works best; however, great care has to be taken with their application. Before the spraying begins, cover those parts of the head that you do not want sprayed — ears and forehead. Spraying a little at one time and combing it out immediately seems to give the best results.

✓ **Shoe polish:** The best, most inexpensive, and easiest to obtain is white shoe polish. Apply with a toothbrush or sponge applicator and comb out immediately. (Incidentally, if your actor has short light brown or blonde hair and you want it darker, use brown or black shoe polish with the same application.)

✓ **Powder or cornstarch:** The least expensive and the hardest to control is powder or cornstarch. If the hair is touched, it comes out in clouds! Setting it with hair spray defeats the purpose as the white disappears. If your actors are careful not to touch their hair, this can work.

Slick idea

If the look you're after is severe or smooth to the head, a great thing to use is Knox gelatin. Mix one package with one-third cup hot water. Allow it to stand for several minutes, and then heat it up in a microwave until it's clear. When it is cool, comb through the hair and set it in the style you want. Allow it to air dry or use a hair dryer. This works well for creating spikes, too. When the rehearsal/performance is over, all you have to do is wash the hair. It does no harm; it can even improve one's hair!

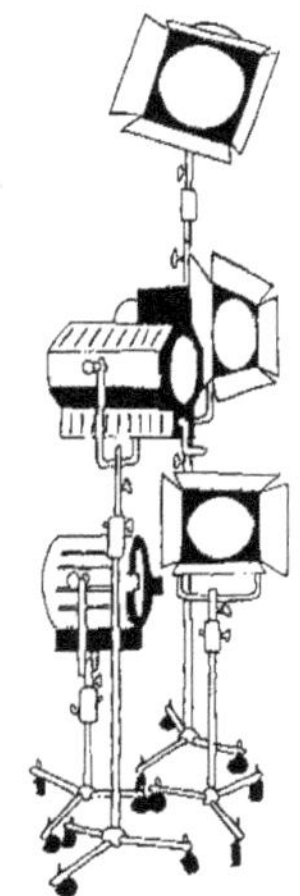

In my first appearance with a speaking role, I was playing an older woman. Of course, I not only had the stereotypical bent back but also powdered hair. All old women past thirty-five had gray hair, right? When I walked on-stage for the first time, I was preceded and followed by a halo of white "smoke." Needless to say, the audience loved it. In my naïveté I thought it was my acting!

. . . .

The second time I did *The Taming of the Shrew*, Kate had beautiful blond hair, so a brown wig was a necessity. I blocked the introduction scene between Kate and Petruchio to be physical. The young woman playing Kate was very strong, so there was a great deal of pulling and shoving. The night of our performance, having done the show for the English classes six times in addition to several rehearsals without any problems, the wig came off as Kate and Petruchio rolled around on the ground.

After Baptista asked how things were going, Petruchio picked himself up, with wig in hand and started to leave. His parting words were, "Sunday comes apace — We will have rings and wigs and things in fine array, And kiss me Kate, we will be married o' Sunday."

Great ad-libbing, but what a horrible experience for Kate! The third time I did *Taming*, again Kate was a blond, but this time we dyed her hair! She was a tiny thing and Petruchio tossed and turned her around the stage like a circus strongman act. I didn't want her to worry about a headpiece.

Wigs

Wigs are another way of creating hairstyles. If the student's hair can't be styled or colored, using wigs can be a blessing. Of course, they are expensive and should be used only as a last resort.

To avoid problems, make sure the wig fits securely. It is very upsetting for actors to have their hair fall off during a performance!! Wearing old, clean pantyhose over their hair makes a good surface for anchoring the wig.

Final note

Yes, there is something very magical about the hair and makeup room. Many schools have a makeup crew who put the makeup on each actor. I suggest you have one person in charge of the makeup room that can:

✓ Help with setting the makeup out;

✓ Assist the actors with putting their own makeup on (if necessary); and

✓ Clean up.

It's important for the students to be together before the show opens, and to actually do their own hair and makeup. They can help each other rather than having a crew assigned to supervise. The look then becomes their own, which helps begin the transformation from student to character in the play. Becoming aware of the hair and makeup basics is a must if any of your actors want to continue with theatre in the future.

Character Pictures with No Makeup

These actors created their characters from within with the help of costumes. The pictures were taken without makeup. The captions describe what makeup was added to complete the characters after these photos were taken.

Tom Jones: A wild Irishman named Fitzpatrick. We added brown eyeliner and eyebrow pencil, making the eyebrows very bushy. We added a bit of rouge to show that he might have imbibed just a bit too much!

Tom Jones: Partridge, the barber and storyteller who had brown eyeliner and eyebrow pencil. His hair was always unruly, and when he cavorted with a lady, he came on-stage with a touch of lipstick.

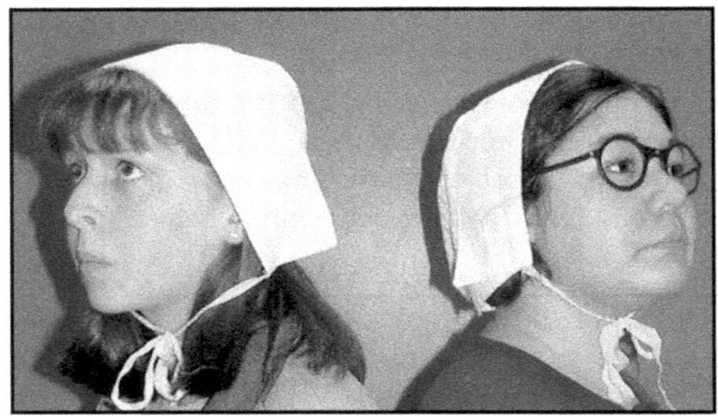

Tom Jones: Two no-nonsense teachers, Thawackum and Square, who accentuated their characters with eyeliner, mascara, as well as brownish cheeks for Thawackum and red rosy cheeks for Square.

Hurricane Smith and the Garden of the Golden Monkey: Hurricane, a brave man who was raised by a Gorilla, crashes a plane in the jungle and saves everyone from the evil Gutman and Cobra Woman. We lined his eyes with brown liner and added a bit of rouge and a fake beard when he played his father.

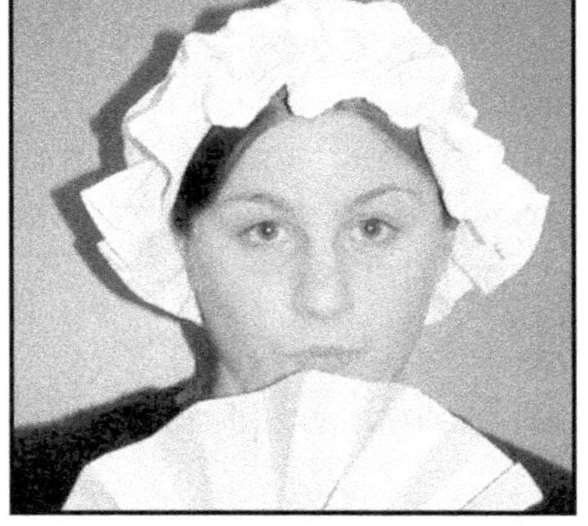

Tom Jones: Miss Western, a lady of uncertain age, who tries to raise Sofia to be a proper young lady. She always hit everyone over the head with her fan when the mood struck her. We used a light pink rouge, brown eyeliner, mascara, and red lipstick (which was put on to make her lips small and cupid-like).

Example 23: Character pictures with no makeup

David and Lisa: Carlos, a street-wise punk who wore military fatigues and a backwards cap. His makeup was dark brown liner and brown eye shadow. We even added a scar.

David and Lisa: David, the young man who is afraid to be touched. He was dressed completely according to *Gentlemen's Quarterly* , with not a hair out of place We accented his eyes and eyebrows with brown pencil. As he was a redhead, he had plenty of color in his cheeks already.

David and Lisa: Timmy, a very shy, introverted boy. With brown eyeliner, very rosy cheeks, and glasses we made him look like a loser.

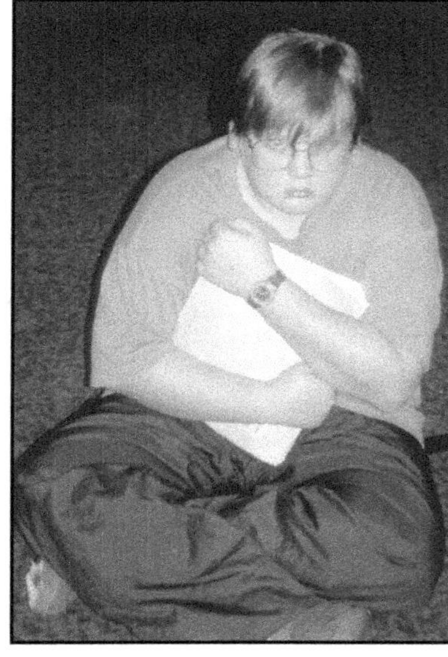

A Murder Is Announced: Miss Marple, a delightful older lady who is into everyone else's business. We tried and somewhat succeeded in using the latex aging described in Mr. Corson's book — it took hours, and I never spent that much time again.

Example 23: Character pictures with no makeup

Here and Now

This play takes place on the bare stage. A group of actors are rehearsing a play, loosely based on actual experiments in a Connecticut high school where students, teachers, and parents met for sessions in a human relations group called "Here and Now." As the actors work on the play, their identification with the characters becomes stronger, and as the confessions and tensions of their parts surface, their own hang ups emerge. This is a play within a play. The actors had to not only change clothes very fast (in less than 30 seconds between scenes) but had to change characters as well — from teenage actors to people in the play — so makeup wasn't an option. We concentrated on costumes and hairstyles, along with characterization.

Claire, one of the parents of the group. A prim and proper woman whose son is on drugs and will not admit it.

Jerry, a young rebel who is hostile, bright, and not liked by his peers. We lined his eyes with brown liner. He did not shave during the week of the play in order to get more of a "tough" look.

Kim, a rebel who resents authority, is aggressive and will try anything once.

Example 23: Character pictures with no makeup

Character Pictures with Little Makeup

These characters, too, were created from within with the help of costumes, hairstyles, and basic makeup (brown eyeliner and mascara for the boys; brown eyeliner, mascara, a coral dry rouge, and a coral lipstick for the girls, unless otherwise noted.)

David and Lisa: Sandra, a very heavy little girl. We dressed her in loose-fitting muumuus (the girl was not heavy) and used hair to help with the illusion of heaviness. Her cheeks were very pink and the lipstick a messy red.

Is There a Comic in the House? Phil, Deliah's straight man, relaxed, casual, and very much in love with Deliah.

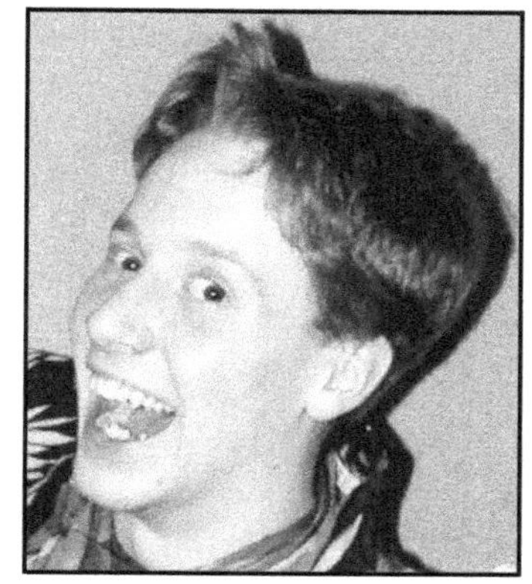

Is There a Comic in the House? Zack Zany — the name says it all! He was not only a vocally loud character but was visually loud as well. We used brown eyeliner on brows and eyes, combed his red hair up with gel, and dressed him in loud, Hawaiian shirts.

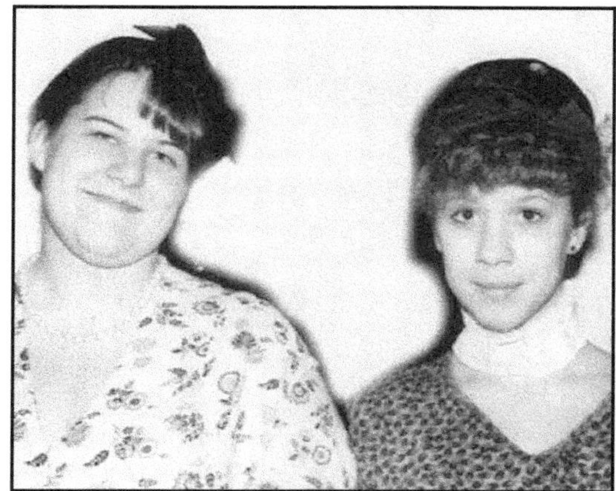

Arsenic and Old Lace: Martha and Abby

Is There a Comic in the House? Deliah, a rather wacky comic. She wore a great deal of red rouge, garish purple eye shadow, exaggerated eyebrows, and very red lipstick. Her character was patterned after Gracie Allen, George Burns' partner.

Example 24: Character pictures with little makeup

Fame: A teacher. By combing his hair back from the forehead and adding a mustache, he looked the part.

The Diary of Anne Frank: Mr. Dussel. We accomplished his age with the use of the hair brushed away from the face, slight graying at the temples, wire rimmed glasses, and the sour look on his face.

The Uninvited: Pam, a young, intelligent, and enthusiastic woman.

Terror by Gaslight: Opal, an innocent but flirtatious maid.

The Bat: Lizzie, maid who is loud, scared, and screams at the drop of a hat. Again, we used her hair to give the physical feature of being a wild woman.

Example 24: Character pictures with little makeup

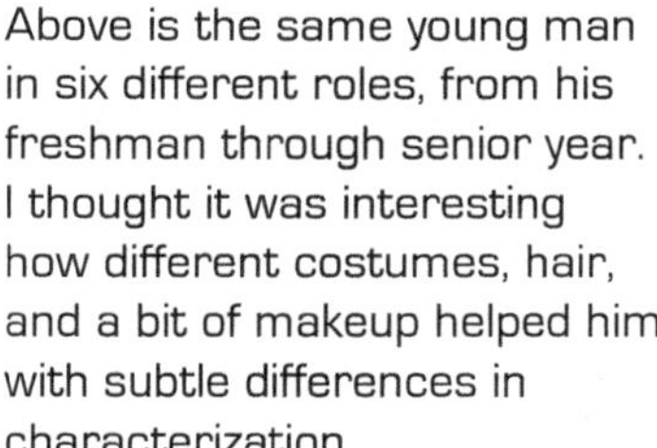

Above is the same young man in six different roles, from his freshman through senior year. I thought it was interesting how different costumes, hair, and a bit of makeup helped him with subtle differences in characterization.

Example 24: Character pictures with little makeup

Age Makeup

These pictures represent students who went further than the basics by following Richard Corson's book, *Stage Makeup*. They worked with the nasal labial fold (the sneer line from your nose to your mouth), the under-eye circles, crow's-feet, and sagging cheeks, following the principles of highlights and shadow. After looking at their faces, I want to especially call attention to their body language — what is each portraying? Did we need to go to this extreme, or would the makeup basics (eye liner, mascara, rouge, and lipstick) with proper hairdos and costumes have been enough?

A Tomb with a View: Agatha, a cook in a very strange household where someone is chained up in the basement and howls like a dog! By putting her hair in the scarf, we communicated that she was a worker and that this took place some time ago.

"One of the mighty pirates from *The Pirates of Penzance* (a local community production). If you have a chorus such as the pirates and do not have enough men, it is possible to cast women in the roles — provided they do not have any speaking lines. Work with their face and hair, and costume them in loose-fitting garments. Using a crepe hair beard and clown white to create the mustache, eyebrows, and sideburns in addition to a scarf to pull hair off the face, I became a man!

The Mystery of the Black Abbot: Monkey Puttler, a Police sergeant from Scotland Yard. We stressed his eyes and body — trying to emulate that of an ape and the illusion of age. Wearing the hat helped to hide the youthful hairline.

Example 25: Age Makeup

Ten Little Indians: Miss Emily Brent, a very cold old maid. Again we stressed hair.

The Bat: Cornelia, a woman who was single by choice and did not believe in ghosts or any such twaddle. Hair and physical stature again were stressed.

Web of Murder: Nora, the housekeeper, much derided by her sister. She is a poor spinster who has a very large secret. Her hairdo was very severe, which matched her outward personality.

David and Lisa: Mrs. Clemens, David's mother who is very concerned with appearances. Her makeup was very light with age lines. We stressed the under eye and the nasal labial. By her dress, hairdo, and jewelry, we were able to achieve a good illusion. She is not a woman who wanted anyone to know her real age. She is extremely protective of her son and hasn't much time for her husband. She wants to look good, no matter the expense.

Example 25: Age Makeup

Stylized Makeup

The makeup for the majority of these students was your basic clown. The animals were designed by the students themselves using *The Mask of Reality.*

Annabelle Broome: Annabelle, the good witch whose desire is to be dressed completely in pink with her pink hair. She wears a pink wig, and we added an upturned nose, done with nose putty, the only time I ever used it. During most of the show she was dressed in a gray costume. At the end of the show, she gets her wish and is dressed completely in pink.

Annabelle Broome: Mable, the head of the Witches' Union. Her special talent is roaring, "Silence!" and thunder is heard. Her makeup was black, white, and shades of red.

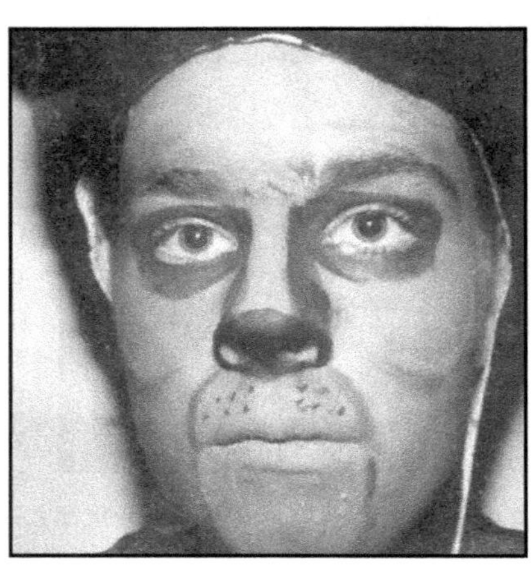

Goldilocks and the Christmas Bears: Papa Bear. We did not use any base. The eyes and the side of the nose were outlined in brown as well as the cheeks and nasal labial. The tip of the nose was black along with the small whiskers and the eyebrows. A touch of white highlighted the cheeks.

Annabelle Broome: A cat we added to the play — don't all witches have cats? She started out with a white base, used black for the eyes and whiskers, and red for the mouth and nose. She also outlined her eyes with black liner.

Example 26: Stylized Makeup

Annabelle Broome: Maud, the sleepy witch who moves when needed. We used a white base, blue mouth and eyes, and black eye brows.

A sad puppy done in brown for the upper part of the face, black around the eyes, eyebrows, nose and mouth, and the rest white. Again, we used not only the makeup but also the girl's hair to complete the transformation. This is the same girl who had to wear the large donkey head. You can see by her expression how much more she could have added to the donkey role if we had taken the head away.

"The same makeup described above but because she smiled she became a happy puppy!

The Near-Sighted Dragon and the Far-Sighted Knight: One of the stupid guards. We used basic clown make-up as well as the actresses' hair.

Example 26: Stylized Makeup

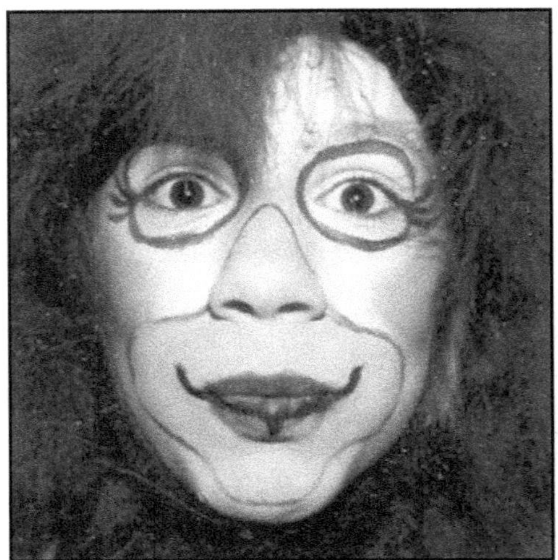

Goldilocks and the Christmas Bears: Mrs. Jay, also a nervous individual — always squawking and running around. She started out with a white base, rouged lips and cheeks, outlined the beak and eyes with brown, and filled in the beak with yellow. She added a brown line over her rouged lips to accentuate her mouth.

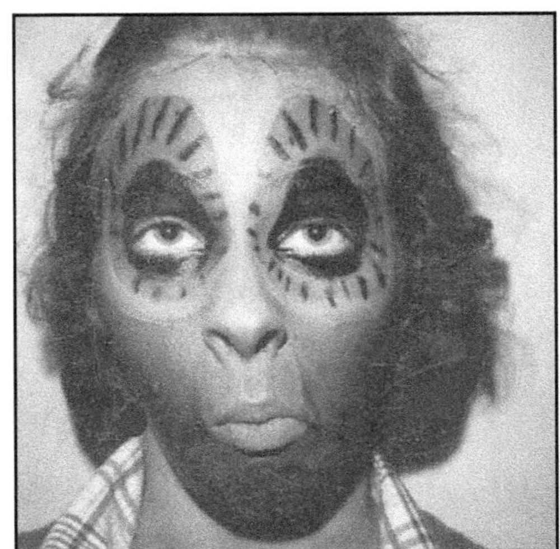

Winnie the Pooh: Owl, the wise and somewhat nervous individual. She was done in black and two shades of brown.

A Midsummer Night's Dream: Titania with glittery eye shadow/costume and lovely long hair.

Cinderella: Portia, one of the ugly stepsisters. Again we used basic clown makeup and made use of her hair as well.

Example 26: Stylized Makeup

Chapter 19
Set

Before I discuss anything about set, I want to make it clear that although most directors spend hours and hours on their sets, it is the least important aspect of technical theatre. Why? You have created interesting, believable characters who are appropriately dressed and tell a story. You have made sure they can be seen and have those props, makeup, and hairdos that help them tell the story. You have concentrated the majority of your technical efforts on publicity and costumes. Remember that your audience has come to be entertained as well as see their child, next door neighbor, and/or friend, not to see the most glorious or magnificent set. They will accept any convention you want to use as they did with lighting, so with what energy you have left, create a simplified setting using some basic set pieces.

How to construct the basic components of stage scenery are covered in a must-have book, *Stage Construction* by Bill Raoul. Another helpful book is *Self-Supporting Scenery for Children's Theatre and Grown-Ups, Too* by James Hull Miller.

Good set design is simple, lightweight, and easy to move and store. Remember that stage scenery is not built as one would build a house or a shop project. You may need to compensate for your theatre inadequacies as well as the fact that you might not have your stage, gym, or multi-purpose room at your disposal for the entire duration of the play. First, you need to know some backstage lingo.

Backdrop: A piece of scenic canvas the length of your stage times the height of your opening that hangs in a vertical position at the rear of a scene. It is painted to represent whatever you need, from a street scene or house to a forest or plain. Curtains secured at the rear of a scene can also be a backdrop.

Flat: A lightweight wood frame covered with muslin or canvas resembling an artist's canvas. The standard size is twelve feet high by four feet wide. Flats most often represent solid walls, with the four-foot side placed on the floor. However, if the flat is placed the other way, with the twelve-foot side on the floor, the flat can be used as cut down scenery or profile scenery (types of simplified scenery) or a ground row.

Hard Flats: These are the same as the flats described above. The only difference is that instead of being covered with muslin or canvas, they are covered with a hard surface such as wood paneling (the preferred is called luan

— a three-layer plywood made from coarse grained tropical wood also known as Philippine Mahogany) or hardboard. These are much easier to make, take less time to construct, are more durable, can be repainted more often, and cost less than the canvas or muslin counterpart. They are considerably heavier than the basic flat.

Platforms and Stairs: Every drama department needs a set of stairs four feet high and at least two four-foot by eight-foot platforms. Platforms give you levels to make the set much more interesting to use and view. Of course you need to have steps leading up to the raised level. Both the platforms and stairs can be made out of plywood. Legs may be added to make them as tall as you need.

Simplified Scenery: The general term used to explain why you don't have a full set. There are many variations of this type of scenery. Four are explained below: **Stage draperies, Music Department Sound Shells, Cut Down Scenery,** and **Suggested Scenery**.

Working with your required technical aspects

Start with your *3rd Read-Through: Required Technical Aspects* form (page 235) and your floor plan in hand (you have already done most of your work in Chapter 4 when you decided on your concept). Most school drama directors do not have the facilities or the budget for elaborate scenery. You must create, with a good script, the mood of the play and the statement you want to make about the play (your concept) with whatever you put on your stage. Remember, too, that the set design for any play must also respect the author's intent. Scenery should not overshadow or detract from the total presentation. If scenery is badly done or inappropriate, it will take away from your production.

Two choices for your set

A full, complete set

This consists of stage scenery constructed to run from the curtain line Stage Right to the curtain line Stage Left with little or no interruption. Special flats are built that have openings for doors and windows.

There are variations and degrees of full settings. Typical is the box set, which attempts to enclose the acting area to resemble a realistic room. Three walls are created with flats. The fourth wall is imaginary as it is the curtain line that the audience sees through.

Expensive settings have been designed for Shakespeare's plays; however, his plays are most successfully done on a bare stage because the language creates its own settings. On the other hand, a poor script is not necessarily improved by the use of magnificent sets.

There are many fine books printed on how to design, build, paint, and decorate such a set (see the Further Reading section).

The Bat: This was our full set. The main color was red, with blue-, yellow-, and ochre-striped wallpaper.

There are six conditions that must be met before you should consider a full set. Consider whether you have:

- A sufficient budget (must include cost of lumber, muslin, glue, plywood, sizing, paint, etc).
- Expertise in the area of set design or someone outside who can assist you.
- Adequate time to design and build the set.
- Ample space for building and/or painting.
- Proper tools and equipment.
- A play that would suffer if a complete set wasn't used.

If any one of the six conditions can't be met, consider one of the following ideas.

Simplified setting

You are designing a fragment of a complete set which suggests there is more to the set than is really there. Start with a bare stage and add minimal set pieces, stressing innovation, ingenuity, creativity, and low cost. The first thing you must decide is which of the four types of simplified settings is best for you:

Stage draperies

Draperies give the illusion of walls. School stages are usually equipped with curtains on the acting area. These generally are inside the stage opening and surround the acting area. Using these curtains, many sets are possible. Add a couch, table, and chairs and the scene becomes a living room. The period of the play can be depicted by the costumes. By adding selected set pieces, the setting can resemble almost any locale. Keep in mind:

- The curtains must be clean;
- The openings for the doors and windows must be big enough for people to go through or look through without disturbing the set; and
- The length of each curtain should be exactly the same.

Remember that anything you put on the stage makes a statement.

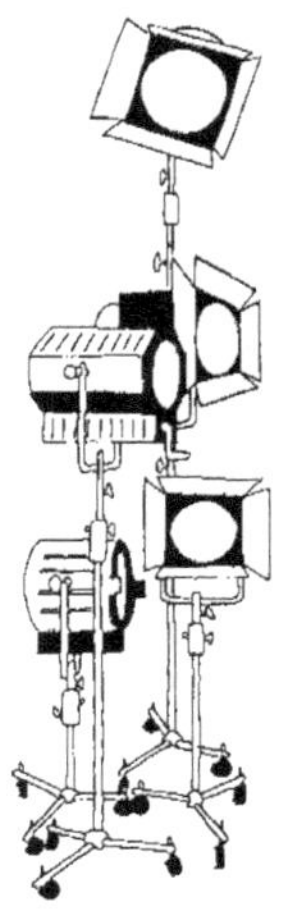

I was doing a cutting for a theatre festival of *Feiffer's People* that had many characters and many settings. I decided to use stage draperies and use boxes for furniture. As the acting area was surrounded by black, I thought that brightly-colored boxes would look interesting and add color to the set. Well, was I wrong!

The adjudicator said that our play became a play about colored boxes and how many ways they could be put together. That was all he could focus on! Had I chosen not to have such colorful boxes (but rather painted them gray or brown), everyone could have focused on the play and characters, not the scenery. I had done the unforgivable. After that, when I chose to use stage draperies, I always looked at what I put on the stage for the actors to use as set pieces and asked myself, "Do I pay attention to the set? Or am I more interested in the characters?"

The Importance of Being Earnest: In front of the stage curtains we added platforms, stairs, and couches borrowed from the teacher's lounge.

Music department's sound shell

These shells can provide solid walls in a hurry. These are placed in front of the existing curtains and then furniture is added. It allows for only two exits and entrances, but it does give the illusion of solidarity.

Cut-down scenery

Cut-down scenery is a type of simplified setting which takes its forms from the architectural features of the room such as a window, doors, and/or cabinets that are normal height. The walls are short, approximately four feet high — a flat placed horizontally instead of perpendicularly if you have any — saving material and effort. The general effect suggests solidity, although there are short walls. These walls plus doors, windows, etc. are placed in front of the back wall and/or draperies.

Catch Me if You Can: As the dance troupe was using the theatre for their spring performance we did not have the time or the luxury to create the required interior set. We used three sound shells and added furniture, a hanging lamp, pictures, and stapled wallpaper on flat surfaces.

Stalag 17 used cut-down scenery with a standard window and door. One night during rehearsal the cast took black paint and painted graffiti on the wall and table. The SS officer was our German teacher who was extremely intimidating. The bunk beds we were lucky enough to borrow from a church camp, mattresses and all. We hung various pictures a la Betty Grable on them. This is the show I mentioned in Chapter 1 that we had to take down the night before we opened!

Suggested settings

Suggested settings are key or important pieces of scenery that are required by the plot of the play. You would usually think first in terms of an entire room, and then remove all that you consider non-essential. Next, select that piece of scenery you will use. The selective piece of scenery will suggest the room and the furnishings will complete it. The scenery and the furniture chosen must be selected to say something about the play. Sometimes furniture alone can function as a set design.

The Curious Savage requires a set of fancy doors and bookcases located up center. Most directors choose to fill the entire stage with scenery that is not needed. By choosing only the doors, a director can establish one major architectural detail which gives the viewer a feeling of a large house. How the doors are finished will also tell us a great deal about the home. Of course, chairs, tables, and a couch will be added.

Night of January 16th: We had the witness chair on a small platform in front of a short wall attached to the judge's bench. The wall hid the platform and stairs the judge had to climb to get to the podium. We borrowed the school rostrum and flag.

110 in the Shade: Tom Valach designed this gazebo that represented the park outside of town.

This was the wagon — a four-foot by eight-foot platform with wheels — that had two sets. One side was the outside of the sheriff's office that portrayed the town, and the other side was the inside of the office. All we did was turn the platform around. This platform and the gazebo pictured above were all we used for the setting of *110 in the Shade*.

Tom Valach selected a door as the major feature for *The Imaginary Invalid.* Our concept was like Argon's mind — full of nothing but cotton! So how do we soften the door? We had lots of green damask (donated by the local fabric store), so Tom used it as our wall. It was draped to give a formal French look. Along with the green fabric, we painted the door a light pink and outlined it in a deep rose. We also decided that all props would be soft sculpture, made out of muslin and stuffed — medicine bottles, mirrors, injection needle, etc. We even padded the screen.

If you have not yet made up your mind, read on. The remainder of this chapter looks at five specific ways to use suggested scenery. There are a variety of ways to create suggested scenery using boxes, frames, arches and doorways, paper backdrops, cardboard, or any combination of these. The suggestions below are meant to help trigger your imagination. This scenery can also be used to design exteriors and classical theatre.

Boxes

A set of six to nine boxes, eighteen inches on each side, made of half-inch plywood, are a must for any drama department. After the four sides and the top are cut, the bottom can remain open. Glue and screw the box together; we never nail in theatre — nails split the wood, and screws allow you to re-use the wood. The boxes need to be sanded and the corners covered with muslin strips seven inches wide, using wallpaper paste or glue. Two hand holes about five inches by two inches (on opposite sides) should be drilled about three inches from the top so the boxes can be easily moved. You can also put one hand hole in the top, eliminating the two side ones.

Boxes are so versatile and can become anything you want them to be — chairs, tables, benches, (putting two or three together), ground rows (all the boxes lined up together and painted), trees (three to four stacked on top of one another and painted), etc. These boxes also work well for shows needing scene changes. With the four sides, not counting the top, you can have four different settings by rotating them a quarter turn.

Another version of the box is constructed from six pieces of poster cardboard, all the same size (a top, bottom, and four sides) with the settings drawn and painted on the sides and/or the top and bottom. Punch at least twenty holes on the four sides of each piece of cardboard and lace them together.

This works well for designs of walls or trees, but can't be used for chairs.

> *I successfully used this idea for a traveling production of* A Thurber Carnival. *The line drawings in black on white cardboard worked well. The cardboard laid flat when not laced, making traveling easy.*

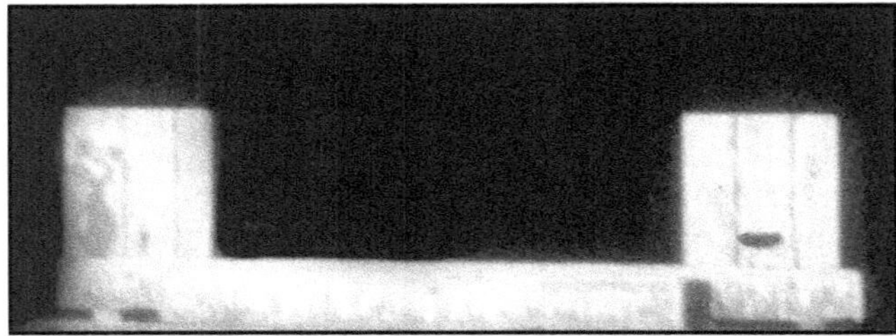

Gold Fever: We needed to establish entrances and exits to buildings, so we used a four-foot by eight-foot platform with a box at each end to establish a door and walls. They were painted a bright yellow that worked well for the grass and flowerpots that were painted on the front of both the platform and boxes. Notice the hand holes.

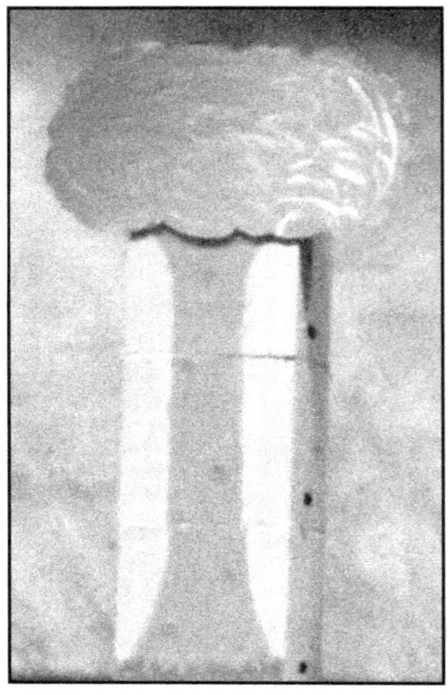

Winnie the Pooh: The same three boxes were used for both the tree — standing one upon another — and the rabbit hole — two boxes supporting the third so Rabbit could crawl in and out. Each side of the boxes was painted differently.

Sacramento, 50 Miles, designed by Tom Valach during his senior year of high school, used an open frame for walls. The rooster costume was rented. The beautiful foliage to the right was a portable wall professionally painted in Portland, Oregon, in the 1920s.

Frames

Frames made of one-inch by four-inch wood or tubing define the outline of walls or buildings. The frames are joined together with hinges to be self-supporting. You will need a carpenter to help with the logistics of the design. They can be open so all you have is a line drawing that is semi-solid, allowing the audience to see inside and out; or they can be filled, giving the illusion of solidity. They can also define entrances and exits. These work extremely well when the requirements of your set call for walls and you don't have flats or the time to make them. These frames have the advantage over regular flats because they:

✓ Are lighter in weight;

✓ Are more easily moved; and

✓ Can be any height you want.

This set is quite fragile and must be moved with care. It is possible to build the frames out of two-by-fours for strength, but this is much harder to support and considerably heavier.

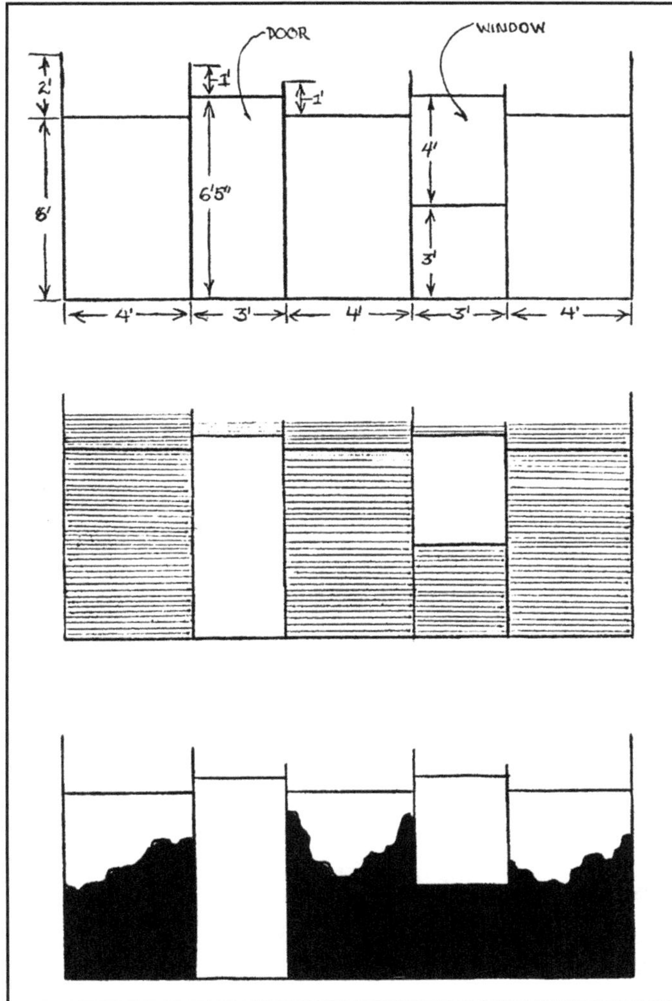

Measurements for a standard set of frames along with two examples of how they may be decorated.

An **open frame** can be used by itself, like a line drawing, to create a set, or you can put another smaller frame inside it to create windows and doors. You then would have a frame within a frame. The size and shape of the frame, doors, and windows depends on the type of play.

A **semi-solid frame** can give the feeling of having a solid house or wall. Use the open frame and string any of the following between the open parts of the frame. (If painting any of the six items below is necessary, it should be done before the yarn, thin rope, etc. is attached as they each have a tendency to sag when wet):

✓ Yarn;

✓ Thin rope;

✓ Clothesline;

✓ Fencing;

✓ Wire; and/or

✓ String.

Or fill the "solid parts" with one of the four suggested light fabrics:

✓ Chiffon;

✓ Netting;

✓ Cheesecloth; and/or

✓ Gossamer (sheer fabric).

Focusing the lights behind the frame enables the audience to see inside the house and the set to become translucent. Focusing the lights in front of the frame makes it look solid. This works very well if you need to go from an exterior to an interior scene.

Solid walls using frames can be created by adding cloth, foam core (a wonderful product that is light and great to paint but expensive), Styrofoam, foam insulation (material that comes in long interlocking strips), one-quarter-inch sheet rock (this is very heavy), or cardboard. Attach the material to the "open" walls, making cutouts for windows and doors.

For *Brigadoon*, we designed walls to represent the houses using the open frame and filling the solid parts with large fencing. They were made to collapse with hinges, thus the town could appear and disappear rapidly.

If a doorway is needed and total realism isn't necessary, building a self-standing doorframe and hanging shower curtains from the top works well. The "door" can be easily opened and closed. This type of setting works extremely well for comedies and plays featuring characters from *Commedia dell'Arte* or farce.

Cut a piece of one-half-inch plywood into a four-foot square. You will need six pieces of pipe (two for the sides, one for the top, one for the bottom, and two extended out at right angles from the door frame) in order to have it stand upright.

The size depends on the opening you want. The pieces of pipe are attached with special pipe connectors called Kee Klamps, using an Allen wrench. These may be purchased through most theatre catalogs. They are expensive, but can be used over and over again. Fasten the bottom pipes to the plywood with a C-type pipe bracket. Attach shower curtains just like on a shower rod. If a solid wall is needed, cloth can be strung, much like floor-length curtains (with a rod pocket at the top) to simulate walls.

A similar kind of frame can be built using plastic plumbing pipe (PVC) and a fabric panel either draped over the pipe or sewn with a rod pocket at the top and the pipe strung through the pocket. It is self-standing, and adding curtains creates the illusion of solid walls.

Arches and doorways

An effective way to provide a setting is to have a set of three or more arches and/or doorways, depending on the size of your acting area. They may be hinged together so that they are self-standing. Construct these openings of plywood, reinforced by one-by-twos and then hinge them together with tight or fixed-pin hinges (hinges either have fixed pins or removable loose pins for easy disassembling). Three doorways/arches seem to work well for balance and storability. Their total length together should be one-third of the stage opening. The style chosen will make a statement about the play. Their design should be drawn on graph paper before any cutting is done.

Inserts, which snap into the openings, make for a completely different setting. An exterior can be easily made into an interior. These frames can also be reversed for more versatility. They are easily moved and stored and can be used for a variety of different sets. They work well in conjunction with a backdrop, boxes, benches and/or banners.

For *And So Ad Infinitum*, arches were designed by John Shaffner for three different sets, as seen in the following pictures:

This is the set for Act I, which takes place with butterflies. We hung colored chiffon in the openings to give a light, airy feel to the set piece.

This setting dealt with the bugs and crawly things. We plugged the holes and hung muslin in front of one of the openings.

This setting was for the ants, a warring group — the red ants against the yellow ants. The arches were plain — stark gray. Tom Valach lit the backdrop from behind so shadows could be seen.

Paper backdrop

If drawing is something you or someone you know can easily execute, and you have a way to attach paper either to the ceiling or back wall, a paper backdrop is a simple and effective way to create a setting. The use of a backdrop is limiting because it relies totally on one's ability to draw, paint — sometimes it is a realistic setting, other times something nonrealistic — and attach. All that is needed is a roll of butcher paper, graph paper, some masking tape, tempera paint, one-by-fours, heavy cord, or "tacky stuff."

Cut strips of the butcher paper the width of the stage to go up to seven feet high, as anything much higher causes a support problem. Tape the pieces together to make one big drop. Make your design as simple as possible on graph paper scale of one inch equaling one foot. Draw your design on the graph paper and transfer the design by putting it on an overhead projector. Project the design on the butcher paper and trace it. Another way to transfer the design is to draw the grid on the backdrop itself. Then paint your design.

After it is painted, attach the one-by-fours along the top of your backdrop with glue. Drill holes about a foot apart so it can be secured with heavy cord or clothesline to the ceiling. If you have nothing to attach it to, instead of using one-by-fours, use the "tacky stuff" grade school teachers use in their classroom. This will not damage the paper. Do not use tape of any kind to secure it — the backdrop will be ruined when it is moved.

Another possibility is to buy a roll of "Tyvek" — what builders use to cover houses before the siding is added. It is waterproof, light, cannot be torn, and is relatively inexpensive. It does have writing on it, but you can use the backside and put a base coat of paint over it before the design is transferred. Proceed as you did with the butcher paper.

During summer school we decided to do *Cinderella* and take it to the children's hospital in Spokane, Washington. As we had no money, we created the set out of objects that were handy. This was our backdrop for the house: just a fireplace and two windows, all done with paint and butcher paper. It was then attached to the existing wall.

A similar idea was used by Missoula's Children's Theatre. The only set piece, a large board with a tablet in the middle, was placed Center Stage. The board was decorated with scrollwork. As each new scene opened, a character came out, pulled the old paper off the tablet, drew the appropriate scene, and the action started.

Cardboard

An inexpensive way to create stage scenery is to use cardboard boxes; usually a refrigerator, mattress, or bicycle carton. They can be used as boxes, cupboards, closets, or bases for such things as caves. They may also be cut apart to be used as walls, ground rows, hills, mountains, bushes, etc.

To make walls, ground rows, or silhouettes, take a large cardboard container, cut off the end, and cut down one side so it will lie flat. Cut it to the desired size and shape. As this is paper, you may want to spray the cardboard with a fire retardant made specifically for paper (check your local Yellow Pages). When painting cardboard, be sure that the back has been painted as well so it will not curl. Reinforce the back with one-by-fours.

Our Sadie Hawkins Jail: We sponsored a yearly Sadie Hawkins dance, and one year we decided to have a jail where, for a certain amount of money, you could be put in jail or bailed out — we did almost anything to raise money! The jail was made out of cardboard, painted, and then braced to stand by itself. The young man in the middle is John Shaffner, the Emmy-winning designer mentioned previously.

Tom Jones: These houses were created and painted by Tom Valach. They are cardboard with one-by-four supports.

Exteriors

Exterior settings are needed occasionally and almost impossible to create realistically. Painting exteriors is an art in itself, so unless you have a scenic artist on staff, try one of the four ideas listed below. They are simple and give the idea of being outside.

Trees

There are several options for creating trees on-stage:

✓ The easiest way to create trees is with a drapery setting. Those curtains at each side of the stage (generally six feet wide) called *legs* work best. Draw them together so they form a long, slender line. If they are attached to a pipe that moves, shift them where you want them. If they cannot be moved, take the curtains down, move them where you want them, and then re-attach them to the pipe.

✓ Trees can also be created by taking brown fabric and stretching it over the curtains discussed above. The fabric should be textured with acrylic paint—it does not chip off.

✓ Trees can be made with a wood frame, chicken wire, and papier mâché.

✓ Real trees can be used.

✓ Ground rows, usually less than three feet high, can be created out of cardboard or quarter-inch plywood, Styrofoam, or foam core. A scenic background with foliage, plants, and/or flowers can be painted on them. Cut the outline of what you want with a saw or trim knife, paint, and brace with a wooden triangle made of one-by-fours. Flats set on the stage floor so

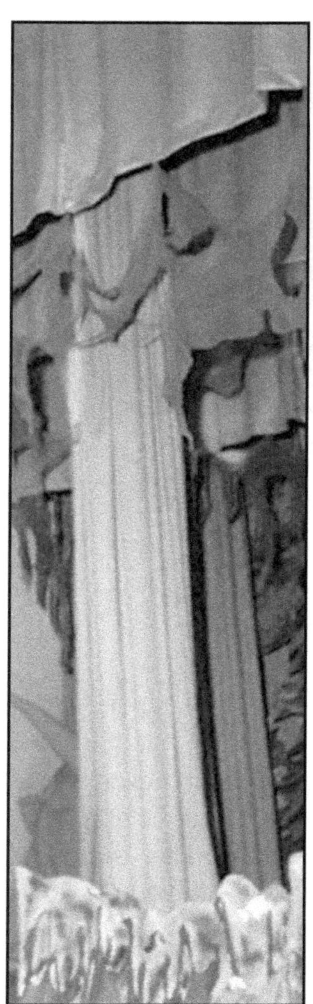

Tree created with a drapery setting.

For *A Midsummer Night's Dream,* we created our magic forest using real aspens, painting them silver, and adding twinkling lights, silver Christmas ornaments, glitter, and ribbon. Above them was a teaser made of black plastic. Christmas lights were strung on top of the teaser along with glittery, four-inch wide, wire-edged ribbon and mini mirror balls. Over the top of that we added glittery silver garland. Attached to the back of the black plastic were groups of black netting with glitter glued to them. The netting hung down below the teaser in irregular bunches. At the base of the trees were weeds picked out of gardens and then painted green, brown, gold, and red with glitter glued on. The platforms in the back were covered with black plastic.

Winnie the Pooh: The tree is brown fabric with some texture. The leaves are explained later as "Winnie the Pooh foliage."

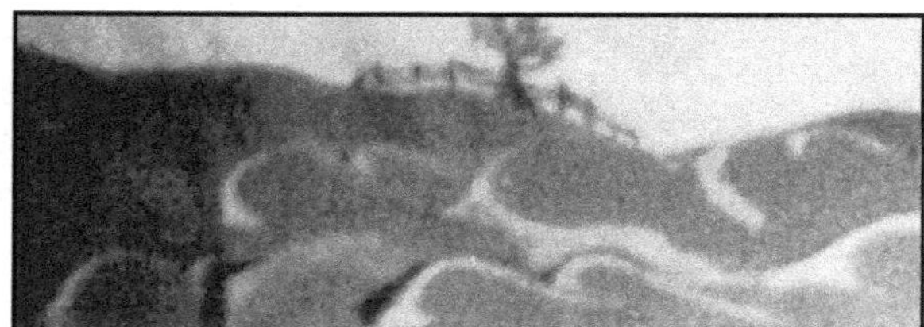

110 in the Shade: We used a cardboard ground row to represent the dried-up land. We painted it dark brown with cream highlights.

they are low and long can also be used. Just add plywood to the flat to create the outline you need, cover with muslin, paint, and brace.

✓ Green or brown fabric attached to two pieces of irregular circular plywood. Consider the plywood a cross-section of the tree. Attach the fabric around the edge of the plywood so that it forms the contour of the tree trunk. Do not attach the fabric all the way around; leave enough space so a weight can be put on the piece of plywood that is placed on the floor. Hang the other piece of plywood (attached to the other end of your fabric) from the ceiling with wire. Green fabric can be gathered and stapled onto one-by-three pieces of lumber. Add white paint to give dimension and hang from the ceiling.

This is another Tom Valach design for *Merry Wives of Windsor*. As this play deals with not only the woods but also a house, fabric was rolled up into tubes with the back open and attached to curved pieces of plywood, which were, in turn, attached to the floor and ceiling. These gathered tubes then became either walls, pillars, or trees, depending on the scene. One of the characters tried to hide behind these pillars, which added much to the humor, as there was no way he could be hidden. The costumes were rented from our university. For the interiors, we used chiffon fabric in several colors and draped it (using staples) on a one-by-four attached to the ceiling.

Mung

Mung is cheesecloth dyed dark green that hangs down around your acting area and looks like moss, fingers, cobwebs, or foliage. Buy enough cheesecloth to measure at least three times the width of the theatre opening. Dye the cheesecloth — a washing machine seems to work the best. Line dry so you do not get too much shrinkage and the cloth does not twist. After it is dried, cut it in two-and-a-half-foot wide strips, as long as the material runs. Rip these strips widthwise (not all the way across — leave a strip on one end to hold it all together) about every six inches. It now is ready to be attached to a curtain, ceiling, tree, ground row, flowers, board, etc. The more there is of it, the better the stage looks. A similar effect can be achieved with nylon netting and/or tobacco cloth. However these are more expensive.

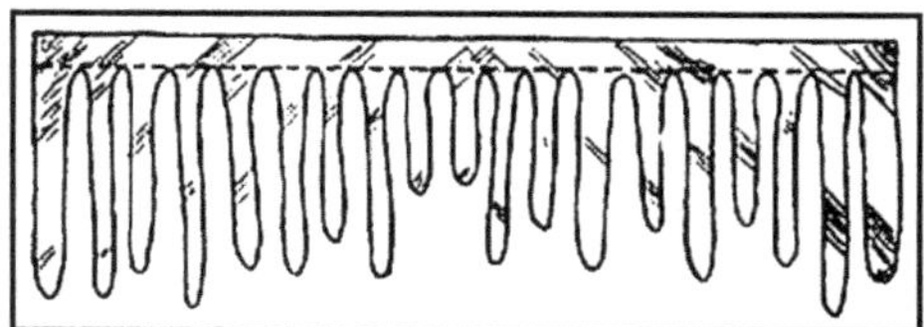

The basic pattern of mung.

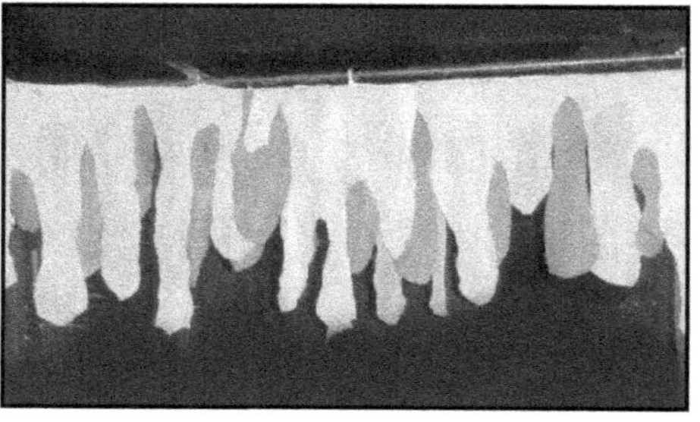

This is Tom Valach's version of mung. This foliage is dyed cheesecloth (several shades of green) that is ironed, cut out, and attached to one-by-fours, which were then attached to the ceiling.

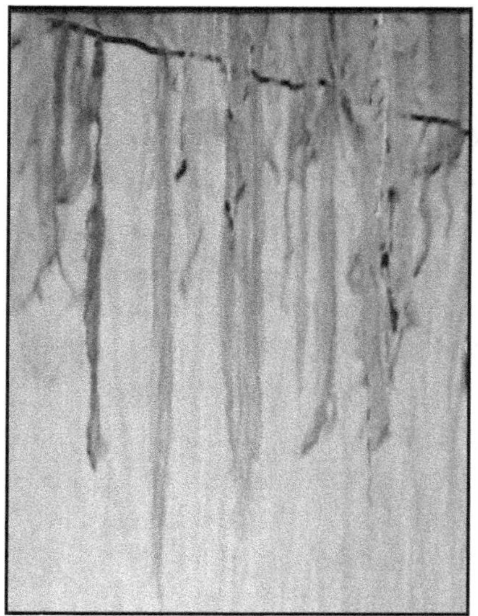

Two more examples of mung.

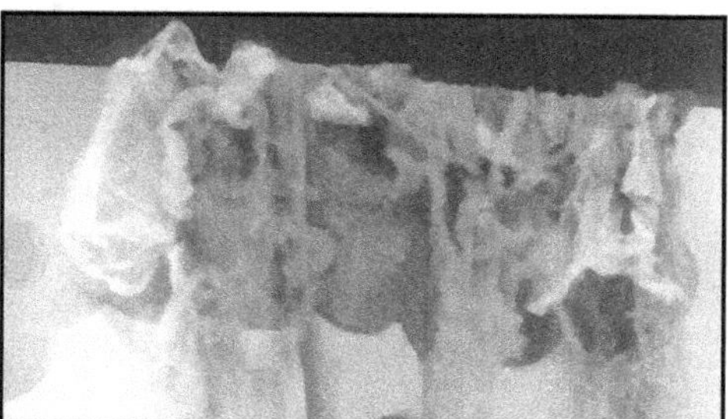

Gook made from netting, cheesecloth, and muslin knotted together and attached to the back of the flat.

Gook

Gook is composed of strips of various types and colors of cloth tied and knotted together to look like a rope. This works extremely well if a major change is needed in thirty seconds or less. Attach the ropes to the back of the set piece and/or wall. Throw them over the clean set and it becomes messy. It then only takes one to two people to throw these ropes back over the wall, and the set is clean.

Winnie the Pooh foliage

Similar to mung, this foliage uses a different technique. The basic material is muslin, but old sheets or any white material can work. This fabric should be four-feet by six-feet wide and three times the length of the stage opening. The fabric can be in several pieces and sewed together at a later date. Dye the fabric the green you want in a washing machine. Line dry the fabric in folds so as not to get many wrinkles in it.

When it is dry, lay the fabric out flat with a drop cloth or other protective covering underneath it. Using a nylon brush and bleach, paint the wide outline of leaves on the fabric. Do not drip the bleach because it will bleach the color out. Much of the dye either totally fades out or becomes a much lighter color. After the entire piece of fabric is painted, sew together if needed, and then cut around the leaves on the bottom. Cut holes in the top of the greenery and attach it to a pipe. Do not wash (as much of the color will wash out), but do air the material out — the bleach has a very strong odor.

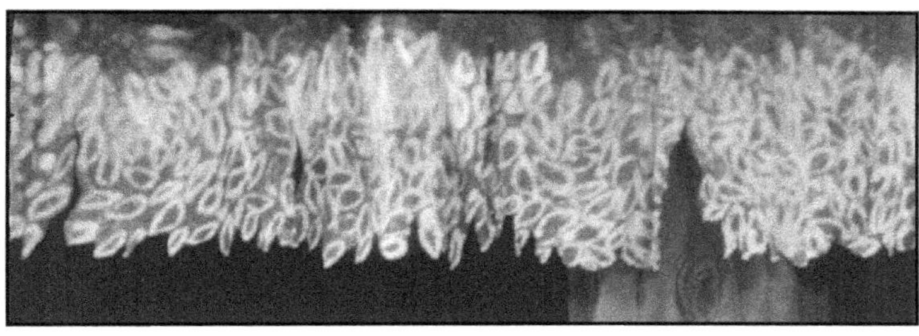

Winnie the Pooh foliage.

Classical theatre

If your decision is to do one of the classics, there are two things you will need to make your job easy: banners and benches. Banners can be made from strips of plain colored fabric: muslin, sheeting, and/or gossamer, a non-woven inexpensive fabric. They are approximately four feet wide and seven to nine feet high. They can be hung in the back of your acting area, from ceiling to the floor, or they may be self-standing, whatever your expertise allows. Using two boxes and a music stand will work. Put the two boxes, one on top of the other. On top of these place a music stand, extended as far as it will go. Attach the fabric to the music stand with tape or "tacky stuff." Depending on the width of your stage, you can have three to five banners. Anything you want to decorate these with is fine. Emblems can be added to these as well as trim. They can even serve as entrances and exits.

Note:
Whether you are building flats, benches, or boxes, make them universal. This means that whatever you build this year, you can add to next year, and everything will fit together. In three to four years you will have enough stock scenery to do almost any set you want.

Benches, depending on the style and height, can serve as tables or chairs — the furniture most often needed in classical theatre. Simple benches work best, as we can accept them for any style. Even taking boxes and painting them to look like benches works well. Many good technical theatre books have excellent diagrams for the building of benches, depending on the style you wish to use.

Set crew

When you have made your decision as to what kind of set you will be using, think about the students who will help you create it. Recruiting your set crew along with your tryouts can help immeasurably, just as you did with all the other crews. Before the prospective students sign up, give them general information of what you require of the crew (see Chapter 6).

The nitty-gritty

Places to find set pieces

There are many places to find set pieces. Remember to give complimentary tickets to those who donate anything for your show, acknowledge them in the program, and write thank you notes. Eleven places to look are listed below:

- ✓ Apartment buildings often have a storage room of old furniture that might be borrowed;
- ✓ The city dump;
- ✓ Rummage sales;
- ✓ Secondhand stores;

- ✓ Your school's teachers' lounge and/or lost-and-found department often has something that can be used;
- ✓ Window displays at businesses and supermarkets. They are usually more than willing to help if care is taken with their merchandise. If they cannot lend anything, they may have helpful hints;
- ✓ Local furniture stores. They often are willing to loan chairs/tables;
- ✓ The music department. Most any high school music department has risers/platforms. These platforms give your set levels, and the shell can become a box set. These platforms/risers may need to be padded with old carpet as they can be noisy;
- ✓ The Industrial Arts department usually includes a unit on how to build stairs. If asked, they might donate the stairs to the drama department;
- ✓ Students have great ingenuity. They are not afraid to look in attics, ask their next-door neighbors, or even the superintendent of schools if they know there is something they can use; or
- ✓ Think, too, of not being so literal with the set design. Possibly a plumbing or wire shop has enough of either pipes or wire to create an interesting set. Look at what is manufactured in your town. Sometimes you'll find things that can create an interesting set.

  A children's theatre production of The Little Prince *used children's playground equipment (which was manufactured in the town) for its set. Entrances were made on the elephant slide and trips were taken on the merry-go-round.*

Paint and brushes

As mentioned above, these settings need to be painted. Interior latex or acrylic paint is suggested for permanent sets. It is relatively easily to clean up. Purchasing straight white latex and universal colorants to make tints of color works well. Medium to dark tint bases should be used if a deeper color is desired; adding colorant to straight white latex cannot make deep colors. Of course, you can also pick a color already in stock and have the store mix it for you.

Before purchasing any paint, check each paint store for their mismatched paint. Often they have a color you can use, and they will either give you the paint free or charge a minimal amount, saving you money.

Tempera's main advantage is that it washes off easily; however, for a permanent set it is too fragile as colors rub off. It works well for temporary sets made of cardboard or butcher paper.

Buying scenic paint from a theatre catalog may be worth the expense. It can be diluted generally three-to-one, covers almost anything, cleans up easily, and is made to be used under theatre lights. One gallon usually covers what three gallons of regular paint would.

When purchasing brushes, do not buy the expensive bristle type. Often with school productions, the paint is not washed out of them and they are ruined. I found buying the foam type of brushes worked just fine. They were not expensive, put the paint on smoothly, and if they were not cleaned up they could be thrown away without any guilt! Using rollers speeds up the job of painting, giving good coverage.

Textures

After your basic coat of paint is on your walls, you will need to over-paint and create a textured look. Why? Because it:

✓ Hides defects in your solid wall;

✓ Provides richness to the wall's surface; and

✓ Enhances your overall color effect.

You want to break up the long expanse of one solid color. It is not a long, involved process! There are many types of textures. Check your local paint stores for a variety of ideas, from using patterned rollers and stencils to specialty brushes and rags.

Decide which texture you want to use (two are discussed below). Next, pick a color that is either lighter or darker than the one you painted on your wall. Always experiment first on a test piece of cloth or board that has been painted with your background color. What you are after is something akin to a speckled look. You do not want a specific pattern, but rather an overall hint of another color. After you feel confident, you and your students are ready to go to work. As your students work with one of these techniques, be sure that they blend their work so that all the painting matches. The two techniques below are easy and quick. They get the job done in the least amount of time. If you are near a larger city you might check out Lowe's or Home Depot. They frequently give classes on faux finishes, and you might pick up some great tips.

Sponging

Start with a sea sponge, available at art supply, hobby, or paint stores. Dip it into the selected paint. Squeeze the paint out of it so that when handling the sponge the paint does not drip. Blot or dab the sponge lightly onto your surface. Always start doing it with a light hand. You can always add, but subtracting is very difficult. Again, you want an all-over hint of color, so do not be afraid to go back over your work and touch up. You can also use two colors — a lighter and darker version of the base coat — for more interest. The important thing is to step back from your work from time to time and see the result. Go out into the audience. Remember, your audience is not sitting on the stage. Be sure to turn on your stage lights. Often you will catch things that you cannot see with the work lights.

Schlepitchka

This very strange name stands for the texture I used the most. It requires a feather duster. You will be doing the same thing as you did with your sponge: dipping it into the paint, squeezing out the extra paint, and then either slapping it on your wall or using a turning motion thrusting it into the wall.

No, No, Nanette: This wall treatment, used in Act III at the lodge, was painted by Joyce Hanson, the set designer and high school senior. She did it in yellow, green, and purple as it was a lighthearted musical.

Remember, too, that you will want to constantly change the side of the sponge or the feather duster. You are not after sameness, but rather an overall indistinguishable pattern. If putting the sponge or feather duster directly into the paint can is not working for you, get a tray, put your paint in it, and lightly dip the sponge or feather duster into the tray. Wring out any extra paint before you start painting. You will get much more control that way.

Three-dimensional shaping or decorations

After the painting has been done, money and time can be spent on decorations or shaping to give frames, boxes, or any other set pieces the appearance of being three-dimensional. Add one of the following:

- ✓ Carpet/carpet pad — can become stone or bricks;
- ✓ Christmas garland — adds brilliance;
- ✓ Felt, rope, and string — are effective as woodcarving, metal grillwork, and wood molding;
- ✓ Papier mâché — works well for rocks, bricks, or tops of columns; or
- ✓ Wire — suspends decorative elements in mid-air, creating chandeliers or candlesticks.

The final final note

There is no substitute for experience when working on any technical area, but do not be afraid to experiment. When you have some free time, take classes: learn everything you can. Check out the books in the Further Reading section, go to the Internet, and make friends at your local college or university. Always keep in mind that the technical aspects of theatre are ever changing. Never underestimate your ability to create and, finally, never forget to use your imagination.

Encore

Chapter 20
Drama Class

You've now produced your first play, very successfully I might add, but one thing you're probably asking yourself is "What do I do with my drama class that meets every day?" Never fear, here are several wonderful suggestions for your classroom. Obviously, in no way is this everything a drama course should include, but rather ten fun activities to begin your quarter/semester classes.

Successful games and activities using large groups

A great way to start any major drama activity is with large groups. You don't want your students to be put on the spot. Yes, several of these activities do have one person "on the spot," but he or she is working with the whole group. The difference is the approach. These activities are considered games rather than assignments. As with any game there are several basic principles. I insisted my drama students follow these three simple rules:

✓ No breaking character.

✓ No saying, "I can't," but rather, "I'll try."

✓ There is no right or wrong way to create any of these games as long as you follow the techniques I have explained.

Many of the following activities involve improvisation, which can be thought of as an "on the spot" or "off the cuff" spontaneous activity spoken or written without prior preparation. As well as being wonderful introduction games, these activities are also great for refocusing a group that has become scattered or one that has become bored. The activities in this chapter would also work well in a rehearsal setting.

A great two-minute improvisation game to start your drama class

In advance, make up a list of about fifty brief, short openers (bits of dialogue) that could be used to start improvised scenes. Write each opener on a card and keep them in a 3 x 5 card box so they can be used over and over. Here are some good examples:

What's in the box? A puppy?
It's snowing! Let's go sledding.
You're late. I will have to tell Dad.
How's your brother?
Ouch! That hurts. Stop it!
Go away. I'm tired.
It's dark in here. I'm scared.
Here's a dime. Go buy some candy.
Don't forget it's my birthday.
I'm lost. Help me.
I dare you! I double dare you!
You're sick. I'm telling Mom
Help me! I'm falling.
Shhhh. Did you hear that?
Trick or treat!
John? Tom? Pete?
I saw that! Stop it now!
There, there. Stop crying.
What's that you're eating? Bugs?
I hate your guts.
A shark! Run for your lives.
Haven't I seen you somewhere before?
Gotcha! Third time's the best!
Is this your house?
This is for you. Congrats
Answer the door. Now!
There's something in my eye.
Stand up. It's now your turn.
I'm blind. What did you do?
Catch.
Who was that man?
Close your eyes. You're it!
Have you seen my kitty? He ran away last night.
Where's my teddy bear? You stole it!
It's empty. Where did you put it?
Next! Finally!
The baby's coming!

On the day you introduce this activity, begin by seeing what your students know about improvisation. Ask students what the word *improvisation* means, making sure they realize that improv games increase creativity, besides being fun to play.

Then discuss the Do's of improvisation:

✓ Take cues from your scene partner.

✓ Be spontaneous.

✓ Make your partner look good.

Next discuss the Don'ts of improvisation:

✓ Don't negate. *Always* answer yes.

✓ Don't be a ham. This is a dialogue, not a monologue.

✓ Don't ignore or deny your scene partner.

✓ Don't change the storyline. Always use the words given on the card. You are not to plot the story in advance.

✓ Don't respond with a question — acting is doing, not telling.

Demonstrate the *Don'ts.* Select one student to read a card to you and you negate. The students will immediately see that the story goes nowhere. If you need to demonstrate the *Dos,* select another student and proceed.

Depending on the class and your time frame, you can go around the room and have every student either read a card or react so everyone gets a chance to "play." Then explain to the students that starting tomorrow when the bell rings, one student (you decide where to start in the class, usually based on the seating chart) will pick a card and the student seated next to the student who pulled the card will react. They are to keep the scene going for two minutes, allowing you to take roll and get ready for the rest of the class period. Usually the first couple of weeks your students are much more comfortable doing this at their desks, but if you prefer, they can get up in front of the class and perform their improvisation.

After several weeks add a new element, which will get them up in front of the class. Set up a simple playing area in the front of the room by putting two chairs side-by-side in the playing area. The first actor will sit in a chair and perform some activity in pantomime, such as reading a book, feeding birds, etc. The second actor will enter and start the improvisation by using one of the short openers listed on page 230.

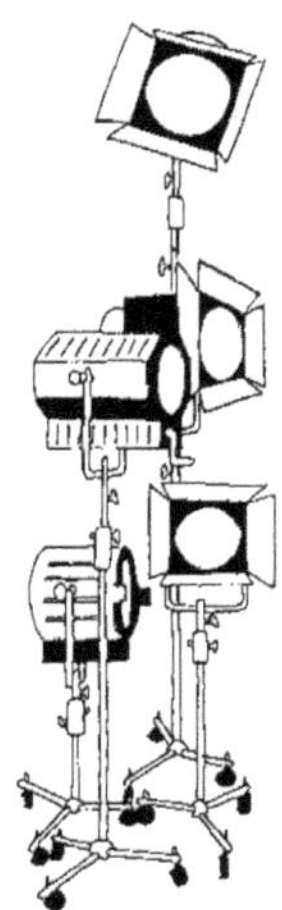

I have recently returned to the classroom teaching the over fifty crowd at the University of Montana's Continuing Education program, primarily using these activities. Everyone needs to feel comfortable before they embark on acting. I use these opening cards every time my class meets.

One of my students was a wonderful older lady from Sweden who had a great sense of humor and fun. My students and I always looked forward to her contributions to the class. When her partner read from the improv card, "He's dead," she replied without hesitation, "I know, I shot him!" It brought the class to a standstill with laughter and clapping. Of course there was nowhere to go and the improv ended!

Clap hands

The second check mark on page 79 is the description of this great game. When using it in the classroom, play the game with the whole class first and then divide the class into two groups of twelve to fifteen. Have them sit in two circles and play. To make it a bit more competitive, when a person messes up, he or she is eliminated from the game. When each group is down to six, have them join together and see who the top two players are.

Most deaths in a minute

Select ten to twelve students, let them separate into two teams, and line up in front of the class. Choose two students from the audience as counters. The teams compete for the greatest number of deaths (making sure to be creative) they can act out in one minute. Each death must be different and unique.

To catch a thief

After your students have formed a circle and closed their eyes, walk around the circle tapping one student on the back. I often walk around the circle several times before I select the specific student. After you have finished walking around the room, say, "Whoever I touched has my school keys from my desk drawer. Now open your eyes and everyone look and feel guilty." Then go around the circle asking each student if he or she took the keys. They are all to answer "no." Afterwards, have the group try to guess who stole the keys. This might be fun to do several times or once each day for several days.

Alien, cow, tiger

Once again, the class forms a circle. There are three things a player can be:

- ✓ An alien: hold your index fingers up next to your head as little antennae and say "bleep bleep," bending inwards into the circle.
- ✓ A cow: bending forward, hold your right hand on your tummy and say "moo."
- ✓ A tiger: reach forward with your hands imitating claws and growl.

Each player decides to become one of the three. The students do not share their decision. The ultimate goal is for everyone to become the same. When you say "go," everyone is to be their chosen animal. Repeat this until everyone is in sync. Do not spend more than about three minutes on this — hopefully that is long enough. You might even have the class invent their own animals or things.

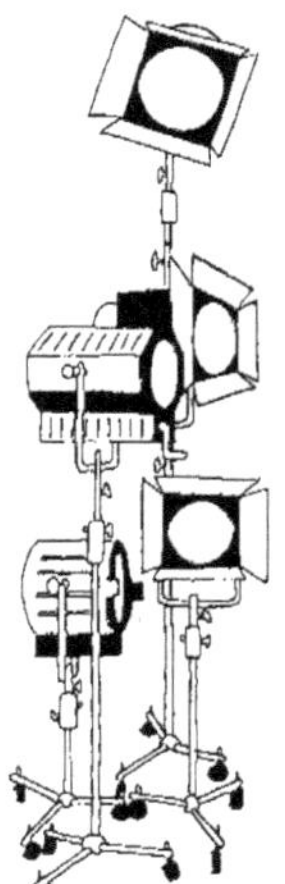

> In my over fifty class I tried this once with great success. However, I tried it again with another class and had one obstinate person who *absolutely* would not change from being a tiger — everyone had better be a tiger or else! Needless to say, the game was unsuccessfully over in less than three minutes.

Who started the motion

This time your students are standing in a circle. Explain that someone is going to be "it" and send them out of the room. When that person is gone, someone else volunteers to start a motion. It can be hand clapping, head nodding, winking, bending, or any kind of appropriate movement. No vocal sounds. They do have to change the movement every thirty seconds. It can be a slight change, going from a big nodding of the head to a smaller nod. It could be a jerkier movement changing to a much smoother one. It could be any type of change. You may have to side coach, giving the volunteer the thirty seconds warning.

As soon as the volunteer starts the motion, the entire circle must join in immediately and the "it" person comes back and stands in the middle of the circle.

The goal of the circle is to protect the volunteer by everyone in the circle changing the motion each time the volunteer initiates a change without looking directly at the volunteer. The "it" person's job is to figure out who the volunteer is. The "it" person will be given three guesses. If he or she figures it out, that's great. If after three tries the volunteer is exposed, he or she becomes "it" and goes out of the room. Another volunteer begins his or her movement, and the process is repeated.

Pass the tennis ball

This game sounds easy but actually requires real concentration. Have your class form a circle and ask for a volunteer to be in the middle. Ask the volunteer to close his or her eyes. Then pass a tennis ball clockwise around the circle. The reason for having the volunteer's eyes closed is so he or she won't know who has the ball when the volunteer calls "stop."

When the volunteer calls "stop," the person holding the tennis ball has to call out a letter in the alphabet — A, B, C, etc. Do not allow the tougher letters such as X or Z. Start passing the tennis ball around the circle while the volunteer has to name six nouns (no proper names, places, or things) starting with that letter.

The goal for the volunteer is to name six nouns before the ball comes back to the person who called the letter. If the volunteer cannot name six nouns with no help from fellow students, he or she changes places with the person who called out the letter. If the volunteer names six, on the sixth noun the ball will stop and whoever has the ball becomes the volunteer. You may have to keep track of all the letters called. You do not want to have a letter called twice. As your students become better players, increase the number of words required.

Kindergarten class

Select twelve actors. Eleven will be kindergarteners and one will be the teacher who is telling the story of *Goldilocks and the Three Bears*. As with the previous improvisations, the actors maintain their characters throughout the scene.

Characters and objectives

Teacher: (male or female) to have students sit quietly and listen to the story

Child A: (female) to make the teacher comment on what a polite child she is

Child B: (male) to get the teacher to let him go to the restroom

Child C: (male or female) to listen to the story

Child D: (male and female) to be helpful to the teacher

Child E: (male) to play with the car in his pocket

Child F: (male or female) to sit close to and get the attention of Child A

Child G: (male) to get Child E in trouble without getting in trouble himself

Child H: (male or female) to get Child C to look at him

Child I: (female) to give a piece of candy to Child D in order to make Child D like her

Child J: (male or female) to get a piece of candy from Child I

Child K: (female) to show Child F and Child H pictures of her puppy

You will need a chair for the actor who plays the teacher and eleven name tags for the students. The children will sit on the floor. Either take the group out of the room and whisper privately to each actor his or her character and objective or have them select a card with the information written on it. *They are not to share the information with their fellow actors.* By the way they act, their objectives should become obvious.

Just before starting the scene, send the teacher and those who are the audience out of the room. Address the actors playing the children as follows:

"One last point: you are all frightened of the school principal because he is very tall and has a deep voice. None of you want to be sent to the office under any circumstances. Play your objectives carefully so you don't cause the teacher to send you to the office. If the teacher tells you to go to the office, you must leave the scene and stand outside in the hall until the improvisation is over."

Next, go outside, send the audience back into the classroom, and speak to the actor portraying the teacher as follows:

"The children are all frightened of the principal. They do not want to be sent to the office. If a child provokes you, you may threaten to send him or her to the office. You don't really want to send anyone there. But, if necessary, you may do so. When you tell a child to go to the office, that actor will leave the scene."

Seat the children on the floor around the teacher to begin the scene. During the improvisation you may want to call on a student from the audience to enter the scene as the principal. This actor has a message for the teacher and could then ask about the behavior of the students. Freeze the scene for discussion if the actors overreact at any time, especially to the entrance of the principal.

Following the improvisation, you may want to have the actors describe how they felt during the scene and how the audience felt by asking these questions:

✓ Were the actors playing children able to draw on their own memories to help them interpret the roles accurately and honestly?

✓ Did the actors actually feel the experience of being a kindergartener in class? Or were they acting throughout the scene?

✓ Did the actor playing the teacher experience any genuine emotions during the scene? What were these emotions?

✓ What actions on the part of the teacher and/or the children seemed realistic and believable?

✓ What was each actor's objective?

Trip to New York

Set up chairs to suggest a bus. Place a desk in one corner for the ticket seller. Choose twelve students who will be taking the bus. They are to create an improvisation based on a character and an objective you will give them (see examples below).

Either take the group out of the room and whisper privately to each actor their character and objective or have them select a card with the written information that you have prepared ahead of time and put in your card file box. *The actors are not to share the information with their fellow actors.* By the way, if the actors create their characters, their objectives should become obvious.

Character and objective

Teenage Girl: to meet her boyfriend, who her parents do not like

Cool Guy: to make people think he's a rich Yankee fan whose flight to New York was canceled

Nervous Woman: to meet her online boyfriend for the first time and is embarrassed to tell anyone

Middle-Aged Man or Woman: to be a stage actor in New York

Old Person: (male or female) to visit his or her favorite grandchildren

Weird Person: (male or female) to convince people that the end of the world is near

Upset Man: to return home without the job he was counting on

Young Person: (male of female) to audition at Juilliard

Nervous Person: (male or female) to skip town before he or she is arrested

Weird Person: (male or female) to go to the Le Cordon Bleu School to become a world-renowned pastry chef

Undercover Agent: (male or female) to identify and arrest a suspect

Eight-Year-Old Kid: (male or female) to wait for his or her mother, who never arrives

All the characters are waiting to get on the bus going somewhere except for the Undercover Agent and the Eight-Year-Old Kid. However, the Undercover Agent must buy a ticket to protect his or her cover. The actors must maintain their character and objective throughout the scene.

Select two more students in the class to be part of the scene, one as a ticket seller (objective: to sell tickets) and one as a security guard (objective: to maintain law and order). Next determine the actors' order of entry into the scene. The scene should not end until you stop it. Your actors must avoid any action that might force an early conclusion, such as a bomb or bus failure.

Before you begin the scene, urge your actors to concentrate on playing their objectives as realistically as possible — no stereotypes. The scene opens with the ticket seller, security guard, and Eight-Year-Old Kid seated on a chair waiting for his or her parent. Call "places" to initiate the improvisation and "curtain" to end it.

Following the improvisation, let the audience share what they observed about the actors' characters and motives. Use similar questions to those you asked after "Kindergarten class." Next, the actors need to state their characters and their individual objectives as well as any approaches they used to achieve that objective. If the audience does not understand the character or objective, discuss ways the scene or actor could have improved.

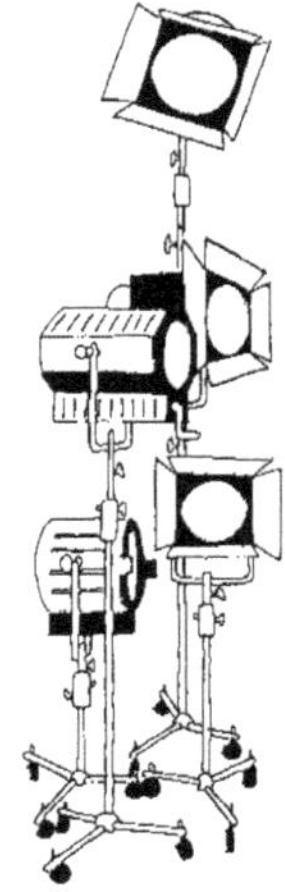

> In any of these improvisations, be alert for overacting or lack of concentration. If necessary, freeze the action to call attention to such faults. Large group improvisations can be a marvelous success, a dismal failure, or any number of things in between. Allow a good scene to run for about ten minutes. A poor one should be cut short.

Students creating their own large group improvisation

Now give your students the opportunity to create their own large group improvisation. This will take several days, depending on your class' ability.

Divide the class into two or three groups of eight to ten students, depending upon class size. Have each group prepare an improvisation in which *every* member must portray a character with an objective. Instruct each group to decide first on a suitable location for its scene. Then they should come up with characters that could fit into that scene.

If any group has trouble thinking of a suitable setting, you will need to be ready with suggestions. Here are some settings that can easily accommodate large groups:

- ✓ Beach: an easy scene to develop; actors enter one at a time, starting with the lifeguard
- ✓ Courtroom: lots of character possibilities — judge, defendant, prosecutor, defense attorney, bailiff, clerk/recorder, witnesses; group can even select a jury from the rest of the class
- ✓ Funeral parlor: begin with the director of the establishment alone with the deceased; have the other actors enter one at a time or in pairs
- ✓ Murder scene: living room of an old mansion; ten suspects and a detective a la Agatha Christie
- ✓ Play rehearsal: this would depend on whether your students have had prior theatre involvement and have some firsthand experience of play rehearsals to draw from
- ✓ School bus: driver and any number of students; all kinds of opportunities for interesting interplay of characters and objectives
- ✓ Wedding reception: a difficult and challenging scene, clear-cut relationships must be established beforehand

Once the scene and characters have been determined, select a group leader who will coordinate casting by helping the actors choose characters and objectives. The leader makes sure there are conflicts that must be resolved and then decides in what order the actors are to enter into the scene. Each actor writes down his or her character's name and objective, which is then put in a hat. When the improv is over, each objective is revealed to the audience.

If possible, you could use a stage for these presentations and invite a small audience. Focus your evaluation on characterization and use of objectives.

Evaluation

Several things I know you are wondering about are: "What do I do with those students who are just watching the activity? I need to make this an educational experience for them too. I want them to pay attention, becoming a part of the whole process of theatre by being a good, informed audience. I want them to answer the questions after the 'Kindergarten class' constructively."

We need to teach our students to view acting with a critical eye when watching fellow actors. The downfall is that sometimes our students become overly critical or very generous. Criticism is so helpful and much needed in the arts, but learning how to do it takes practice as well as acceptance.

Tips for improvement

Praise sandwich

One way to start the process of criticism is by having constructive feedback called a *praise sandwich.* The bread is the praise and the filling is the criticism. Always start and end with the "good stuff" just as you do when you make a sandwich.

Student Evaluation Form

Another way to criticize is to use a form that your students in the audience fill out. I have included a sample Student Evaluation Form on page 260.

Epilogue:

Additional Resources

12 Weeks of Production
Check List

As soon as school starts

(After your first year, do these in the spring for the following year.)

- ❑ Set dates for production
- ❑ Requisition building use
- ❑ Start viewing and reading plays
  (You will be doing this in the summer as well.)
- ❑ Fill out 1st read-through forms on each play viewed or read

12 weeks before production

- ❑ Select several plays you want to consider
  - ❑ Fill out 2nd read-through forms on each play
    (characterization and concept)
- ❑ Select your play
- ❑ Get administrative approval
- ❑ Order scripts
- ❑ Pay royalty

Word of Caution: Calendar adjustments are required if the show is a musical.

11 weeks before production

- ❑ Fill out 3rd read-through forms (deal with your technical aspects)
- ❑ Come up with costume and set design
- ❑ Make tentative rehearsal schedule
- ❑ Put together and print tryout information sheets
- ❑ Make and print tryout poster

10 weeks before production

- ❑ Distribute the tryout sheets and/or scripts —
  make them available to everyone
- ❑ Hang up tryout posters
- ❑ Continue working on the design of the show

9 weeks before production

- ❑ Continue working on the design of the show
- ❑ Rest up

8 weeks before production

- ❑ Hold tryouts
- ❑ Assign roles
- ❑ Assign crews
- ❑ Rehearse
    - ❑ Read-through
    - ❑ Blocking
    - ❑ Blocking
- ❑ Work on set and costumes

7 weeks before production

- ❑ Rehearse
    - ❑ Blocking
    - ❑ Blocking
    - ❑ Catch-up blocking
    - ❑ Off-book
- ❑ Check publicity
- ❑ Work on set and costumes

6 weeks before production

- ❑ Rehearse
    - ❑ Off-book
    - ❑ Off-book
    - ❑ Off-book
    - ❑ Working
- ❑ 1st costume check on characters

5 weeks before production

- ❑ Rehearse
  - ❑ Working
  - ❑ Off-book
  - ❑ Working
  - ❑ Working
- ❑ Finalize and print tickets
- ❑ Prop check
- ❑ Program check

4 weeks before production

- ❑ Rehearse
  - ❑ Working
  - ❑ Working
  - ❑ Working
  - ❑ Working
- ❑ 2nd Costume check
- ❑ Finalize and print poster
- ❑ Add sound to all rehearsals
- ❑ Makeup check

3 weeks before production

- ❑ Rehearse
  - ❑ Working
  - ❑ Working
  - ❑ Working
  - ❑ 1st full run-through
- ❑ Finalize props
- ❑ Makeup check
- ❑ Publicity
  - ❑ Check assembly schedule and see if you can use some time to advertise your play
  - ❑ Deliver posters around town
  - ❑ Schedule the "Sneak Preview" and notify the English Department
  - ❑ Send out PSAs
- ❑ Finalize set
- ❑ Focus the lights (if applicable)
- ❑ Schedule photographer for cast picture

2 weeks before production

- ❑ Rehearse
  - ❑ Act I Dress
  - ❑ Act II Dress
  - ❑ Act I Dress
  - ❑ Act II Dress
- ❑ Actors in makeup
- ❑ Add lights
- ❑ Arrange for ticket seller, cash box, and ushers
- ❑ Buy gift for student assistant

Week of production

- ❑ Rehearse
  - ❑ Full Show with everything
  - ❑ Full Show with everything
  - ❑ Full Show with everything
- ❑ Order "Break your leg" cake
- ❑ In the School
  - ❑ Hang up posters
  - ❑ Put announcements in daily bulletin
  - ❑ Use PA system for short announcements
  - ❑ Present Sneak Preview for English classes
- ❑ *Performance*
- ❑ *Performance*
- ❑ Strike

The week after production

- ❑ Write thank you notes
- ❑ Return borrowed items
- ❑ Get some much-needed rest

1st Play Read-Through Form

Name of play________________________________ **Publisher**______________________

Author____ **Royalty**_________________

Comments: What is the play about?

Type of play: Comedy____ Drama_____ Farce____ Musical____

Length: 1 Act____ 2 Act____ 3 Act____ Other_____

Scenes: 1 2 3 4 5 6 more____

Setting: Interior____ Exterior_____

Where:____

When: Future____ Present_____ Past_____

Time: Year_____ Spring ____ Summer_____ Fall____ Winter____

Time span: ___________ (minutes-years)

Cast: Men_____ Women_____

Types: Adults_____ Students_____ Character_____Children_____ Other_____

Does it have: Walls____ Doors____ Windows____ Fireplace____ Chairs_____ Tables_____
Platforms_____ Staircase____ Bookshelves____ ***OR***
_____ Can be done on a blank stage just using curtains, suggesting walls, doors, and windows

Costumes:

_____Period (clothes which are from a different time period than we live in now)

_____Modern (clothes which we wear today)

_____Special (elaborate)

General feeling

What did you feel after reading it? Did you like it? Was it stupid, great, funny, touching, exciting, wordy, dream-like, full of remembrances, light as a feather, or fluffy? (Don't mull this over, just jot down your initial impression. this often becomes your concept or idea for the show. First impressions are seldom wrong.)

What color(s) do you see the play in, if any?

2nd Play Read-Through Form

Character Analysis/Costume Card

Play______________________________**Character's Name** _________________________

Description of character in the script:____

Gender: Male_____ Female_____ Either_____

Description of costume in the script:____

Age:_____ **Occupation:** ____

Character's relationship with others:

Married to__________ Single_____ Divorced from __________ Enemy of __________

Friend of________________ Father of______________ Mother of______________

Brother of______________ Sister of______________

Time period of the play:____

When do they appear in the play?

Act 1/Scenes _____ Act 2/Scenes _____ Act 3/Scenes _____

Act 4/Scenes _____ Act 5/Scenes _____

Time span of character's involvement:

Minutes_____ Hours_____ Days _____ Weeks_____ Months_____ Years_____

Adjectives (list at least 2):____

Character's want or goal in life:____

____

Character's actions: Act Silly_____ Cry_____ Dance_____ Die_____ Fight_____ Kiss_____

Laugh_____ Recite poetry_____ Scream_____ Shout_____ Sing_____ Fall_____

Jump_____ Lounge/ Pose_____Run_____ Sit_____ Walk_____ Other_____

Size of role: Large_____ Medium_____ Small_____

Importance to plot: Major_____ Minor_____

Is there a line or phrase that describes the character?____________________________

____

Does the character need to change clothes? Yes_____ No_____

Why?:____

If the character needs to change costumes, can any of the following be used?

Apron_____ Blouse_____ Coat_____ Gloves_____ Hat_____ Purse _____

Shawl_____ Shirt_____ Skirt_____ Sweater_____ Tie_____ Vest_____

Other____

3rd Play Read-Through Form

Required Technical Aspects: ____________________

What do you need?	Yes	How many?	Why?
Furniture			
Benches			
Stools			
Tables			
Chairs/Couch			
Other			
Props			
Hand props (books, umbrellas, papers, etc.)			
Set props (drinking glasses, plates, baskets, food, maps, pictures, etc.)			
Lamps			
Music			
Special effects/ lighting			
Platforms/levels			
Set — Doors, Curtains, Stairs, Windows, Walls			
Anything else?			

Floor Plan Template

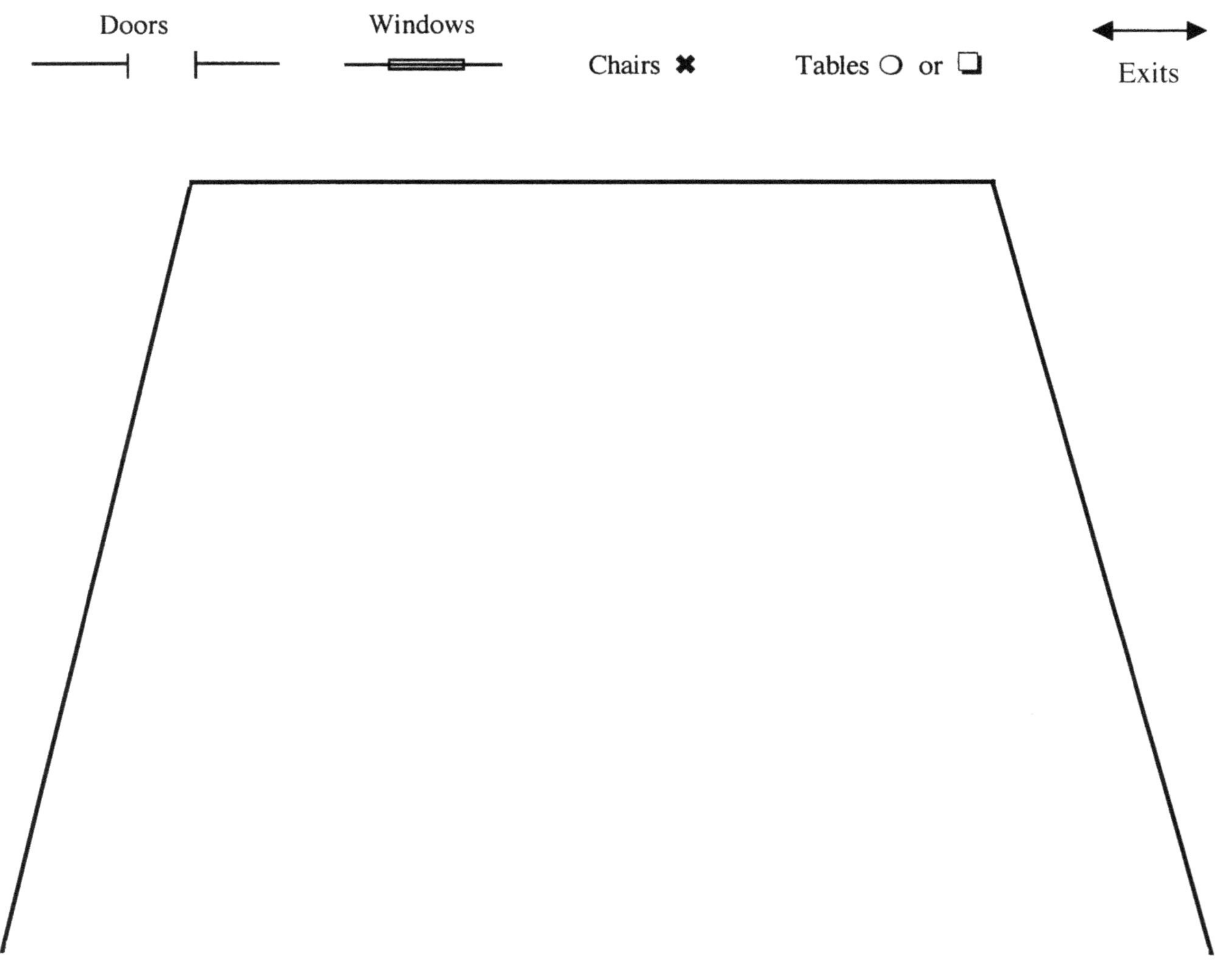

Curtain Line

Basic Rehearsal Schedule

Event	Date	Time	Segments	Technical
Tryouts				
Read-through				
Blocking				
Blocking				
Blocking				
Blocking				
Catch-up blocking				
Off Book				Publicity check
Off Book				
Open				Costume check
Off Book				
Working				
Working				Tickets done
Off Book				Props check
Working				Program check
Working				
Working				
Working				Costume check
Working				Poster done, add sound
Working				Props done, makeup check, add sound
Working				Props done, makeup done, add sound
Working				Props, program done, add sound
Working				Props done, makeup check
1st full run-through				Costumes done
Act 1				Add lights, makeup
Act 2				Add lights, makeup
Act 1				Everything
Act 2				Everything
Full Show				Everything
Full Show				Everything
Full Show				Everything
Performance				Everything
Performance				Everything
Performance				Everything

Tryout Information Sheet

Name________________________________ ❑ Senior ❑ Junior ❑ Sophomore ❑ Freshman

Address____**Phone**_______________

Classes

Commitments Monday-Thursday

After School (2-6 PM) Please include dates.

After Supper (6-9 PM) Please include dates.

Previous experience — list on the back

Special talents (only list those that you can do and would be willing to do, please)

❑ singing ❑ dancing ❑ playing instruments ❑ photography ❑ sewing ❑ drawing

❑ computer graphics ❑ video ❑ carpentry ❑ other_________________________

Part you're interested in. If you write down a specific character, *I will only consider you for that specific role and no other.*

❑ **Any** ❑ **Small** ❑ **Specific**_____________________________________

Parent Letter/Theatre Contract

Dear Parents,

The Drama Department is thrilled to have your child in our upcoming production of

____ on __________________________.

He or she is required to be at the following rehearsals:

✓		From	To	Date
	Mondays			
	Tuesdays			
	Wednesdays			
	Thursdays			
	Fridays			
	Saturdays			
	Everyone will be needed			

Would you and your child please sign and date the top copy of this letter, keep it for your records and return the other two copies to the Drama Department? This means:

✓ Both you *and* your child understand the commitment he or she has made to our production.
✓ He or she will be at all of his or her rehearsals

A complete rehearsal schedule has been enclosed for your information. Thank you very much.

Sincerely,

Theatre Director

Parent signature __________________________________ Date __________________

Student signature _________________________________ Date __________________

Character Analysis #1

Your Name: ______________________________ Character's Name: ______________________

1. What are your goals or aspirations?

2. What are the obstacles to the successful achievement of these goals?

3. What events or conditions prior to the play's beginning are important for understanding your motives and objectives in the play?

4. How do you react to these obstacles?

5. List your characteristics.

Character Analysis #2

Your Name: ______________________________Character's Name:______________________

List please:

A. What does your character do?

B. What does your character say?

C. What do the other characters say about you?

D. What does your character want?

Character Analysis #3

Your Name: ______________________________Character's Name:______________________

1. What is/are your character's:
   - A. Greatest fear (tangible or intangible)?
   - B. Happiest moment?
   - C. Saddest moment?
   - D. Most ashamed of (a deed or aspect of your appearance or personality)?
   - E. Most proud of?
   - F. Strongest want (long-range goal or desire)?
   - G. Loves?
   - H. Hates?
   - I. Virtue?
   - J. Fault?
   - K. Most treasured possession?
   - L. Feelings about mother?
   - M. Feelings about father?
   - N. Feelings about self?
   - O. Feelings about sex?

2. Tell about a childhood memory your character has:

3. Write three sentences about your character's opinion on any subject:

4. Write a brief outline (should include opening, main action, climax, and conclusion) of two incidents from your character's life that could become stories on two separate sheets of paper.

Character Analysis #4

Your Name: ______________________________ Character's Name: ______________________

Do not answer any question with just the answer — tell me *why*.
All answers must be in first person. Use extra paper if needed.

1. How does the title of the play relate to your character?

2. What is your character's main sense of urgency? What strong impulse motivates your character to act? (In *Romeo and Juliet*, Juliet's sense of urgency is shown when she becomes impatient with the nurse for not telling her immediately about the plan for marrying Romeo.)

3. What is your character's secret? Why? (Having a secret always adds a sense of mystery to a character.)

4. Tell me two things about your character's family.

5. What is your character's leading center? (The head? The heart? The stomach?) Why? You should gesture with your character's leading center.

6. What color do you associate with your character? Why? (You might associate a sweet character with pink/baby blue.)

7. What object do you associate with your character? Why? (You might associate an egg-beater with a character who is a "bubble brain.")

8. What animal do you associate with your character? Why? (You might associate a happy-go-lucky character with a puppy.)

9. If your character saw the play, what reaction might he or she have? On a separate sheet of paper write a brief outline (should include opening, main action, climax, and conclusion) of one incident from your character's life that could become a story.

10. Does your character have a sense of humor? Is this sense of humor used in a positive or negative way?

11. In real life, would you or would you not be your character's friend? Why or why not?

12. What are your character's two major wants, desires, and/or life objectives, and how does your character go about achieving them?

13. What is your character's major objective for each scene in which he or she appears? (Please list on a separate sheet of paper each scene and the objective). These also can be stated as, "I want ______from this scene"). How does your character go about achieving those major objectives?

14. Has your character changed by the end of the play? If not, why? If so, in what ways?

Shakespeare Character Analysis

Your Name: ______________________________Character's Name:______________________

1. Who is your character?

2. How old is your character?

3. What is your character dressed like?

4. Is your character married? To whom?

4. What is your character's occupation?

5. Where is your character?

6. In general terms, tell me about the plot of the play (just a couple of sentences).

7. What is your character talking about? (This is a paraphrase.)

8. List what prop, color, food, and animal your character would use/be and justify.

    Prop:

    Color:

    Food:

    Animal:

9. Is there a famous quote in your solo/scene? Restate — telling me its significance.

General Insert Form

Your Name: ______________________________ Character's Name: ______________________

1. If you could go anywhere in the world for free, where would you go and why?

2. What other roles have you had? (Name the role and the play.)

3. What other school activities are you involved in?

4. What occupation do you see yourself having in the future?

5. If you could change anything in the world, what would it be and why?

6. If you were granted three wishes, what would you wish for and why?

7. Seniors: Tell me about your post-graduation plans and goals.

Student Evaluation Form

An evaluation form for students to critique their classmates

Name ______________________________

Please rate the selected actor in the following areas on a scale from EX (excellent), VG (very good), G (good), S (satisfactory), P (poor). Please try to be as honest as possible.

Process

Effort ______________________________

Level of Personal Challenge and Risk Taking ______________________________

Cooperation with Everyone ______________________________

Product

Character Development ______________________________

Energy ______________________________

Concentration and Focus ______________________________

Ensemble/Teamwork ______________________________

Who Were They? ______________________________

What Was Their Objective? ______________________________

Write at least one thoughtful sentence about the student's performance:

____

____

____

Glossary

Act Curtain: The curtain that divides the acting area from the audience.

Ad-lib: The presence of mind by another actor to improvise when something doesn't go as planned.

Amateur: One who works in the theatre without pay.

Apron: Part of the stage projecting into the audience; in front of the act curtain.

Aside: Lines spoken by an actor to the audience, not noticed by other characters on-stage.

Audition: Process where the director of a production asks actors or performers to show him or her what they can do (how they would play a specific role).

Backdrop: A piece of fabric, painted or plain, that hangs at the rear of a scene. Curtains secured at the rear of a scene can also be a backdrop.

Backstage: Portion of theatre not included in the auditorium and stage proper. It is that part of the stage which is out of sight of the audience.

Bit Part: Role with very few lines and little action.

Blank: Mental fade-out causing lines or business to be forgotten.

Blocking: Putting actions to the words in the script.

Bomb: A theatrical dud.

Borders: Narrow, horizontal masking pieces — usually curtains (see masking below) — normally in neutral colors that hide the lighting instruments from the audience and provide an upper limit to the scenery. Often used in conjunction with legs. Also called a teaser.

Build: To bring a scene to climax by increasing volume, emphasis, pace, or intensity.

Center Stage: The very middle of the stage.

Character Part: Role depicting an unusual individual.

Chorus: Group of singers, dancers, or speakers working in unison.

Clear Stage: Command to leave stage.

Close In: Move closer together.

Concept: The broad idea or theme of a play.

Counter: Balancing move in opposite direction to make all actors seen.

Cover: To attempt to hide mistakes in lines or action. Also, to block another character from the audience's view.

Crepe Hair: Wool-like substance used for making beards.

Cue: Last words of a speech signaling when another actor speaks or enters. It also is an instruction given by the stage manager for either lights, set, or props to take some action (turn lights out, move set piece, or place prop where actors can access it).

Cue Sheet: Organized list which outlines when changes of lights, sounds, sets, etc. are needed.

Curtain Call: At the end of a performance, the acknowledgment of applause by audience for the actors; the bows.

Curtain Up: The signal for the cast and crew that a scene or act is ready to begin.

Curtain Line: Imaginary line where act curtain hangs between audience and stage. Also, the last line of a play.

Cutting: A play cut to time, with scenes in original order, with no additions, alterations, or substitutions, and without character or gender changes.

Cyclorama (Cyc): A plain cloth, curtain, or wall filling the rear of the stage. The term is often loosely applied to a blue-dyed cloth at the rear of the stage that may be curved at the ends.

Director: One who plans and directs the play for production.

Downstage: Toward the audience.

Dramatis Personae: Latin, meaning persons in the play.

Ellipsoidal Lights: Lighting instruments with adjustable focal length. They have an elliptical reflector (a shape like a stretched circle with slightly longer, flatter sides), a lamp, shutters, and lens.

Ensemble: An acting group; normally used to describe actors who work together with no one outperforming the others.

Fake: To seem to be doing something without doing it.

Featured: Billing secondary only to the star role.

Flats: Frames of one-by-four lumber, covered with lightweight canvas or heavy muslin and painted, that form the walls of the set and are relatively easy to move. There are also door flats, window flats, fireplace flats, etc. Today they are being replaced with a similar frame covered with wood rather than cloth called *hard flats* or *TV flats*.

Flies: Space directly above the stage where scenery is raised. This is an extension of the stage walls to allow scenery to be flown up until it is out of sight of the audience.

Flop: Theatre production that fails.

Fly Bars: Movable pipes or metal bars where scenery and lighting instruments can be attached for flying above the stage. They can also be called *battens*.

Focus: To center attention on something.

Fourth Wall: The imaginary side of the scenery design (room) that faces the audience.

Fresnels: (Pronounced "Fray-nell") Lighting instruments that produce an even, soft-edged beam of light through a Fresnel lens. The lens is a series of stepped concentric circles on the front and pebbled on the back and is named after its French inventor, Augustin Jean Fresnel (1788-1827), who developed the lens for French lighthouses so that they could be seen further out to sea. He achieved a longer focal length with less glass than a standard plano-convex lens.

Full Set: Use of entire stage to create a naturalistic setting of a complete room built from flats (with only the side nearest the audience — fourth wall — missing).

Gels: Gelatin (gel in sheets) was used to provide colored lights on-stage. It is now made of a non-flammable plastic and comes in sheets that cover approximately six lights, and costs about five dollars per sheet.

Give Stage: Move to less important position.

Gobo: Stands for Graphical Optical Black-Out. It is short for Go-Between, as the gobo goes between the lamp and the lens. It is a thin metal plate etched to produce a design, which can then be projected by an ellipsoidal. There are hundreds of gobo designs available — common examples are foliage, windows, and scenic (neon signs, cityscapes, etc.).

Grease Paint: Mixture of grease and coloring, used in theatrical makeup.

Green Room: Lounge near stage used by actors, author, and director.

Grips: Stagehands.

Grouping: Arranging characters for meaningful and emotional interest in the play.

Gypsy: A dancer who goes from musical show to musical show, often in the chorus.

Ham: Someone who overplays their part with voice, body, and facial expressions — but thinks he or she is good.

Headliner: Star or leading player.

Hold: Keep position without moving.

House: Where the audience sits. It also can be called *out front*.

Improvisation: Short bit with lines and action created by actor; often used as a rehearsal exercise.

In the Red: Losing money on the show.

Jury: First-night audience.

Juvenile: Player of youthful roles.

Kill: To eliminate a piece of scenery or property from set, or to black out the lights.

Knockout: Sure-fire hit.

Lead: Actor playing the most prominent or important part.

Legs: Long, slender drapes set as masking piece at the sides of the acting area Upstage of the act curtain. Usually set up in pairs across the stage and used in conjunction with borders to frame the audience's view of the play. Some say the phrase *break a leg* means to take an extra bow from the legs after a successful performance. Also called tormentors.

Levels: Acting areas placed higher than stage level.

Lines: Speeches of the play.

Masking: Neutral material (black) stage curtains or designed scenery that defines the performance area and conceals the backstage area.

Monolog: Protracted speech by one person.

Offstage: Area of the stage not enclosed by set. Can also be referred to as *backstage*.

On-stage: Portion of stage enclosed by a set and visible to audience. Also called the *performance area*.

Open Up: Turn more toward audience.

Pace: Timing of lines and action.

Packing the House: Filling the theatre for a performance.

Panning: Unfavorable reviewing.

PAR: (Parabolic Aluminized Reflector) A lamp containing a filament, reflector, and lens in one sealed unit. Used to produce a high-intensity, narrow beam of light. PAR lamps are available in many different sizes and powers. PAR sizes available include 16, 36, 38, 56, and 64. (The number refers to the diameter of the lens, in eighths of an inch). The most common for theatre use are PAR 64s rated at 1000W, although other wattages are available. 110V PAR lamps are often used for touring groups due to the increased light output.

Pick Up Cues: To begin speaking immediately on the last word of the previous speaker for rapid speech.

Pipes: Horizontal metal tubes hung above the stage and/or above the audience to which lighting instruments and scenery, etc. may be suspended. They can also be called *battens.*

Pit: The orchestra area — in modern theatres it is located below and in front of the stage.

Places: Signal for cast to get where they need to be at the opening of the show, act, or scene.

Plant: Person stationed in audience who has function in play; or a line, idea, or character that significantly foreshadows some important element coming later in the play.

Position: Actor's place on-stage as set by director.

Prompt Book: Script marked with directions and cues for use by your student assistant.

Properties/Props: All objects including furnishing, set dressings, and items large and small that cannot be classified as scenery, lights, or costumes.

Quick Study: One who can memorize a part quickly.

Rake: Gradual slope of auditorium or stage floor. In the auditorium, the slope is toward the stage. On the stage, the slope is toward the audience.

Repertory: Collection of plays that are familiar to a group of actors and may be readily performed.

Revue: A type of multi-act theatrical entertainment that combines music, dance, and sketches.

Ring Down: Close front curtain, often in emergency.

Royalty: The money you pay to the author and/or publisher for the right to perform a play.

Run: Length of engagement.

Run-Through: To rehearse a play without stopping.

Scene: Division of an act; usually refers to short section where there is change of characters.

Script: Typewritten or printed copy of play.

Shoestring Production: A production with minimum financial expenditure. Generally, school productions would fall under this term.

Shutter: A metal blade that can be used to shape the edge of the light beam. Shutters (normally four) are located at the center of the instrument.

Sides: Pages of manuscript paper holding just one actor's lines and cues.

Sightlines: The areas of the stage that can be viewed from different areas of the audience.

Sitting on their Hands: Slang for an unresponsive audience.

SRO: Standing Room Only.

Stage Directions: Instruction in script of play.

Stage Fright: The fear that takes place when actors are on-stage.

Stagehands: Helpers backstage who work with the technical aspect of a production: moving scenery, props, etc.

Stage Left: Actor's left when facing audience.

Stage Manager: Person responsible for play in production; calls cues from the cue sheet for actors, lights, sound, set changes.

Stage Right: Actor's right when facing audience.

Stage Whisper: Giving the illusion of whispering but speaking loud enough for audience to hear.

Steal a Scene: To call attention to yourself when it should be elsewhere.

Stock Company: Company that performs a new play every week.

Strike: Call given to stage crew to remove scenery or dismantle the set, remove it from the stage, and put everything away.

Tableau: Living picture posed by players who are frozen in place.

Take a call: Bow before audience.

Take Stage: Move into stronger stage position.

Tech Director: Person responsible for all production/technical crews.

Theatrical Lighting: Using stage lights to not only light your actors but also create lighting effects.

Topping Cues: Pitching voice higher or louder than cues.

Trap door: Opening in stage floor.

Trouper: Seasoned actor who works for play's best interest.

Turn in, Turn out: Turn your body toward or away from others.

Typecasting: Actors playing themselves.

Understudy: Actor capable of playing another's role in an emergency.

Upstage: Toward rear stage.

Upstaging: Moving upstage to gain audience's attention, thus compelling cast to turn toward that actor and away from the audience.

Visibility Lighting: Using whatever lighting is available to make sure your actors can be seen.

Walk-on: A small acting role with no lines.

Wardrobe: Costumes and articles of dress for production.

Watts: Unit of electrical power derived from the current of electricity multiplied by the voltage at which the current is delivered. Stage lighting equipment is rated in watts. This refers to the amount of power required to light the lamp. A higher wattage lamp requires more power and gives a brighter light output.

Wings: Space at either side of stage, behind the scenes (offstage/backstage).

Works Lights: High-wattage lights used in an acting area when the stage or auditorium lighting is not on. They are like regular lights — the bulbs screw into the socket, have no special effect, and just light the area.

Currently there is a wonderful web site with technical terms called Glossary of Technical Theatre Terms: www.theatrecrafts.com/glossary.

Further Reading

Bruder, Melissa, Lee Michael Cohn, Madeleine Olnek, Nathaniel Pollack, and Robert Previto. *A Practical Handbook for the Actor.* New York: Random House, 1986.

Campbell, Drew. *Technical Theatre for Nontechnical People.* New York: Allworth Press, 1999.

Corey, Irene. *The Mask of Reality.* Louisville: Anchorage Press Plays, 1968.

Corson, Richard, and James Glavan. *Stage Makeup.* 9th ed. Boston: Allyn and Bacon, 2000.

Feder, Happy Jack. *Mime Time.* Colorado Springs: Meriwether Publishing, 1992.

Grote, David. *Play Directing in the School.* Colorado Springs: Meriwether Publishing, 1997.

Isbell, Tom. *Lessons: The Craft of Acting.* Colorado Springs: Meriwether Publishing, 2006.

Jackson, Sheila. *Costumes for the Stage.* Chicago: New Amsterdam Books, 1990.

Jones, Justine, and Mary Ann Kelley. *Improv Ideas.* Colorado Springs: Meriwether Publishing, 2006.

Juracek, Judy. *Soft Surfaces.* New York: W. W. Norton and Company, 2000.

Levin, Irina and Igor Levin. *The Stanislavsky Secret.* Colorado Springs: Meriwether Publishing, 2002.

Lord, William H. *Stagecraft 1.* Colorado Springs: Meriwether Publishing, 2000.

Lounsbury, Warren C., and Norman C. Boulanger. *Theatre Backstage from A to Z.* Seattle: University of Washington Press, 1999.

Miller, James Hull. *Self-Supporting Scenery for Children's Theater and Grown-Ups, Too.* Colorado Springs: Meriwether Publishing, 1988.

———. *Small Stage Sets on Tour.* Colorado Springs: Meriwether Publishing, 1987.

———. *Stage Lighting in the Boondocks.* Colorado Springs: Meriwether Publishing, 1995.

Novelly, Maria C. *Theatre Games for Young Performers.* Colorado Springs: Meriwether Publishing, 1985.

Parker, W. Oren, and R. Craig Wolf. *Scene Design and Stage Lighting.* Belmont, CA: Wadsworth Publishing Company, 1996.

Pectal, Lynn. *Designing and Drawing for the Theatre.* Columbus: McGraw-Hill, 1994.

Raoul, Bill. *Stock Scenery Construction: A Handbook.* Louisville: Broadway Press, 1998.

Rogers, Barb. *Costuming Made Easy.* Colorado Springs: Meriwether Publishing, 1999.

——. *Instant Period Costumes.* Colorado Springs: Meriwether Publishing, 2001.

——. *Costumes, Accessories, Props, and Stage Illusions Made Easy.* Colorado Springs: Meriwether Publishing, 2005.

Spolin, Viola. *Improvisation for the Theatre.* Evanston, IL: Northwestern University Press, 1983.

Sweet, Harvey. *Handbook of Scenery, Properties, and Lighting.* Vol. 1. Boston: Allyn and Bacon, 1995.

——. *Handbook of Scenery, Properties, and Lighting.* Vol. 2. Boston: Allyn and Bacon, 1995.

Swift, Charles L. *Introduction to Stage Lighting.* Colorado Springs: Meriwether Publishing, 2004.

Walker, Mark. *Creative Costumes for Any Occasion.* Deerfield Beach, FL: Liberty Pub Co, 1984.

Zimmerman, Suzi. *More Theatre Games for Young Performers.* Colorado Springs: Meriwether Publishing, 2004.

About the Author

During her thirty-seven years as a drama teacher, Margaret produced much more than great shows – she inspired many of her students to become theatre professionals. A few of her "kids" are now nationally known Broadway actors, film stars, and backstage technicians. Among them are Kathleen McNenny, a Broadway actress; Scott Michael Campbell, a television and film actor; Tom Valach, a freelance designer in the Twin Cities; and John Shaffner, an Emmy Award-Winning designer and chairman and CEO of the Academy of Television Arts and Sciences (Emmys) from 2008 to 2011.

When Margaret retired, the high school auditorium where she taught was renamed in her honor. She continues to teach acting privately and to the over fifty crowd for MOLLI (Montana Osher Lifelong Learning Institute) as well as at the Missoula Children's Theatre Fine Arts Camp. When her time permits she accepts acting roles at the Missoula Community Theatre where she works with former students.

She served as the Montana State Thespian Director from 1972 to 1992, establishing the yearly state convention in partnership with the University of Montana. Her students performed on the main stage at two International Thespian Conferences.

She has directed over 190 productions from children's theatre to full-blown musicals like *The Music Man* with a cast of 300.

Margaret graduated from Macalester College with a B.A. in Theatre and Speech and earned an M.A. in Direction from the University of Montana.

When she isn't acting or teaching she enjoys living in her restored Victorian home in Missoula with her husband of forty-six years and their "children" Sissi, a Hungarian Puli, and Daphne, a fourteen-pound domestic shorthair cat. She also does blogging for Contemporary Drama Service: http://contemporarydrama newsletter.contemporarydrama.com/ You can visit her web site at margaretfjohnson.com

"Everything it takes to make a great theatrical production," she says, "is what it takes to make a great life: caring for others, accepting each other for who we are, being responsible and dependable, but most important of all, being proud of what we do."

www.ingramcontent.com/pod-product-compliance
Lightning Source LLC
Chambersburg PA
CBHW062016090426
42811CB00005B/874

* 9 7 8 1 5 6 6 0 8 2 5 3 2 *